0108860

N199
1195
RAA
(Wee)

LESSER EVIL
AND THE
GREATER GOOD

HAROLD BRIDGES LIBRARY
S. MARTIN'S COLLEGE
LANCASTER

Books are to be returned on or before
the last date below.

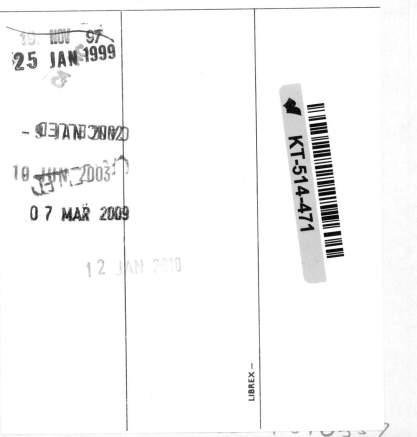

19. NOV 97
25 JAN 1999

- CANCELLED

10 JUN 2003

0 7 MAR 2009

12 JAN 2010

KT-514-471

LIBREX —

THE
LESSER EVIL
AND THE
GREATER GOOD

The Theory and Politics of
Social Diversity

edited by
Jeffrey Weeks

Rivers Oram Press

First published in 1994 by
Rivers Oram Press
144 Hemingford Road, London N1 1DE

Published in the USA by
Paul and Company
Post Office Box 442, Concord, MA 01742

Set in 10/12pt Palatino by EXCEPT*detail* Ltd, Southport
and printed in Great Britain
by T.J. Press (Padstow) Ltd, Padstow, Cornwall

Designed by Lesley Stewart

This edition copyright © Jeffrey Weeks, 1994

The articles are copyright © 1994 Chetan Bhatt, John Bird,
Peter Jowers, Ernesto Laclau, Rosemary McKechnie, Frank Mort,
Anne Phillips, Anna Marie Smith, Judith Squires, Jem Thomas,
Simon Thompson, Sean Watson, Jeffrey Weeks, Ian Welsh

No part of this book may be reproduced in any form without
permission from the publishers except for the quotation of brief
passages in criticism

British Library Cataloguing in Publication Data
A catalogue record for this book is available from the British Library

ISBN 1-85489-054-9
ISBN 1-85489-055-7 pbk

Contents

Part 3: The Politics of Solidarity

Acknowledgements

This book had its origins in a seminar series held at the University of the West of England, Bristol, during the academic year 1991–92. On behalf of the contributors to that series, and to this book, I would like to thank Professor Peter Glasner, Dean of the Faculty of Economics and Social Science, for his support for the seminars and for this book project. I must also thank Helen Robbins and Lesley Gander, and their colleagues on the administrative staff of the faculty, for their practical support of the project during its various stages.

The seminars and the book grew out of the discussions of the Social Diversity Study Group, and I owe a personal debt to its members for the stimulating discussions we had in the preparation of the project, from which I benefitted enormously. I especially have to thank them for their patient responses to my nagging as we worked on the book. I would also like to thank all those who took part in the seminar discussions; the papers in the book have gained greatly from their interventions

But the greatest debt is owed to the contributors to the seminar series and to this book. I have enjoyed working with them; and I hope our readers will enjoy the results.

Anne Phillips's chapter, 'Pluralism, Solidarity and Change' has also been published in an extended version in her book *Democracy and Change*, and the editor and publishers would like to thank Polity Press and Pennsylvania State University Press for permission to include the essay in this volume.

Jeffrey Weeks

vii

List of Contributors

Chetan Bhatt has worked in the voluntary sector, latterly around HIV and AIDS, for the past decade. He has recently completed a research project on right-wing religious movements.

John Bird is Principal Lecturer in Sociology at the University of the West of England, Bristol. His recent research interests have been in the area of expanding opportunities in higher education, especially for members of minority ethnic communities, and he has conducted major research for the Department of Employment in this area.

Peter Jowers is a Senior Lecturer in Politics at the University of the West of England, Bristol. His research interests include modern political and social theory, and world music.

Ernesto Laclau is a Professor in the Department of Government, and Director of the Centre for Theoretical Studies in the Humanities and Social Sciences, University of Essex. He is the author of *Politics and Ideology in Marxist Theory*, *Hegemony and Socialist Strategy* (with Chantal Mouffe), and *New Reflections on the Revolution of our Time* (1990).

Rosemary McKechnie is a social anthropologist, and was most recently a Research Officer at the Joint Department of General

Practice and Primary Care, St Bartholomew's and Royal London Hospital Medical School, University of London.

Frank Mort teaches cultural studies at the University of Portsmouth, and has also taught in the Department of History, University of Michigan, Ann Arbor, US. He is the author of *Dangerous Sexualities* (1987), and *Cultures of Consumption* (forthcoming). He is currently working on a study of consumption in post-war Britain.

Anne Phillips is Professor of Politics at London Guildhall University. She is author of *Engendering Democracy* (1991) and *Democracy and Change* (1993), and editor of *Feminism and Equality* (1987) and *Destabilizing Theory: Contemporary Feminist Debates* (with Michèle Barrett, 1992).

Anna Marie Smith is an Assistant Professor in the Department of Government at Cornell University. A revised edition of her PhD thesis, entitled *New Right Discourse on Race and Sexuality: Britain, 1968–1990*, will be published in 1994. She is a former member of Outrage! and Feminists against Censorship.

Judith Squires is a Lecturer in Politics at the University of Bristol. She is editor of the journal *New Formations*, editor of *Principled Positions: Postmodernism and the Rediscovery of Value* (1993), and co-editor of *Space and Place: Theories of Identity and Location* (1994).

Jem Thomas is head of the School of Sociology at the University of the West of England, Bristol. He is currently completing a major study of Max Weber and the value question.

Simon Thompson is a Lecturer in Politics at the University of the West of England, Bristol. He is completing a study of contemporary liberal thought.

Sean Watson is a Lecturer in Sociology at the University of the West of England, Bristol. He is completing a PhD on contemporary policing.

Ian Welsh is a Senior Lecturer in Sociology and pathway leader of the MSc Ecology and Society course at the University of the West of England, Bristol. His book on the nuclear power industry in Britain will be published in 1994.

Jeffrey Weeks is Professor of Social Relations and Director of the Centre for Social and Economic Research at the University of the West of England, Bristol. His most recent book was *Against Nature: Essays on History, Sexuality and Identity* (Rivers Oram Press 1991). He is now completing a study of sexual values, and a major project on the voluntary sector response to HIV and AIDS.

Introduction
The Lesser Evil and the Greater Good

Jeffrey Weeks

Heterogeneity, diversity, difference, pluralism, hybridity, flux, reflexivity, contingency—words such as these, and the lexicon continues to grow, dominate some of the most creative work in social and political theory today. Their meanings may be contested, and their implications struggled over—and this book reflects some of those challenges and theoretical and political agonisings—but they signify a profound shift in the ways in which we theorise, and politically engage with, some of the key assumptions of our culture. The founding solidities of History, Progress, Reason, Science, Identity, Community, Solidarity, even 'the social' itself, have crumbled as their dubious roots have been explored, and their complex histories and frequently murky implications have been deconstructed and recon- structed, interred and resurrected, and deconstructed all over again. And we are left with—what?

First of all, we have a world in radical transition, marked by apparently ever increasing complexity, variety and moral pluralism, which radical social and political theory is attempt- ing to grasp, or understand, or perhaps even construct. The ways we characterise these shifts vary—'disorganised capitalism', 'high' or 'post' 'modernity'—but that the pace and quality of change is accelerating seems to be a given. Second, we have an efflorescence of frequently discordant claims from individual and collective subjects who have either been denied a voice, or are refinding one, or who are reaffirming their claims against those who would challenge their historical

1

dominance and legitimacy—with incalculable consequences. Thirdly, we have an oscillation between the seductive delights of absolute relativism, where everything seems acceptable because it exists, and the search for universal standards, however minimal. Thus the three themes which are interrogated in this book: contingency, pluralism, and solidarity.

None of these terms has a single, straightforward meaning, as the essays in this book illustrate, but they do have broad areas of reference. 'Contingency' stands for a sense that the meanings and values of the world are not there waiting, passively, for discovery by the ardent theorist or scientific investigator. Nor are they subject to immutable laws, either of nature or of society or history. There are no foundational givens, no immanent truths to social existence. On the contrary, the social and cultural world is radically indeterminate, in the sense that it has no pregiven meaning, and our understanding of it is a product of the complex intersection of specific histories, discursive formations and political articulations, and the reflexive ordering of human life, which provide the web of meanings. The logic of contingency is a logic of absence, of no single logic that pertains to all social phenomena. That does not mean that everything is accidental, nor that understanding, meaning or values are impossible. What it does mean is that we cannot assume the inevitability of links between one phenomenon and another, nor the likely outcome of the intersection of one element and another. For some, this opens the pathway to despair at worst, and political pessimism at best. Some of that pessimism is reflected in this collection. For others, contingency opens the way to a truer freedom, for the exploration of possibilities which the 'settled pessimism' of our time have occluded.

Pluralism is a more familiar term, though again a fiercely contested one. It refers both to the infinite variety of individual values and goals, and to the complexities of social belongings, in a culture where sub-groups and subcultures, interest groups, communities, identities and social movements proliferate, offering a density of possible belongings, and a potentially explosive tangle of obligations and antagonisms. At one level, it is descriptive of an ever more complex, and conflictual, world;

2

INTRODUCTION

at another, it offers a value to be achieved, a way of living with difference and diversity.

So where does that leave the third term, solidarity? The problem with social diversity is that while it opens up the possibility of individuals and groups developing a greater sense of identity and belonging in their specific cultural 'homes', whether these are organised around nation, ethnicity, race, gender, sexual preference or whatever, the sense of a wider belonging to the *polis* or even the community of the human race is often obliterated. Whether through what often seems an inevitable sectarianism, at its worst leading to the horrors of 'ethnic cleansing', or through a sort of exhaustion at wider commitments that the struggle to achieve a cultural identity that reflects your own needs and desires often requires, the specific triumphs over the general, the relative over the universal. In the market place of conflicting identities and belongings, the possibilities of a broader identity is often forgotten. To put it another way, in rightly pursuing a politics of the lesser evil, learning to live with difference, and consequently ways of life that we may deeply disapprove of, is it still possible or desirable to pursue a politics of the greater good? Solidarity is a term which suggest that, whilst not forgetting the fact and value of diversity, there are common interests that can be articulated which complement and sometimes transcend the specific interest. But realising such a goal remains perhaps the greatest challenge facing the theory and politics of social diversity.

This book grew out of a special seminar series held at the University of the West of England, Bristol, during the academic year 1991-2, designed to explore these themes. It was orga-nised by the Social Diversity Study Group, a group of resear-chers in sociology and politics based in the Faculty of Economics and Social Science, which over the previous year had been meeting to discuss the challenge to social and political theory, and political practice, posed by the new theorisation of, and political practice around, difference and diversity. The seminar series had the general title of 'Contingency and Solidarity', a reference to Richard Rorty's famous book, *Contingency, Irony and Solidarity*, which has been a key reference point for many of these debates in recent years (and which is discussed in more detail in Simon Thompson's essay below). Ernesto Laclau,

3

whose own work has been central to a rethinking of what is meant by post-Marxism, and the formulation of what he has called a 'radical and plural democracy', gave the first paper in the series. He was followed by the other speakers included in this book. The authors have taken the opportunity of this book to rewrite their papers, and in one or two cases to write on different topics. But all of them have addressed the common themes of this project: to rethink the implications of the recognition of the significance of social diversity for the ways we formulate theory and practise politics. Their voices are individual, and occasionally discordant. That, however, like this book, reflects a wider commitment to a theory and politics that is dialogical, open to debate and respectful of difference.

The theoretical reference points of the essays are similarly varied. There are the giants of nineteenth and twentieth-century thought: Kant, Weber, Durkheim, Freud (but rarely, it is worth noting, Marx). There are also some of the most influential writers of today: Laclau, Rorty, Lyotard, Foucault, Beck, Giddens, Butler, Bauman, and others; post-Marxists, post-liberals, poststructuralists, and postmodernists, perhaps (though all these labels are disputable), but not, whatever their abstractions, post-political. On the contrary, the theoretical engagements are closely linked in these essays to an active rethinking of politics, refracted through, and reflecting on, the impact especially of the new social movements and identity politics of the past generation, around race and ethnicity, gender, lesbian and gay politics, environmentalism, and the politics of HIV and AIDS. The theorists of contingency and difference are not vocalising in a political void. They are attempting to come to terms with a world where the challenge to the inherited traditions and monolithic solidities of (an often imagined) past are crumbling, and where forceful new particularisms both undermine, and underline, the need for wider solidarities.

In Part 1 of the book, the logic of contingency is explored through the work of several key thinkers. In his essay on 'Values, diversity and social theory' Jem Thomas concentrates on the work of Max Weber, whose curiously modern feel is powerfully evoked. Contemporary views about diversity and contingency can be traced to counterparts in Weber's work, just as the influence of Nietzsche is as obvious there as in the writings of Michel Foucault. Weber is as preoccupied with the non-realist character of knowledge as any postmodern thinker, and like them he teeters on the brink of relativism, however much he strives to repudiate it. Weber's work and influence, in other words, anticipates and encapsulates many of the dilemmas and opportunities we face today—which is no doubt why, of all the 'founding fathers' of sociology it is Weber who today seems a key point of reference.

For Weber, Jem Thomas argues, values are irredeemably plural in two related ways. First of all, human societies display an extraordinary range of value variation, even in relatively short periods of time. Second, each of us has a number of coexisting values, but we are unable, either in our personal or our political lives, to rank them in any unchallengeable fashion. This poses fundamental problems for our attempts to understand social existence. The concepts in which knowledge is expressed are dependent on our values, and values change. They are themselves contingent, expressions of our own personal preferences, which also change. As Jem Thomas puts it: 'Progress, rationalisation, development, dialectic are always *relative* to our current point of view and that point of view is simply contingent, a given historical fact, not a necessary one.' In Weber's words: 'there are no absolute norms of historical interest.' So does this make social knowledge merely a fiction?

Weber tried to get round this by stressing the core value of science—the pursuit of truth—but in a way, Thomas argues, which undermines the is/ought distinction which is central to his work. Ultimately, therefore, Weber's views are subjective, plural and ethical. Jem Thomas himself queries that subjectivity, arguing that: 'If we want to see fact as more subjective than positivism allowed, the very same move brings us to see value as more objective than positivism allowed.' But it is the subjectivism about value, rather than a critical attitude towards it, that resonates most closely with key contemporary social and political theory.

This is made clear in Simon Thompson's discussion of the 'ironist liberalism' of Richard Rorty. Rorty's e
central liberal values is explicitly twinned with a
universality and rational basis of such values.

rational and irrational are rejected by Rorty as 'clumsy and obsolete'. He denies the need for any foundational basis for values. But that does not make a viable liberal political theory impossible. On the contrary, the radical contingency of all beliefs and values gives us a freedom to shape what could be, rather than fruitlessly attempt to reach an elusive 'truth'. That does not mean that preferences or alignments are purely arbitrary. For Rorty the liberal-social democratic world view is more desirable than any other: less arbitrary, giving greater individual autonomy and freedom of choice, and more likely to be more beneficial, or at least cause less humiliation, to a greater number of people than any other. The liberal position, whatever its transparent limitations, offers a possibility of a more caring and inclusive community that can broaden to include the whole of humanity.

The justification for a liberal politics would therefore appear to be ultimately pragmatic, and dependent on us liberals being able to persuade others of its transparent merits. The problem, of course, is that to others it seems just a new form of the classical patterns of Western hegemony. Unlike older forms, it is not absolutist in the sense that it assumes that reason or the hidden ruses of history can justify it. Nor is it intolerant of difference. On the contrary, it seeks to embrace toleration of diversity as a key element of the liberal enterprise. But the 'we' that Rorty evokes as the bearer of these liberal values can, as Simon Thompson points out, seem exclusive to those outside its bonds. The question of who constitutes the 'we' was a source of debate between Rorty and Foucault. For Rorty, the 'we' was constituted in an already existing tradition of liberal thought; for Foucault, a 'we' had to be constituted through the shaping of new meanings and imaginings. Perhaps, however, as Thompson suggests, this is a false polarity: 'we can accept that thinking occurs within traditions of thought, whilst allowing the possibility that this process of thought can change the tradition in which it is located'. If this is the case, then one can begin to define the possibilities of a pluralistic world that can be inclusive, without denying the particular experience and desires of those who may have had the historic misfortune (to some people at least) of living outside the liberal tradition.

The difficulty of finding this balance provides the organising principle of Part 2 of the book. Rosemary McKechnie and Ian Welsh, in their case studies of a gay community faced by the threat of HIV and AIDS, and a planet confronted by the rush of global environmental change, engage with recent sociological theories concerning 'risk' and trust relations, especially in the work of Ulrich Beck and Anthony Giddens. Whilst accepting much of these writers' arguments about the centrality of such concepts in high modernity, McKechnie and Welsh place greater emphasis on the moral critique and the transformative possibilities of the new social movements. They counterpose the imaginative possibilities of activist discourses to the abstractness of expert systems, and stress the significance of what they term 'intermediate collectivities' in creating an awareness of risk and the context for developing trust relations:

> We believe the construction of personal narratives, the self-identification that permits individuals to form significant shared associations within which they can take a meaningful 'risk position', are constituted through a much wider base than scientific formulation of risk.

So, for example, the gay community has contextualised scientific definitions of risk, and made them meaningful to the specific history of that community, without stigmatising activities which are integral to the identities shaped within it. That pioneering activity is rooted in a complex history of self-activity which provides a filter through which risk can be measured.

The creativity of the new social movements, and the value of the social identities they simultaneously create and are shaped by, provide the possibilities of a radicalised pluralism that goes beyond the easy platitudes of traditional liberal pluralism. In particular, by recognising the inequalities of power that give rise to the new movements, the new pluralism presses for a wider definition of belonging, and therefore of the 'public sphere' where differences can be negotiated. As Judith Squires says in her chapter: 'what might conceivably make a pluralism radical is an awareness of the existence of structural oppression and the need to positively act to overcome them.' But defining the public arena where this can happen is more difficult. In her discussion of the image of the city as a public space, Judith Squires powerfully dissects the conflicting forces at play: the celebration of the city as an arena for individuality, diversity, and spectacle, accompanied by a search for order and discipline. Desire and fear dance in a perpetual dialectic, where the city is both an opportunity and a threat. On the one hand we have the aspiration for inclusion, for individual and collective self-realisation in a wider belonging. On the other, there is the wish for homogeneity, and therefore for the exclusion of those who might disrupt the city's desired order. This is the classic dilemma faced by the politics of pluralism. In confronting it, Judith Squires argues for a 'grammar of conduct' which would provide rules for the use of public space, and therefore of living together in difference, rules based on the acknowledgement of the power dichotomies that underlie conflict.

But what if those in power are constitutionally (in every sense of the term) bound by a fear of diversity, and by a disciplining duty? In his chapter, Sean Watson poses the controversial and deeply unsettling question of whether ontological trust and acceptance of diversity must always be based on the paranoia of policing. Quoting serving police officers, Watson sees policing as a self-enclosed, fear driven guardian of boundaries: 'we're here to represent the society and safeguard morals.' But the definitions of society are narrow, and the morals are those of the dominant group, and of the police themselves, manning the barricades against difference and diversity, especially racial and sexual difference.

It has become an anthroplogical cliché that outgroups are frequently associated with dirt, disease, and moral contagion. Sean Watson seeks to show the *affective force* with which the fear and loathing of the other is generated in the police forces. Drawing on the post-Lacanian psychoanalytically inflected work of Slavoj Zizek, Watson argues that for the police, the world is full of threatening objects, emanating from everywhere in their moral and cognitive universe. The affective loathing directed at criminals, new age travellers, homosexuals, ethnic minorities etc., is a manifestation, Watson argues, of internal antagonisms in the police subject, which in turn is a product of the contradictory positioning of the police within incommensurable world views. They are enjoined simultaneously to maintain the Queens' peace, and to maintain the Rule of Law; but the former frequently involves ignoring the latter, especially when threatened disruption comes from those who do not conform to the norms of the culture. By their very position as guardians of order, their identity as members of the police is shaped by the rejection of the other. They are compelled to battle against complexity, ambiguity and contradiction; yet their very identity depends on the constant recreation of the threatening other.

In his essay, John Bird takes up several of these themes—exclusion, fear of the other, 'pleasure in hatred'—in relation to racism and ethnic hatred. Drawing on a wide range of theoretical sources, including Emile Durkheim, Zigmunt Bauman and the psychoanalytical work of Melanie Klein, Bird traces the ambiguities of community and the prevalence of intolerance towards difference. Following Klein in counterposing the schizoid position of infancy, with its characteristic tendency of splitting the good and bad object, to the depressive state, which entails an ability to live with fluidity, he stresses that the former is never entirely given up, leaving open the ever-present possibility of falling back into it. Ethnic cleansing in Bosnia and elsewhere represents the all too bloody evidence of this today. There is nothing inevitable about this, Bird argues; the process of reparation offers a route to the mutual toleration of difference. But living with uncertainty demands, in Bauman's phrase, 'nerves of steel'. John Bird sees little in the current forms of postmodern politics—neo-liberalism, the politics of desire, and the politics of fear—to reassure him that we have such steely resolve.

Chetan Bhatt, in his exploration of the new politics of race and ethnicity, develops this theme: 'It would appear that rather than living in an age of ambivalence and uncertainty, we are living in one of multitudinous, murderous certainties.' He points out that a politics of difference can be right-wing and reactionary as often as it is progressive. The new translocal identities around religions, Islamic and Hindu in particular, are framed within a Manichean conflict of West and non-West, offering a new foundationalism and transcendent truths that eschew the compromises and relativisms of western liberalism. The characteristic forms they take evoke ancient truths and

9

traditions, but Bhatt sees them as deeply modern phenomena, dependent not on ancient texts or sanctified tradition but on new modes of electronic communication to provide an identity that goes beyond regional or national identities, or indeed well established forms of religious accommodation. Like the progressive new social movements more readily recognised in the West, the new religious movements focus on the body and sexuality, and on the modes of cultural reproduction. But their project is not to acknowledge or come to terms with diversity, but to subsume it. The lesson of Chetan Bhatt's vivid analysis is clear: a politics based on the simple acceptance of diversity and difference forgets that social differences are continually remade, and that that remaking can as often lead to the universalising of the particular, and the positing of new absolutisms, as it does to the politics of toleration and acceptance of human variety.

Pluralism, then, is not enough; but the alternatives are equally problematic. The hazardous theoretical and political task of going beyond a simple pluralism whilst holding on to its central concerns, provides the context for Part 3 of the book, on the politics of solidarity. Ernesto Laclau opens this discussion with a subtle and original explanation of why 'empty signifiers' matter to contemporary politics.

An empty signifier points to an absence, something which is evoked as a desirable goal ('community', 'order', 'solidarity'), but which is transparently not present, otherwise there would be no purpose in political and social struggle to achieve it. It is a space that can be filled by political articulation of various differences and identities, establishing chains of equivalence across disparate particularisms. This articulation can only be made, however, across limits that signal the impossibility of achieving it within existing frameworks. That, in turn, relies on the meanings that can be constructed to bridge the chasm of difference. But what shapes the possibility of such a construction? Laclau rejects the notion that there is any predetermined social and political force that can take the lead in what is a hegemonic struggle—a struggle for the shaping of meaning so that what is fundamentally contingent can appear, temporarily at least, as a natural order of things. But particular groups—for example a workers' movement, but it could be another—

assume a leading position, embodying the hopes and aspirations of others, filling the absence by a new set of meanings, because of 'the unevenness of the social', and the unevenness of power in social relations.

Politics is possible, and necessary because of the absence of any pre-ordained pattern of social meanings and unification in a world of complexity and difference. Just as there is no pre-given social force embodying universal aspirations, which can achieve hegemony, so there is no pre-given unity in the social which predestines the possibility of successful social harmony. That fact, however, provides the space for democratic politics— a space, we could add, where the empty signifier 'solidarity' becomes a political possibility, to be articulated across a multitude of differences.

In his chapter on the recent work of Jean-François Lyotard, the pioneering theorist of postmodernity, Peter Jowers examines the possibilities of the aestheticisation of politics. In a detailed study of Lyotard's concept of the sublime, and its roots in Kantian aesthetics, Jowers indicates the profound importance of creativity and imagination when facing the challenges of our times. The intensified feeling embraced by the concept of the sublime forces radical interrogation of the world. It is a negative critical point, disruptive of any finality and generic closure, which Lyotard views with horror. Its very formlessness makes it resistant to power. Yet at the same time, it opens up the possibilities of inventiveness and imaginative responses to the world: sublimity emerges by way of fear and anxiety and issues in joy. The search for the political good, for a working consensus to overcome diversity, is rejected by Lyotard, because it threatens closure, a closing off of possibilities. Instead, he seeks a politics of the 'lesser evil' which can live with the creative possibilities of heterogeneity.

Frank Mort's essay is concerned with the developmental possibilities of one aspect of the heterogeneous politics of today, the recent emergence of a 'queer politics' around homosexuality. In part a reaction to the accommodatory nature of lesbian and gay politics of the past generation, with its over-reliance on the idea of fixed homosexual identities and on social integration, in part a radicalisation of that identity-politics and a return to the transgressive politics of early gay liberation in

THE LESSER EVIL AND THE GREATER GOOD

the early 1970s, Mort's queer politics simultaneously plays with, and challenges, notions of cultural identity. Its emphasis on the fluidity of identity and the creative possibilities of transgression suggests the wider possibilities of forms of politics which go beyond the settled forms of Western democracy. But at the same time, Frank Mort shows the limitations of sexual politics in the forms in which they are expressed. In many ways, he suggests (though each party might be surprised at the argument), queer politics echoes the difficulties of the progressive social democratic agenda of the 1960s. Both had the same problem: of how to construct a broader political base to support what are essentially the values of a progressive middle class constituency. The challenge remains, Frank Mort argues, of developing a language of politics that can command broad support for complex pluralist values across multiple social constituencies.

Anna Marie Smith takes up the challenge in her study of the 'hegemony politics' in the work of Ernesto Laclau, Chantal Mouffe and Judith Butler. Their interests and work seem on the surface quite disparate. Laclau and Mouffe's work has been directed towards drawing out the most democratic aspects of the Marxist tradition in order to shape a political theory suited to the complexities of contemporary identity games. Judith Butler has concentrated on the disruptive possibilities of gender politics. But, Anna Marie Smith argues, all three are ultimately concerned with the sites in which hegemony, as the contingent articulation of disparate elements into viable con-testatory political and cultural identities, can be organised. In such an endeavour, sexuality and gender are key sites, as Chetan Bhatt and Frank Mort also argue in their essays. The implications of such arguments are enormous. Identities are not fixed essences, locked into eternal difference. They are fluid possibilities, the elements of which can be reassembled in new political and cultural conditions. Politics is not, therefore, a power struggle between natural subjects. It is a struggle for the very articulation of identity, in which the possibilities remain open for political values which can validate both diversity and solidarity.

In the final essay in the book, Anne Phillips re-evaluates and illuminates the whole pluralist debate, and her conclusions are particularly pertinent to this debate. Difference as such might be an irredeemable element of social life, but that does not mean that particular differences are inevitably intractable: 'While difference must be recognised and equality guaranteed, none of the difference is set in stone.' But to move away from the 'enclave' politics that difference encourages requires more than a simple celebration of diversity. It requires a recognition of the asymmetries of power that have made difference both intractable and divisive; and it requires an articulation of broader concepts of justice and toleration in which a politics of mutual challenge opens the way to wider solidarities. This does not mean a fruitless aspiration towards homogeneity, where difference will disappear. Nor does it presuppose that mutual understanding will necessarily bring shared ideals. The challenge is to avoid the absolutisation of difference, whilst respecting human diversity, of working towards a framework of values which sustains our differences whilst affirming what we have, and need, in common. As Anne Phillips concludes: 'What distinguishes a radical perspective on democracy is not its anticipation of future homogeneity and consensus, but its commitment to a politics of solidarity and challenge and change.'

The essays in this book illustrate the complexities of the challenges facing a theory and politics of social diversity. But they also suggest the opportunities for a new political imaginary, which can hold in balance a respect for difference and a recognition of common concerns: the lesser evil *and* the greater good.

PART 1

The Logic of Contingency

(1)

Values, Diversity and Social Theory

Jem Thomas

This chapter is concerned with the themes of social diversity and contingency in a particular context: the context of Max Weber's theory of value.

Value and Diversity

All human societies exhibit diversity. Even the most small-scale and technologically primitive have a division of labour based on age and sex. That, in its turn, gives rise to a world in which people have different life histories and differently gendered identities; in short, a world of individuals. What has made social diversity an issue with regard to advanced industrial societies is a feeling that the sheer quantitative extent of diversity, the *range* of different trajectories life in our world can take, has reached a point of some sort of world historical importance. Taylor has recently put this by suggesting that there may be different kinds of life, each of which realises values incommensurably. Moving from one sort of life to the other could not be seen as gain or loss, just as a sort of blank incomprehension of one's own past.[1] On this sort of view, diversity, rather than rationality or reification, is what is most typical of the contemporary world and marks the rough passage from modernity to postmodernity. As the remark by Taylor indicates, it has become common to refer to this world historical significance of diversity as incommensurability.[2] This is a term I am not especially happy with. Since Donald Davidson's classic paper on conceptual schemes,[3] it is hard to see that it can be given any tolerably precise degree of meaning. Nevertheless, for our purposes here, we can suggest a core meaning to the effect that 'diversity' and 'incommensurability' both relate to the fact that values are somehow irredeemably *plural*, in two related senses:

- First, human societies display an extraordinary range of value variation in even relatively short periods of time. We prize equality, our own ancestors would have found it contemptible; we prize sexual satisfaction, early Christians and late pagans prized lifelong virginity, and so on.

- Second, each of us has several values: courage, kindness, health, peace, rationality, long life and more, can all simultaneously be goods for us. However, we are unable, either in our personal lives or in our politics, to *rank* them in some incontrovertible way. Even if there were some scheme which told me, say, always to prefer kindness to courage (whatever that would mean), then the first point, about variation across time and between groups, guarantees that I know someone else will hold equally firmly to the conviction that the appropriate decision scheme ranks the values the *other* way.

It follows from the conjunction of these two points that the rational settlement of value disputes is, at best, a highly restricted option. It is not entirely abolished; for if we both agree, say, that we hold human life sacred, then we get somewhere in the discussion of capital punishment or abortion. But as these examples indicate, the 'somewhere' is not really very far. Because we are so often likely to appeal to different values and because we are also inclined to think that there is no compelling reason for all persons to rank this one before that one, then we are all inclined to agree that some disputes just cannot be settled rationally and, instead, *power* comes into play and one view is simply enforced.

So much is this the case, that some postmodern theorists now claim that that is *all* that there is. 'Rational' debates are either just rationalisations, or, worse, the rules of rational discourse are just the very means by which power expresses itself and secures the victory of some group over another. In the prose of Jean-François Lyotard:

> Power is not only good performativity, but also effective verification and good verdicts. It legitimates science and the law on the basis of their efficiency, and legitimates this efficiency on the basis of science and law.[4]

As he says elsewhere in the same text, knowledge and power are simply two sides of the same question: it is the person with power who decides what knowledge is and who decides what it is that needs to be decided.[5]

A question that arises here, however, is what it is that values, on this view actually *are*. Sociologists often write as though values were *ideas*; Martin Albrow, for instance, talks in this same context of sociologists showing how value-ideas guide people's conduct, as if having a value were roughly equivalent to having a concept of liberty, justice or whatever.[6] But seeing values as ideas does not square with the account of incommensurability I have just sketched. If values are concepts, there is no immediately obvious reason why we shouldn't have a rational settlement of conceptual (i.e. value) disputes. Instead, the diversity thesis about the impossibility of ranking values suggests, much more strongly, that a value is something akin to a *want* or a *like*. This is first and foremost a metaphor. My valuing liberty is akin to my liking cheese. We cannot rationally arbitrate between value conflicts for the same reason we cannot rationally arbitrate between the person who likes cauliflower and the person (me) who loathes it. The very idea of rational arbitration seems out of place. Either you like cauliflower or you don't; either you prize liberty or you do not. There is more, on this view, however, than metaphor. Value statements are not just akin to want statements, they can be recast into them. So, 'I value peace' can be rewritten as, 'I want it to be that there is no war'; or, 'We should keep our promises' becomes, 'I want it to be there is promise-keeping.' Something like Christianity appears in Nietzsche, a main source for this view of value, as nothing more than a disguised expression of envy, resentment, spite and other pathological states of desire. Perhaps the best known version of this view of value statements is A.J. Ayer's. He implied that the statement 'Stealing is wrong' can be translated as 'Stealing: boo!' and 'God is good' becomes 'Hurrah for God!'[7] Accordingly, this has sometimes been called the boo-hurrah theory of ethics; I shall more conventionally refer to it as *non-cognitivism*; that is to say, statements of value are not cognitive statements, statements of knowledge about the world.

What I want to argue here centres around Weber and has three main elements:

- That this (non-cognitivism) is the view of value that Weber adopted;
- That, for various reasons, he sought to build a sociological method around it;
- That the view is false or at least open to serious question.

The principal difficulty for this view of value is fairly obvious. It is that the *phenomenology* of value is not at all as the theory implies. Our experience of value is not a bit like our experience of wanting. For instance, one of our commonest experiences is that of a conflict between our obligations and our desires. There is something we think we *ought* to do and something that we would *rather* do. Whichever way it works out, it doesn't feel at all like the equally common conflict between two desires *tout court*. They do not feel the same, precisely because we have a sense of obligation in the first case and not in the second. Supporters of this sort of account of value can deal with this problem in a number of ways.

One way is to say that the feeling of obligation, and the concomitant sense that we *recognise* value as the source of the obligation, is simply an *error*. J.L. Mackie, for example, argued just this.[8] We think we are responding to values which place us under some sort of obligation but we are just mistaken. Mackie and his supporters are inclined to suggest that this error is functional. Our moral life operates better if we think we are reacting to objective values rather than projecting our subjective wishes onto the world. This is a powerful argument but has an odd consequence. For if that is so, then value theory, by exposing the error *as* an error, in fact undermines our moral life; moral philosophy therefore becomes immoral.

A second tack is the classic Durkheimian one, again a sort

of error theory. Our experience of value, on this view, is indeed typified by externality and constraint, unlike our simple desires. It is wrong though to assume therefore that value is in any way objective; rather the sense of externality and constraint associated with our moral phenomenology is disguised social pressure. Once again though, there is an odd consequence: the theory is left quite unable to account for the moral sense of a prophet or reformer who is, by definition, at odds with prevailing social pressures yet is central to any historical account of the development and change in value systems.

On the whole, Weber avoided both of these kinds of difficulty. However, he had quite different problems, which are also the result of his adherence to the view that values are a bit like desires, or that value statements can be recast as desire statements. Whilst he was committed to the non-cognitivist view of value,

● he was *also* committed to the view that value had epistemological as well as axiological significance; and
● he seems to have thought that truth is a value, which raises special problems about doing science.

I shall look at each in turn.

Weber, Value and Epistemology

Weber was a committed anti-realist.[9] Both his Kantian and his historicist inheritance are at work here. Reality is never directly knowable, only sense data are. Further though, the realm of sense data, facts, is both extensionally and intensionally infinite. That is to say we can endlessly uncover new facts about the universe and we can endlessly discover new properties of known facts. This is not a point about the infinity of the universe, so much as a point about the way the mind apprehends it: there is no logical limit to how many distinctions we can draw, how many subdivisions we can make and so on. If that is the case, then realism must be wrong; our knowledge cannot be simply a reflection of a structure in the world. If we divide the world into two genders, male and female, then those concepts *create* an ordering of facts, they do not reflect a structure that is pregiven. This, the lack of any pregiven structure (perhaps it would be better to say the impossibility of knowing any such), is referred to by Weber as the 'irrationality of the concrete'. It is the irrationality of the concrete, the absence of pregiven patterning to the infinite mass of actual and potential sense data, which undermines any project for accounting for sociological categories by simple reference to what is allegedly *there*. In Weber's words, 'the absolute irrationality of every concrete manifold is a conclusive epistemological proof of the complete absurdity of the idea of the "reflection" of reality by any science.'[10]

Now, if the realm of potential facts is infinite and our knowledge is clearly finite, then our knowledge must be an artifact. That is, our knowledge must work by some sort of selection of what is significant. This was a commonplace idea in *fin-de-siècle* neo-Kantian philosophy. The crucial question becomes what the *criterion* of selection is and what *sort* of an artifact our knowledge is.

For Weber, the artifactual character of knowledge is especially marked in the social sciences, for two reasons:

(a) Social science is above all concerned with *meaning* and Weber largely seems to follow Rickert in linking meaning to values.[11] To borrow an example from Geertz,[12] the distinction between a twitch and a wink is the agent's intention to communicate something, what Weber called the 'actual existing meaning'.[13] But that is comprehensible only in relation to rules which embody and express the *value* we ascribe to communication and intimacy. This concern with meaning, though, raised a set of strategic concerns for Weber. Could the meaning of the act include something not intended by the agent, not an 'actual existing meaning' but an imputed one? If it could include that, how far would social science be able to speak of the 'real' meaning of the state, say, or legitimacy, where 'real' has some sense of 'true' or 'valid' beyond what either individual or typical actors might think? On the whole, Weber allowed the first two senses of meaning whilst disallowing the third.

(b) Social science is concerned with uniqueness and diversity. There are plenty of things that are human phenomena and which could be expressed as universal laws. The point is we are not very interested in them. Our interest is always in what is *distinctive*, in what marks something out for attention. Most especially, of course, we are interested in the lineaments of what we now call *modernity*, the hallmarks of our own historically unique selfhood: who we are, what our troubles are, etc. Diversity, like any other feature of the world is not just given. We find it because we seek it out; we seek it out because it has a special value for us.

Weber's solution to these issues about the artifactual character of our knowledge is well known: social scientific concepts are *ideal types* and ideal types are constructed in relation to values. An ideal type is not a method we choose, like choosing between structured and semi-structured interviews; it is the form of all valid social scientific concepts. The only alternative would be for social science to be a sort of list of random and unusual facts, like those books that schoolboys enjoy about how high fleas hop and what town has the longest name. Even then the very term 'unusual' points to some sort of ideal type construction. Our social sciences are *not* like that because our data are organised around our values. It is important to recognise what Weber meant here, though his own accounts are infuriatingly imprecise. Take an example like bureaucracy; it is not just that our values incline us to be interested in bureaucracy rather than some other phenomenon. That is true enough, but further our very ability to tease out the elements that enable us to identify a phenomenon as a bureaucracy is a matter of value-relevance. Further still, Weber tells us that bureaucracy as an ideal type has six main characteristics, each of those in turn is selected from the infinite mass of potential data by their relevance to values, as is each element of each of the six characteristics and so on.[14] A concept like *writing*, which is one of the elements of one of the characteristics, is itself a complex social scientific concept and is therefore itself a selection from the irrational and infinite mass of real and potential data.

It follows from this that we can have as many ideal types as we can have values: we can have a proletarian sociology, a feminist sociology, a gay sociology and so on. Notice, again, it is not just that our different values lead us to have different areas

23

of interest: feminists are more interested in domestic violence than in discounting Treasury bonds or whatever. Rather it is that we can have different ideal types of what look remarkably like the same thing. We can have feminist, catholic, proletarian ideal types of the family or the state. This has to be so precisely because our concepts are not *reflecting* reality but are artifactually constructing it. This is not at all a state of affairs that Weber regretted. On the contrary, a proliferation of ideal types informed by different values is something which he seems to have been calling for. At a time when the notion of the state and its interests was taken as a self-evident value by many scholars and led some of them to proclaim that there was therefore no room in academic life for those socialists and anarchists who denied the validity of the state and law, Weber declared that:

> My own opinion is exactly the opposite. An anarchist can surely be a good legal scholar...the Archimedean point of his convictions, which is outside the conventions and presuppositions which are so self-evident to us, can equip him to perceive problems in the fundamental postulates of legal theory which escape those who take them for granted.[15]

The conclusion to all this then must be that our social scientific knowledge is massively *contingent*. It is contingent in a double sense:

(a) First, the concepts in which our knowledge is expressed are dependent on our values. The set of concepts we employ now is quite different from that employed at an earlier time. It is not at all necessary that we should go on speaking of class or capitalism, gender or patriarchy. On the contrary, these concepts are contingent on our values; it is just the way we happen to be looking at our social world now. We can readily anticipate that social science in a few years' time will have a set of new concepts which represent not an enrichment or a refinement of our current interests but simply the outcome of a different, emerging range of values. Who, just a few years ago, would have anticipated the recent emergence of new concepts for articulating human relationships to other species? These new concepts, however, do not represent progress in our knowledge, still less an adaptation of social science to new problems; they are the simple sequel to new values.

(b) Second, however, as we have seen, those values themselves are to be understood as contingent phenomena. Like desires or wishes, it is always the case that our values might have been other than they are. I was going to say that our values are contingent on our personal preferences. It is more though that they *are* our personal preferences and there is nothing at all necessary about those. They might be other than they are and indeed they do regularly change.

We should note that some question arises of just what 'contingent' here means. After all, Weber's argument is precisely that there is a necessary and internal connection between our values and our knowledge which looks, at least at first glance, like the very opposite of contingency. However, the point is that it is not, for Weber, the structure of the world that necessarily determines our concepts but rather our conceptual knowledge embodies our acts of valuation. Yet since our values are non-cognitive, then neither our concepts nor our values are the shape that they are because of any necessary dependence on the world. Instead, all our statements expressing what the world is, and what in it is to be prized, depend on some subjective state of the utterer. There are other senses of contingency in Weber's work too that could usefully be drawn out: the role he was prepared to ascribe to chance, the way in which he held causal statements to depend on the imaginative construction of counterfactual conditionals, the fact that interpretive understanding was, for him, partly intuitive. None of these, however, is as important as the fact that what, in Hegel, was the necessary unfolding of actual human mind in history is, in Weber, just a *play* of ideal types. Progress, rationalisation, development, dialectic are always *relative* to our current point of view and that point of view is simply contingent, a given historical fact, not a necessary one. In Weber's words, it is just the case that 'there are no absolute norms of historical interest.'[16]

Why then is our social science not just a Babel of conflicting voices? Why is it that for Weber the proletarian or feminist sociologies are still, in fact, just tendencies within what remains *one* sociology? Partly because Weber used the notion of a shared value in a very broad sense. Different tendencies in sociology still manage to agree on what sorts of issues matter—if they disagree about the issues, well, those disagreements occur just *because* we share certain common concerns.

That answer is a thin one though. Rickert had indeed thought that social science was possible as *knowledge*, if and only if there is some such thing as objective value. Weber's abandonment of it leaves sociology looking dangerously like fiction. Barry Hindess has attacked Weber for turning sociologists and historians into 'authors of plausible stories...nothing more'.[17] Facts must be interpreted and interpretation occurs along value lines, each sees what is in his own heart,[18] it is a sort of fiction. Weber ended one of his essays with a famous metaphor: our interest in social and historical data is like a powerful beam of light cast into the darkness. The beam moves on, leaving what once was under a searching gaze lost in twilight.[19] We do not just outgrow older science, we shrug it off, abandon its premises; it comes to be of antiquarian interest only.

Weber and Value Freedom

The only thing that preserves us from the full force of the relativism implicit in the previous points about value-relevance and moving searchlights is Weber's well known principle of *value-freedom*. There are all sorts of ways we can understand this principle: accepting that our concepts are 'coloured' by our values whilst denying that our values are shaped by the 'facts'; or, outlining a state of affairs whilst eschewing any comment on its desirability; or, again, refusing to concede that certain practical policies follow inevitably from particular scientific insights. Weber adhered to all of these versions of value-freedom. However, the way I want to construe Weber's notion of value-freedom here derives from his late essay 'Science as a Vocation'. It is that as scientists, our commitment to truth takes precedence over our other value commitments. In short, calling yourself a social scientist is to accept a ranking of values which places truth first. Marxists, Anarchists, Christians or whoever, in so far as they are social scientists, are equally committed to the ideal of truth; that is, to evidence gathering, logical deduction, testing, refutation and so on.

The problem is at once apparent. For Weber there is an assumption here that there is only *one* set of canons of science (in spite of his own methodological dualism). The Marxist, Anarchist etc., will have different values, different concepts and different models but *not*, for Weber, ultimately different conceptions of science. Were they to do so some much more intractable incommensurability would set in. Curiously, most discussions of value-freedom ignore this point, preferring to stress how hard it is to avoid attitudes of praise or blame, one of the more minor aspects of the issue. Weber would be deeply vulnerable here to the argument mentioned above and common among Foucauldians and other postmodernists to the effect that the canons of science are never neutral but are just the way groups express their search for domination.

We can make Weber's dilemma still more acute though. Weber followed the neo-Kantians in seeing truth itself as a *value*. But if it is a value, our commitment to it is, on the account of value I am ascribing to Weber, at once contingent and personal.

Weber seems to have been aware of this, at least dimly. He seems to want to say that we should be committed to truth and to rational procedures just because we are scientists and, well, that is what scientists *do*. If not, we are doing something else, fiction, artistic creation, propaganda, *something* but whatever it is, it is *not* science.[20]

Now that seems to me an extraordinarily weak argument; perhaps it was meant as a transcendental argument—*if* what we are doing is to count as science, *then*....However, it doesn't seem to me to work. We might as well argue that murderers ought to kill people because that is what murderers do, or that soldiers ought to obey their orders because that is what soldiers do. It is weak because it avoids two key questions:

- It avoids the question of what the proper obligation of any profession actually is. Professional norms change just because people ask questions like whether or not soldiers ought always to obey their orders.

- It avoids the question of whether one ought to be a murderer, a soldier or a scientist at all. To say we should do X, because we are scientists and scientists do X, simply hedges the question of whether *anyone*, ever, should be a scientist at all.

In passing, we might like to note another weakness to this line of reasoning in Weber. I do not attach too much importance to it but it is fun. Weber's argument is one that deduces an *obligation*, what social scientists ought to do, from an *assertion*, namely of the fact that we are scientists. Y is a scientist therefore Y ought to do what a scientist ought to do. If the argument is valid (and it seems to be), then it would violate the very is/ought, fact/value distinction that Weber's work rests on.[21] Weber justifies his adherence to the is/ought distinction with an argument that violates the is/ought distinction.

Leaving that to one side, the impasse Weber has reached is a sophisticated version of the dilemma that stopped the infant Wittgenstein in the doorway of his room. Why should we tell the truth? Truths are by no means always welcome. If a feminist social scientist investigating education discovered that girls underachieve in some areas not, as she had anticipated, because they are discriminated against but because they are just more stupid than boys, what should she do? Why shouldn't she just suppress her findings? Or fake new, more congenial ones? That would, of course, not be accepted as good *scientific* practice but it might well be good *politics*, especially on Weber's grim view of politics.

The twin essay to 'Science as a Vocation' was 'Politics as a Vocation', though it is now known that the former was written a good year before the latter.[22] The pair can be read as having at their heart this issue of why we might prefer the one set of obligations over the other. Why should we choose the search for valid propositions over the pursuit of power and acceptance of the consequences of political action? In short, the two essays counterpose power and knowledge in a way that is different from Lyotard's postmodern attempt to conflate them. At the same time though, Weber was unable to find rational grounds for preferring the one to the other but that means he was unable to find a rational ground for commitment to the idea of science as truth telling. He left science without foundation. If we think of his view of the scientist as someone who accepts a sort of Kantian imperative to seek out even painful truths, then his own comment on Kantian ethics at once undermines that position:

> ethics is not the only thing in the world that is 'valid'; rather it exists alongside other value-spheres, the values of which can under certain conditions be realised only by one who takes ethical responsibility upon himself. This applies particularly to political action. It would be pusillanimous, in my opinion, to attempt to deny this conflict.[23]

Weber's solution to this dilemma was the Star Trek option. We should boldly go..., we should seek out the daemon who holds the fibres of our being and those who are not manly enough (sic: *männlich*)[24] can make the intellectual sacrifice and run back into the arms of the churches. In general, we should try to live bravely in the light of what we discover to be our deepest values, whether they are intellectual or political. Weber's solution then, is subjective, personal and ethical. He could hardly have had any other solution given that his notion of value (or the one I have attributed to him) is of an inner, personal and subjective state. We do not, however, have to accept that view.

Beyond Weber

What I have claimed amounts to saying that Weberian sociology has a curiously modern feel. Contemporary views about diversity and contingency and of the non-realist character of knowledge can easily be traced to counterparts in Weber. The influence of Nietzsche is present in Weber as much as in Foucault who, indeed, acknowledged his own affinity to Weber. In consequence, Weberian sociology, like much postmodern thought teetered constantly on the brink of relativism, however vehemently he may have repudiated it.[25]

29

He rescued the objectivity of his new science above all by insistence on its adherence to certain scientific norms, acceptance of which was, however, necessarily non-rational. This non-rational terminus to the historical process of rationalisation is the core of the tragic element of Weber's account of modern Western culture.[26] Weber's sociology does not just possess a particular account of value, it rests heavily upon it, for reasons we have seen. It follows then, that if that account of value is vulnerable, so too is the whole of Weberian sociology.

The position to which Weber was committed, at least on my version, has been until recently the dominant position in Anglo-American philosophy. So much so that much of the debate in twentieth-century ethics has been between different versions of the position I have here broadly characterised as 'non-cognitivist': emotivism, prescriptivism, quasi-realism and so on. It is legitimate here to class them all together as they all share a view in common: that it is possible to separate the *descriptive* level from the *evaluative or prescriptive* level of a statement. So if, in ordinary English, I were to say that the 'fire-bombing of Dresden was a nightmare that cost tens of thousands of innocent lives'; then there is, on this view, a purely factual content: that Dresden was indeed bombed, that it was fire-bombed and not bombed some other way, that tens of thousands and not fewer, lives were lost. Each of these is open to check and can be agreed by people whose evaluation of the act as right or wrong might differ most sharply. The idea that there is a strict logical separation between the factual and the evaluative, that the factual is open to intersubjective verification and agreement even when evaluations are sharply contested, is vital to Weber's case. Both his claim that sociology is indeed a science and his view of its social and political role depend on it.[27] He said that,

> It has been and remains true that a systematically correct scientific proof in the social sciences, if it is to achieve its purpose, must be acknowledged as correct even by a Chinese....At the same time, our Chinese can lack a 'sense' for our ethical imperative.[28]

Perhaps the best known defence of this view is Hare's analysis of 'ought' as the principal term of obligation.[29] For him, 'ought' resolves into something a bit like, 'In situation X, do Y'. Its moral content is especially related to the demand for *consistency* and *universalisability*. That is to say, 'In situation X, do Y', involves our accepting something like, 'In situation X^a, X^b, X^c, X^d, still do Y;' (consistency) and also, 'Everyone in situation X, do Y' (universalisability). All this constitutes a powerful and well-argued view. I certainly would not want to deny that value language performs both prescriptive and emotive functions. Nevertheless, there are now quite well established grounds for questioning how far that constitutes the whole story.

A first query centres around the fact that there is a large class of words whose evaluative and descriptive content cannot apparently be separated in this way. It simply is not always possible to offer non-evaluative descriptions that are extensionally equivalent to value terms. Williams gives the example of terms like *coward, lie, brutality, gratitude*. These terms are clearly descriptive but equally clearly have an evaluative function. Williams here follows the Wittgensteinians in rejecting what is implicit in Weber's 'Chinese' example: it might simply be impossible to pick up and use these sorts of concepts unless one *shares* the requisite evaluative interest.[30]

Williams calls terms like these, where there is a certain union of fact and value, 'thick' ethical concepts.[31] Now this is important—the notion of 'thick description' originates in Ryle's philosophy of mind, and has been borrowed by Williams for purposes peculiar to his moral philosophy. But it is also well known in sociology, for it was borrowed by Clifford Geertz for his account of what interpretive understanding is in sociology and anthropology. Geertz's point was that translation out of the 'thick' concepts in which people couch their reasons for acting and construct their social settings is neither possible nor desirable. It would amount to 'changing the subject'.[32] To redescribe a wink as a twitch is to alter or lose its meaning. If a man takes vengeance for a slight to his honour, then we cannot begin to understand or describe the resulting duel or feud without local, 'thick' ethical language. In Taylor's words there is a best account principle at work here.[33] If the best account I can give of myself and others is one couched in a rich language of complex evaluation and description, then that account is 'trumps'. It needs no alteration, it *is* the reality we have to deal with. At this point the ghost of Weber is likely to interject with some asperity that *of course* we must use the actors' reasons for their conduct and that *of course* we must describe their moral stances, that is the whole point of his interpretive sociology and, the ghost is likely to add testily, it remains quite different from *endorsing* the value stances.[34] Such a response, though, misses some of the irony of the situation. Geertz's account of interpretive sociology draws heavily on Weber; Geertz's use of the phrase 'thick description' is an attempt at a gloss on the Weberian concept of '*Verstehen*'. However, in the process, it erodes the fact/value, description/evaluation distinction that elsewhere is central to the Weberian case.

We might go further. If we see value in this way as something embedded in thick descriptions of human reality, then the universalisability principle looks rather different: if I think it is wrong for X to kill Y, there is a prima facie ground for thinking Y would be wrong to kill X. In practice, however, we quite commonly do not think that way at all; our emphasis on consistency and the universal tend to be rules of thumb rather than strict rules. Feminists, for instance, might maintain that a man's murder of his wife and a woman's of her husband are not at all generally equivalent; and defenders of capital punishment are anxious to insist that the execution of a murderer is not at all morally equivalent to the murder itself. We could defend the position here by saying the universalisability of the rule can be preserved by importing some subordinate clause: it is *always* wrong to kill, *unless* a, b, c, and so on.

Might it not be, though, that nothing at all links all bad things together except that they are bad, and nothing at all links all good things together except that they are good?[35] Couldn't value exhibit real diversity too? Why should we suppose that all instances of value should be variations on some theme like promoting utility, giving pleasure or fulfilling a categorical imperative? It might not be possible at all to have a *foundational* account of value in which some single theory or commitment guarantees coherence and unity among values. If we have two purely factual statements: say, Napoleon was defeated at Waterloo and John's shoes are black, we do not demand some *further* way of making them consistent with each other beyond the fact that both are true. Why might it not be the same for the value properties picked out by sociology's thick descriptive language? They are just *there* and the statements describing them are just true. Value, then, is not an inner want projected out on to the world in a more or less consistent fashion but is a *real feature of the world* and has as much consistency or inconsistency as any other real feature of the world. Our moral phenomenology, our feeling that we *respond* to value instead of *imposing* it, is correct after all. Real value is acknowledged and captured in a language that is at once descriptive and evaluative.

This position at once invites the objection that was implicit in Weber's comment about the Chinese. If value properties are 'real' then it is a rum kind of reality, since it is impossible to imagine these properties figuring in a truly objective account of the world: one equally valid for the Chinese, a Martian, an intelligent dolphin or whatever. It is tempting to short circuit the discussion here by saying that the very notion of the ideal type is premised on Weber's recognition that the social sciences simply cannot aspire to that sort of objectivity. Mackie maintained that if value is a property of the world then it can only be a 'queer' property; one could maintain it is only a secondary property, like colour, a property *for us*, not a genuine feature 'out there'.[36]

The difficulty for this kind of objection is that one can make out the same sort of argument for the irreducibility and objectivity of colour terms as for value language.

Suppose we discover that every case of red we encounter has some 'microproperty',[37] let us call it its 'R-texture', which is scientifically detectable and which, we suspect, is what *makes* the object seem red. We could then build an R-texture meter perhaps, which bleeps in the presence of R-texture. Every case of red: strawberries, paint, pillar boxes, disco lights, turns out to have R-texture. Equally everything without R-texture seems to us not red but green or blue or colourless or whatever. Using the R-texture meter even a person blind from birth is able to say, 'This is red' and 'This is not red', accurately. Some people might even come to use the term R-texture as a synonym for red; saying that their new car or frock is *really* R-textured.

Now suppose that after some time scientists in a paint firm discover that a certain shade of grey *also* has R-texture; our blind man with the R-texture meter makes errors, saying, 'This is red' when it is the appropriate shade of grey. All sorts of things might now happen; scientific research might try to improve the R-texture meter, or to investigate and define the R-texture more closely. Surely. though, it is clear that one thing will *not* happen. No-one will start to say that that shade of grey is *really* red; that the blind man is right and we are wrong, that we have been using the term 'red' wrongly and we should have used it to include grey. The reason we would not say that is just that it is not true. Red is red and grey is grey. The word 'red' is irremediably phenomenological; red is how certain things seem to us and grey things do not seem that way.

What I am suggesting is that just the same sort of thing applies to value terms. If someone asserts that 'good' is equivalent to some objective property like maximising utility or promoting health and autonomy, we often do feel that most things that are good do that and that most things that do not do that are not good. Then suppose something we had hitherto regarded as evil turns out to satisfy the description—torturing people furnishes lots of others with intense pleasure and promotes the general good. Would we now say, 'Oh! We made a mistake, torture is really, after all, a good'? Of course not; we should just regard it that there was something amiss in the original argument about what 'good' is. Equally though, just because neither good nor red turn out to be terms that can be recast in some absolute, objectivist language, it does not follow that we can conclude that neither is an objective property. Neither value nor colour is projected onto a neutral world, they are rather how the world is apprehended by creatures like us. As Taylor has said,[38] there is an element of delusion to the view that we could treat all value positions as effectively equal; such objectivism, 'is just not available to us humans'.[39] I am therefore here asserting two things:

- Value is clearly subjective in the sense that if there were such a thing as an 'absolute' description of the universe stripped of all its distinctively human properties, such that intelligent Martians or dolphins would understand it, then neither colour, nor value, nor virtually any other part of the social sciences would figure in it.

34

- Nevertheless, both colour and value are properties of the world. I cannot decide to see red things as grey nor grey things as red; nor can I say, 'It may be red for you but for me it is blue.' Our attempt to do that in the case of value, to suppose we make values up, or that we can say, 'Well, for you it is bad but for me it is good' is a mistake. In that sense, value is an objective and real property.

Conclusion

Weber's position on values, value-freedom and value-relevance was, in fact, complex and sophisticated. Weber repudiated the view that history had or revealed any objective meaning or value. That conclusion was in some ways a despairing one but is in some ways exciting—life can have whatever meanings we give it. What I want to emphasise here is just that this rejection of objective meaning and value in Weber was not the *conclusion* of his studies but one of their *premises*. I have shown that at times he seemed, with his subjectivism about value, to contradict his own premises, most especially the requirement that sociologists practise an interpretive sociology which employs a thick and complex descriptive language. He was committed too, much though he denied it, to a species of relativism mitigated only by a strong conception of scientific truth, which he nevertheless necessarily regarded as unfounded. I have tried to argue that this concedes too much to subjectivism about value. With much of the discussion of value in contemporary sociology, especially postmodern sociology, it is as if we wanted to preserve half the legacy of positivism. Positivism adhered to a strict fact/value distinction. Facts were objective, grounded in observation, values subjective, an expression of attitude or feeling or some other inner state. Now, huge tracts of conventional sociology and philosophy of science has repudiated that notion of 'fact'. Its foundational character, its basis in observation, its intersubjective validity have all been challenged; instead facts are seen as partly relative to theory, observation is at least partly interpretive, and intersubjective agreement is generated by the norms of the scientific community not productive of them. Yet, curiously, though we no longer want to see 'fact' as objective (in quite that sense of an absolute-description-of-the-world), we seem to want to hang on to its counterpart, the absolute subjectivity of value. However, no binary opposition can survive the dissolution of one of its poles. If we want to see fact as more subjective than positivism allowed, the very same move brings us to see value as more objective than positivism allowed. It is not objective in the sense of figuring in *any* description of the world but then neither is anything else; both our scientific knowledge and our experience of value depend on an unalterably *this-sided* point of view. Our sociology, like our literature, our music and other parts of our culture is part of the way we apprehend value and refine our awareness of it.

(2)

Richard Rorty's Ironist Liberalism

Simon Thompson

Lyotard contends that a postmodern world is characterised by an attitude of 'incredulity toward metanarratives'.[1] In such a world narratives 'such as the dialectics of the Spirit, the hermeneutics of meaning, the emancipation of the rational or working subject, or the creation of wealth'[2] can no longer be used to underpin the more particular narratives we use to order our lives. Without such 'discourses of legitimation' or 'meta-narratives' it is impossible to show that our beliefs are 'in touch with how things really are', and that our values are the only ones acceptable to all rational persons. The loss of faith in metanarratives forces us to acknowledge that all beliefs and values are radically contingent.[3]

In this chapter I want to examine the effect of this aspect of what White calls the 'postmodern problematic' on political theory.[4] My guiding question can be expressed as follows: what sort of account can be given of our political values if it is accepted that all such values are contingent? How can we stand by our values if we know that it is impossible to prove their intersubjective validity? I shall focus on the answer which Richard Rorty gives to this question, since with his rejection of what he calls a 'metaphysical' form of liberalism in favour of an 'ironist' liberalism, he claims not only that the inescapability of contingency is not a disadvantage, but, more strongly, that its acceptance can actually help to advance the liberal cause which he seeks to defend. Whilst a metaphysical liberal seeks a foundation for his political values in some sort of meta-

37

narrative—such as one based on 'Nature or Reason or History or the Moral Law',[5] an ironist denies that there is a need for such a foundation. An ironist who is also a liberal is someone 'devoted to social justice' but 'who nevertheless takes her devotion to this cause as merely contingent'.[6] She stands by her political values in spite of her awareness that had she been born in a different place or at a different time, it is likely that she would have been equally attached to other values.

The ironist liberal claims that if we embrace contingency rather than try to evade it, we shall be able to defend a highly attractive liberal politics. This claim is based on a conception of liberal politics which sees 'freedom as the recognition of contingency'.[7] We can see what Rorty means by this remark by looking at his account of the ideal political system he wishes to work toward. He argues that in his 'liberal utopia' the ideal citizen would be 'the sort of person who faces up to the contingency of his or her own most central beliefs and desires—someone sufficiently historicist and nominalist to have abandoned the idea that those central beliefs and desires refer back to something beyond the reach of time and chance'.[8] In this case, he suggests, it would be possible for such a society to 'regard the realization of utopias, and the envisaging of still further utopias, as an endless process—an endless, proliferating realization of Freedom, rather than a convergence toward an already existing Truth'.[9] To take a particular example, Rorty has recently written on what he sees as the connection between 'Feminism and Pragmatism': referring to the possibility of 'a society in which the male–female distinction is no longer of much interest' he argues:

> Feminists who are also pragmatists will not see the formation of such a society as the removal of a set of social constructs and the restoration of the way things were always meant to be. They will see it as the production of a better set of social constructs than the ones presently available, and thus the creation of a new and better sort of human being.[10]

A recognition that the best form of social organisation need not correspond to a pre-existing blueprint, and that the justification of a favoured form of organisation need not be measured up to such a blueprint, provides us with an opportunity to shape our own destinies. In this way, Rorty defends the attractions of a form of liberal politics which embraces contingency.[11]

However, if these are the advantages gained by accepting contingency, we must accept that from the viewpoint of a liberal tempted to seek a metaphysical demonstration of the validity of her political values there are also drawbacks involved in this acceptance of contingency. In particular, such a politics will not be able to show that liberal political values are universally valid or that they are founded on philosophical premises which cannot be rationally disputed. It must be accepted that there are limitations on both the scope and the power of the justification which can be provided for these values.

As far as the scope of justification is concerned, Rorty contends that no non-trivial beliefs and values are universally valid since all significant beliefs and values serve to draw a line between a group that endorses them, and a group which does not. Thus Rorty, following Sellars's analysis of the nature of morality which sees moral statements as a matter of 'we-intentions',[12] argues 'that the force of "us" is, typically, contrastive in the sense that it contrasts with a they which is also made up of human beings—the wrong sort of human beings'.[13] In this way, Rorty is happy to acknowledge that his theory is 'ethnocentric'.

With regard to limitations on the power of the account which can be offered for our political values, Rorty accepts that in place of philosophical justification, an ironist liberal can offer no more than an 'apologetic' for liberal democracy. This he describes as follows:

> By an 'apologetic' I mean a way of describing old institutions and practices in a new, more useful way. To offer an apologetic for our current institutions and practices is not to offer a justification of them, nor is it to defend them against their enemies. Rather it is to suggest ways of speaking that are better suited to them than the ways which are left over from older institutions and practices.[14]

Sometimes Rorty seems to suggest that all that an apologetic can do is to bolster the confidence of those who are already convinced liberals; it cannot expect to persuade anyone else to become a liberal. It is thus no more than preaching to the converted.

In short, Rorty defends a liberal politics which links acceptance of contingency to the possibility of freedom, but which also recognises that in this case there is no guarantee that everyone will come to accept liberal values, and our arguments cannot show that it would be irrational so to reject them. In this paper I hope to make a limited contribution to the critical assessment of ironist liberalism by examining two closely related criticisms of this theory which I refer to as 'irrationalism' and 'ethnocentrism'. The rest of the paper proceeds as follows. I begin by introducing these criticisms of Rorty's theory. I then consider how Rorty might respond to these criticisms. The following section attempts to evaluate the adequacy of these responses, and, where necessary, seeks to improve upon Rorty's own account of these matters. The final part sums up the results of my investigations.

The Criticisms

I believe that two closely linked criticisms of Rorty's ironist liberalism are of particular importance for the purposes of this paper. The first of these argues that since Rorty provides no well grounded reasons for choosing one set of values rather than another, he makes the choice of political values *irrational*. Those advancing such a criticism find it unacceptable to admit, as Popper does, that 'my rationalism is not self-contained, but rests on an irrational faith in the attitude of reasonableness.'[15] The second criticism follows from the first. It argues that since this account gives us no reason to identify with one particular 'we' ('we bourgeois liberals') rather than another, it is unjustifiably *ethnocentric*. To accept this account is to privilege liberal political values over others without good reason. In short, the irrationality of our commitment to particular political values makes us unjustifiably ethnocentric. Let us consider each of these criticisms in a little more detail in this section, before looking more closely at the adequacy of the responses that Rorty can make to each of them in the following two sections.

First, consider the criticism of irrationalism. According to Bernstein, Rorty offers no substantive reasons in favour of liberalism. All he 'is doing is affirming his own idiosyncratic ethnocentric prejudices'.[16] Bernstein claims that on Rorty's account, '[t]here is never a non-trivial *reason* for favoring one vocabulary rather than its incompatible alternatives...Rorty's ironist may in fact think that some beliefs are "worth dying for", but she has nothing to say about why *her* beliefs are worth dying for rather than the strongly held beliefs of the fanatic or fundamentalist.'[17] In this case, if one doesn't find Rorty's redescription of liberalism attractive and congenial, then 'there is nothing more to be said':

> If none of our central beliefs can be even minimally rationally warranted, if there is no (non-trivial) way of distinguishing between relevant and irrelevant considerations for the beliefs we hold, then it looks as if Rorty is telling us that when doubts are raised about one's final vocabulary the only response that is appropriate is 'Here I stand (and I hope that you will also stand here)'.[18]

Bernstein concludes that Rorty's account of the limited and circular nature of justification describes 'a vicious circle—a circle which he breaks by declaring "Here I stand" (full stop)'.[19]

Rorty's critics then argue that not only does he offer no reasons in favour of liberalism, Rorty actually revels in the irrationalism of his position. This argument can begin by noting how Rorty sees language as a medium of persuasion not of truth determination. For example, Lovibond contends that Rorty's claim that language is independent of any kind of 'reality' leads him to develop two conceptions of speech—'as an instrument of psychological manipulation, and...as a weapon'—which can be contrasted with speech as a medium in which we can hope to discover the *truth* of a state of affairs. She argues that Rorty insists that '[w]e must expel from our reflective understanding of "true" and related terms something which has traditionally been central to it: the idea of an expression of faith that, in the long run, others could be brought *by dialogical means* (rather than, say, by force or emotional manipulation) to concur with the position of the speaker'.[20] She concludes that Rorty 'encourages a vision of language as a medium of play and trickery rather than communication, and a tendency to rejoice in the untruthful—even "deceptive"—character of speech in general'.[21]

As evidence of this claim, Rorty's critics cite his declaration that anything can be made to look good by redescription: 'What was glimpsed at the end of the eighteenth century was that anything could be made to look good or bad, important or unimportant, useful or useless by being redescribed.'[22] To take a particular example, Rorty, following Dewey's argument that '[t]he worse or evil is a rejected good', contends that on this view, 'the enslavement of one human tribe by another, or of the human females by the human males, is not an intrinsic evil. The latter is a rejected good, rejected on the the basis of the greater good which feminism is presently making imaginable'.[23] In other words, there is a description under which female enslavement is an evil, and a rival description under which it is a good. An argument for the first description rather than the second can only be a matter of saying 'try thinking of it this way',[24] rather than arguing that female enslavement is an evil no matter how it is described.

This criticism of irrationalism can lead directly to the second criticism of ethnocentrism. If no reasons can be given for valuing, for example, freedom rather than authority, and if language is no more than a medium of rhetorical persuasion (rather than a medium in which reasons can be offered and debated), then to identify with one moral constituency rather than another is to do no more than align oneself arbitrarily with that constituency. This is to be ethnocentric in the worst sense of that term—it is to be prejudiced, parochial and provincial.

There are further problems posed by Rorty's notion of ethnocentrism. In particular, critics have attacked his apparent assumption that when he argues that 'we' should attempt to justify ourselves by contrasting ourselves flatteringly with others, it is clear who 'we' are. For example, Dews argues that 'Rorty notoriously invokes...a bland homogenous "we", whose reference seems to oscillate between, at one extreme, the Western liberal democracies, and at the other, North American professional philosophers.[25] Even in the former case, it has been argued that to refer to 'we *liberals*' is of no help at all. As Bernstein says, '[a]t times Rorty speaks as if "we" all have common intuitions about what liberal democracy means or should mean, but this is really disingenuous'.[26] This is because 'the overwhelming "fact" of contemporary life' appears to be 'the breakdown of moral and political consensus, and the conflicts and incompatibility among competing social practices'.[27] He concludes that '[s]ometimes it seems as if what Rorty means by "we" are "all those who agree with me"'.[28]

If 'we' turn out to be a very small group indeed, then the principles which 'we' enunciate could be highly parochial. In this case, the critics argue, it becomes even more important for Rorty to find a way of discriminating between justified and unjustified forms of ethnocentrism. As Bernstein says:

> Rorty, of course, knows that there are pernicious and benign forms of ethnocentrism. The standard form of intolerance is one where some group takes itself to be the measure of what is 'rational' and excludes some other group whether we speak of 'we Greeks (versus barbarians)', or 'we white South Africans', or 'we white males'. So despite Rorty's manifest plea for toleration, the latent content of what he says can lead to the worst forms of intolerance *unless* he is prepared to distinguish (even locally and historically) pernicious and benign forms of ethnocentric appeal.[29]

In this case, the critics' question then becomes: on what basis could Rorty make such a distinction? Why is liberal ethnocentrism justified, whereas racist ethnocentrism is not? It has already been suggested that as a consequence of Rorty's irrationalism, he can have no recourse to an argument which could show why this might be the case.[30]

Different critics react in different ways to Rorty's ironist liberalism. Some cannot accept the inevitability of contingency, and long for some sort of metaphysical proof of liberal political principles. Others accept contingency, but deny that this implies the need for ethnocentrism. In the first camp,

Habermas sometimes appears to be tempted to reintroduce some sort of metanarrative of 'reason'. He talks, for example, of attempting to trace 'the historical fate of a reason that has been arrested again and again, ideologically misused and distorted, but that also stubbornly raises its voice in every inconspicuous act of communication'.[31]

In the second camp, Foucault denies that any such meta-narrative is necessary. But he rejects any account of the justification of political values which roots that justification in the tradition of the particular community with which 'we' identify:

> I do not appeal to any 'we'—to any 'we's' whose consensus, whose values, whose traditions constitute the framework for a thought and define the conditions in which it can be validated. But the problem is, precisely, to decide if it is in order to assert the principles one recognizes and the values one accepts; or if it is not, rather, necessary to make the future formation of a 'we' possible, by elaborating the question. Because it seems to me that the 'we' must not be previous to the question; it can only be the result—and the necessary temporary result—of the question as it is posed in new terms in which one formulates it.[32]

Here Foucault poses a fundamental challenge to Rorty's whole approach to the justification of political values. He argues that to decide whether one should endorse particular values and principles it is necessary to consider the worth of such values and principles *before* ever identifying with the 'we' who endorses them.

To sum up rather crudely, Rorty's critics argue that his ironist liberalism is indefensible since its account of the justification of political values begins with the irrational declaration: 'Here I stand', and leads to the ethnocentric declaration: 'Here we stand.' These critics argue that since neither of these declarations can be justified, Rorty's ironist liberalism is indefensible. Rorty is certainly aware of these criticisms, and, as one would expect, he believes he can overcome them. In the next section I shall consider what counter-arguments Rorty can offer to these charges, before assessing the adequacy of such counter-arguments in the section after that.

Rorty's Responses

Rorty's general strategy in response to the criticism of irrationalism is to try to undermine the very distinction on which this criticism is based. He argues that distinctions such as that between 'rationality and irrationality' are 'clumsy and obsolete tools—remnants of a vocabulary we should try to replace'.[33] He accepts that his theory does not meet the standard of rationality his critics demand of it. But he argues that this does not mean that his theory is irrational. Rather he contends that it is pointless to call a value 'irrational' if this is judged against a standard of rationality which is, in fact, impossible to achieve.

For example, consider the criticism that Rorty makes the attachment to a conviction a matter of arbitrary choice rather than necessity. He seeks to deflect this criticism by arguing that the distinction between 'mere preference' and something less 'arbitrary' 'presupposes a dubious distinction between necessary, built-in, universal convictions (convictions that it would be "irrational" to reject) and accidental, culturally determined convictions'.[34] If 'necessary' convictions do not exist, there is no point in condemning all actual convictions for being merely 'arbitrary' and 'accidental'.

Rorty makes the same sort of response to this criticism as it is applied to his ethnocentrism. Here critics contend that Rorty offers no reasons to choose 'us' rather than 'them' as the relevant moral constituency for considering questions of justice, and thus he supplies no criteria by which to distinguish between good and bad types of ethnocentrism. In this sort of case he argues that it is unhelpful to judge commitment to a moral constituency as either rational or irrational. He can contend that our identification with a particular group cannot helpfully be called irrational if no such identification could be shown to be rational. In this way, talking of critics of liberalism such as Nietzsche and Loyola, Rorty says that to rule their arguments out of court is not to say that they are wrong in some way (as we would try to say if we believed that some kind of rational justification for liberalism were possible), but '[n]or is it just to say that our preferences conflict with theirs' (as we might say if we accepted that our theory was 'ultimately' irrational). Rather, Rorty contends, '[i]t is to say that the conflict between these men and us is so great that "preferences" is the wrong word'.[35]

To see what Rorty means, consider a couple of particular examples. If we disagree about the best flavour of ice-cream, I would not take your contrary opinion as evidence of madness, unreasonableness, nor even perhaps of poor gastronomic judgement. Here the language of preference seems most appropriate. By contrast, if you disagree with me about the number of chairs in a particular room, then I would think that you were wrong, and I would have to seek some kind of explanation for your mistake. In the simplest sort of case, it may be that you count a sofa as a kind of chair, but I don't; in a more extreme case, having eliminated more straightfoward and more palatable explanations, I might conclude that you *were* irrational. Here the language of rational judgement (and consequently of irrationality) may be appropriate.

But what should I think of a person who does not endorse my fundamental political principles? Rorty contends that if I am a liberal, and you are, for example, a racist, I may discover that you endorse so few of the beliefs and values that are fundamental to my world view that debate between us is useless. Rorty argues that here the gap between us is so great that I cannot take your views seriously—indeed I may even conclude that you are 'mad'.[36] But, he argues, '[w]e do not conclude that Nietzsche and Loyola are crazy because they hold unusual views of certain "fundamental" topics; rather, we conclude this only after extensive attempts at an exchange of political views have made us realize that we are not going to get anywhere'.[37] In this case, neither the language of irrational preference nor rational judgement seems adequate to capture the nature of our disagreement. No commitment to a particular group of persons could be rational in the way that metaphysical liberals would wish it to be, but it does not follow that a commitment to liberalism is merely an arbitrary preference.

In addition to this attempt to evade the criticism of irrationalism as this is applied to ethnocentrism, Rorty does also offer some kind of justification for identifying with 'we liberals', and thus for endorsing the sort of ethnocentrism that 'we liberals' practise. Just as Rorty does make a case in favour of describing female enslavement as an evil rather than a good, so he also makes a case for liberal society over any other form of social organisation. But rather than trying to defend liberalism by reference to any sort of metaphysical claim, he suggests that a case for liberalism can only consist of an invidious comparison between liberal society and others 'leading up to the suggestion that nobody who has experienced both would prefer the latter'.[38] This comparison will simply suggest that the sum of particular pros minus particular cons in liberal society is greater than that in other types of society. As Rorty says, 'I do not know how to "justify" or "defend" social democracy...in a large philosophical way (as opposed to going over the nitty-gritty advantages and disadvantages of the alternatives...people propose)'.[39] In short, although it is impossible to show that a commitment to liberalism is rational or irrational, we can nevertheless try to justify our commitment by developing an invidious contrast between liberal and non-liberal society.

Rorty believes that he can also confute the other criticisms of ethnocentrism which are independent of that which accuses it of irrationalism. With regard to the criticism which contends that his conception of who 'we' are is vague and imprecise, Rorty argues that it is possible to offer a fairly straightfoward account of the group he refers to as 'we'. In general, he suggests, the explication of what he means by 'we' 'is best done by reference to a view of current political dangers and options—for one's sense of such dangers and options determines what sort of social theory one is able to take seriously'.[40] In this case, 'the best way to answer Bernstein's question about who I mean by "we"' is by reference to a 'political credo'. Thus he argues: 'The audience I am addressing when I use the term "we" in the way Bernstein describes is made up of people whom I think of as social democrats'. Such people subscribe to some sufficient proportion of the detailed political credo he outlines. This credo includes an endorsement of an economic system of 'governmentally controlled capitalism plus welfare-statism'; a commitment to 'steady reform along increasingly egalitarian lines'; and an acceptance that 'Soviet imperialism is indeed a threat'.[41]

Turning to the criticism which contends that if 'we' turn out to be a very narrowly defined group, then the principles that 'we' enunciate may be highly parochial, Rorty argues that the ethnocentrism of liberal society is in fact of a particularly mo ally progressive kind. As a more direct reply to the critics' claim that ethnocentrism is parochial and intolerant, he contends that this charge loses much of its force once it is realised that the group he identifies as 'we' is committed to a form of moral progress in which the 'ability to envisage, and desire to prevent, the actual and possible humiliation of others' leads to increasing numbers and types of persons being included in that group.[42] Thus Rorty argues that his ethnocentrism 'is the ethnocentrism of a "we" ("we liberals") which is dedicated to enlarging itself, to creating an ever larger and more variegated *ethnos*'.[43] Rorty argues that one of the chief virtues of liberal society is that it is always striving to increase the number of groups it can identify with (or at least feel able to tolerate). He concludes that since the 'we' he refers to constantly attempts to increase the numbers it classifies as 'we' rather than 'they', it is not parochial and prejudiced as charged.

On the one hand then, Rorty rejects the metaphysicians' hope that liberal values can be shown to be rationally indisputable or universally valid. But, as I have shown, this does not mean that Rorty thinks that nothing can be said for liberalism. It is still possible for the ironist liberal to offer an invidious contrast between liberal and non-liberal societies. On the other hand, in response to Foucault's claim that 'the "we" must not be previous to the question; it can only be the result',[44] Rorty flatly denies that this is possible. He argues, pace Foucault, that it is not possible for a question to precede the formation of a 'we' to whom that question is addressed: 'Foucault seems to be envisaging some sort of simultaneous *creatio ex nihilo* of vocabulary and community. I cannot envisage this. As far as I can see, you can only describe or propose some radical change if you keep a background fixed—if you take some shared descriptions, assumptions, and hopes for granted.'[45] Rorty denies that it is possible for critical enquiry to precede and determine the nature of the 'we' with which one associates oneself.

My Evaluation

I believe that Rorty can successfully counter the criticism of irrationalism in the ways I have mentioned. I accept that it makes no sense to condemn allegiance to a set of political values as irrational if no such allegiance could be shown to be rational in any appropriately strong sense of that word. I also accept Rorty's claim that the best way to defend liberalism is to compare its values, institutions and practices to those of other societies. This need not be quite so prudential as he sometimes seems to suggest. I would argue instead that the ironist liberal can try to defend her political values by means of more substantive arguments. For example, she could attempt to show that such values can effectively order a society in which due respect is shown to all persons, or that they can help to create a society in which people generally feel more fulfilled, and so on. If asked whether the value of respect for persons is universally or objectively valid, I think that the ironist liberal should turn this question back on the critic. She should challenge this critic to show how any value could be given the sort of foundations which he demands of the liberals' values. If the critic can offer no such demonstration—and I believe he will not be able to do so—then his challenge can be dismissed.

However, I would argue that Rorty's responses to the criticisms of ethnocentrism which I have considered are inadequate. I believe that in some respects his account of ethnocentrism must be supplemented and, in other respects, it must in fact be modified. In order to explain the details of my proposals, I shall separate the following discussion into two parts, each of which will focus on a particular question. The first question is as follows: how does Rorty propose to specify the 'we' with which he identifies for the purpose of considering issues of political justice? The second question asks if and how this 'we' can alter in light of its enquiries into such issues.

As far as the first question is concerned, I would argue that unfortunately things are not as simple as Rorty claims. It is not possible to give one definition of the group referred to as 'we' and then leave it at that. There is no one 'we' which can be identified *in abstracto* since the definition required will vary

49

depending on the context and, in particular, according to the purposes for which the definition is required.

To see what I mean, look again at the account I have just summarised of who Rorty means by 'we'. This is defined in the fairly narrow terms of the political credo that Rorty outlined. This 'we' is to be contrasted with a 'they' comprising of other political groups who oppose this credo. 'They' include 'radicals'—characterised by Rorty in terms of a nostalgia for Marxist terminology and a belief that the use of this terminology can make a useful contribution to a dialectical process in which the evils integral to capitalism will ensure its destruction and so lead to the achievement of socialism.[46] Presumably, 'they' also include the neoconservatives whom Rorty 'is astonished, and alarmed' to find himself grouped with,[47] and whom he characterises in terms of their lack of interest in increasing equality.[48]

Putting aside the question of whether such an account of liberalism's opponents is of any use (particularly the crude parody of 'radicals'), my concern here is to point out that this characterisation of 'we' sits ill at ease with other parts of Rorty's account. For example, on one occasion he seems to use the distinction between *us* and *them* to contrast those to whom we owe an explanation of our actions, and those to whom no such explanation is necessary.[49] But, in this case, 'we' must surely include those neoconservatives and radicals with whom we have substantive political disagreements, although they remain our fellow citizens.[50]

In yet other passages, Rorty seems to define the group he refers to as 'we' in other ways. For example, he sometimes sees 'we' in much broader terms, such that it would include neoconservatives and radicals, but still exclude those he tends to call 'fanatics' or 'fundamentalists'. This might draw the line more successfully between those we liberals can engage in profitable political dialogue with and those with whom such dialogue is impossible. (After all, Rorty's defence of liberalism must in part be addressed to radicals and neoconservatives in the hope of persuading them to change their ways.)

Or, to take a final example, consider again how Rorty tries to defuse criticisms of ethnocentrism by suggesting that 'we liberals' try to see previously isolated and alienated groups as fellow citizens 'by imagination, the imaginative ability to see others as fellow sufferers'. He concludes that '[s]olidarity...is created by increasing our sensitivity to the particular details of the pain and humiliation of other, unfamiliar sorts of people'.[51] But what sense does it make to think of neoconservatives and radicals in this way? I already know that they can be hurt and humiliated in much the same way as I (and my fellow liberals) can be. If, by this criterion, they are part of our group, who is left in the other group? Is there any group that the liberal does and should think incapable of suffering pain and humiliation?

I would argue that the general lesson which should be drawn from these considerations is not that it is impossible to define the group with whom one should identify, but rather that different definitions will be appropriate on different occasions. For this reason, the defence of Rorty's ethnocentrism does not require us to choose any particular group—such as a narrowly defined *social democratic we* or a more broadly defined *modern Western we*. Rather, I would argue each of these different versions may be appropriate on different occasions. Rorty argues that 'feelings of solidarity are necessarily a matter of which similarities and dissimilarities strike us as salient, and that such salience is a function of a historically contingent final vocabulary'.[52] I would want to add that what strikes us as salient depends on our present purposes, and that for different purposes, different accounts of who 'we' are will be relevant. If at a particular moment our concern is to undermine the position of the greedy businessmen and shadowy millionaires who threaten the social democratic political project, then the appropriate we will be something like the first, narrower conception. If, however, our present purpose is to help boost the self-confidence of our liberal society, then the appropriate we will be more like the second, wider conception. Thus I would conclude that it is not possible or necessary to try to answer the question of who 'we' are independent of any particular context. In this case, of course, it becomes imperative for the ironist liberal to be quite clear about the identity of the group she refers to as 'we' in each particular context.[53]

The second question I want to consider is as follows: can this 'we' alter in light of its enquiries into issues of political justice? (And if so how can it alter?) This question can be related back to the disagreement between Foucault and Rorty in which the former contended that the identification of a 'we' should not precede an enquiry into which theories and values to endorse, whilst the latter reiterated his claim that the identification of a 'we' *must* precede the formulation of theoretical propositions or the endorsement of political principles.

I would argue that in fact it is not necessary to contend *either* that the identity of the community of enquiry must be established before a choice of principles can be made *or* that a critical enquiry must precede the identification of the community which is intended to endorse the principles which emerge from that enquiry. Rather, the best account of the relationship of these two elements allows for a dialectical interaction to take place between them. In this way it is not necessary to choose either Foucault's assertion of the question to the community or Rorty's contrary assertion of the community to the question. As long as we accept that both question and community are not fixed, so that both can alter in its interaction with the other, we can avoid either horn of this dilemma.

On the one hand, the question can change the community. To see how this might happen, look at Rorty's insistence that a liberal society is characterised by a constant tendency to expand its moral community—that is, to come to see increasing numbers of people as part of the community to whom we must justify ourselves, the group we can call our fellow citizens. Asking the question, 'who feels pain and suffers humiliation?' can help us see that other groups whom we have previously overlooked should be included in our moral constituency. In this way we may come to realise, for example, 'that women and blacks are capable of more than white males had thought'.[54] (Here, it may be noted, Rorty appears to identify 'us' as 'white males'.)

I think that a simple addition to Rorty's account, which is entirely in keeping with the rest of what he says, would greatly help his case here. My proposal is that he should be prepared to accept that in some cases moral progress is achieved by *decreasing* rather than *increasing* the reference of the group referred to as 'we'. Moral progress can be made by dissociating ourselves from persons previously included in our moral constituency, as well as by trying to increase the numbers of those we seek to include in that constituency. We may find that on reflection there may be people previously included in the group thought of as 'we' whom we now think should not be included in that group. For example, we may come to doubt the commitment of neoconservatives to equalising the life chances of the citizens of our society. Or we believe that we can no longer get on with a group that we thought we could tolerate but who turn out not to respect the ground rules of liberal debate. Allowing for the possibility that moral progress might be a matter of *decreasing* the reference of 'we' would ease at least some of the disquiet felt about Rorty's ethnocentrism.[55]

On the other hand, the community can change the question. To continue the previous example, once women are included in liberal males' moral community, then issues may arise which were not previously considered important. For example, the way in which a distinction between public and private realms can be used to perpetuate female subordination may be raised, and issues such as the politics of personal relations may appear on the liberal political agenda. In other cases, it may be that this dialectical interaction of an enquiring group and the nature of the enquiry it undertakes will have rather more radical consequences. Altering the reference of this group may change the sort of questions the group addresses in such a way that the identity of the group may be altered out of all recognition.

In short, if we take into account the possibility of a dialectical interaction of this kind, we are not forced to choose between a rigid ethnocentrism and Foucault's rather abstract alternative. We can accept that thinking occurs within traditions of thought, whilst allowing the possibility that this process of thought can change the tradition in which it is located. I would suggest that a modification to Rorty's theory of this kind would help to deflect much of the criticism that has been directed against it.

Conclusion

In the course of this paper I have shown why I believe that against critics such as Habermas, Rorty successfully argues that it is pointless to criticise ironist liberalism for its alleged irrationalism. He convincingly shifts the burden of proof onto those who seek to show that all rational persons should endorse a particular set of political principles. Furthermore I would argue that he does offer some kind of argument in favour of a liberal politics, although he admits that the kind of justification he can provide is circular—in that it defends liberalism in its own terms—and must end ultimately in a statement of convictions about which no further argument is possible. Again, the burden of proof is with the metaphysical liberal who would seek to go beyond this.

As far as the charge of ethnocentrism goes, however, I believe that critics such as Foucault have—at the very least—identified certain gaps in Rorty's account. I have therefore suggested a couple of ways in which his account could be supplemented or modified. In particular, I have argued that different conceptions of 'we' are needed at different times; and that there can and must be a dialectical interaction between the community of enquiry and the beliefs and principles which it endorses so that, for example, the reference of this 'we' can decrease as well as increase.

In light of all these considerations, I would suggest that ironist liberalism should not be rejected in the name of a metaphysical sort of liberalism. If, as I believe, the latter theory cannot make good its claim to be able to establish liberal political values on universal and rational grounds, then we are left with Rorty's ironist alternative. This is not to say that we must therefore accept that liberalism is parochial and irrationalist. Rather, since no political theory could meet the standards set by methaphysical liberals, it makes little sense to condemn theories which either try and fail to meet such standards or which, as in the case of Rorty's ironist liberalism, never attempt to achieve these standards in the first place.

PART 2

Problems of Pluralism

(3)

Between the Devil and the Deep Green Sea

Defining Risk Societies and Global Threats

Rosemary McKechnie and Ian Welsh

In this chapter we critically review the arrival of 'risk' and 'trust' as issues in social theory in the 1990s through the work of Ulrich Beck[1] and Anthony Giddens.[2] The social, cultural and theoretical implications of HIV/AIDS and global environmental change constitute the focus of this review as these are both areas where issues of 'risk' and 'trust' are central to both identities of resistance and regulatory regimes and practices. Our major concern here is to argue that the formulations of 'risk' and 'trust' offered by Beck and Giddens, whilst appearing to offer a 'new modernity', reassert a narrow scientific rationality as the basis of reflexivity, effectively blocking the way towards radical renewal. If this is accepted then the transformative potential of the social relations which are seen arising from Beck's postulated 'global risk society' lose the radical veneer suggested by these writers. This has the effect of blunting the transformative potential ascribed to new social movements by both writers. We will argue that reflexivity with sufficient diversity to meet the challenges posed by high modernity can only arise through 'new social movements' if the basis of reflexivity is broadened to include explicitly moral challenges to the dominant social order.

Our position is that the globalisation of thinking in relation to risk and trust obscures the importance of difference and diversity in constituting social actors critical of modernity. Further we will argue that the emphasis on globalisation within these particular works, and social science more generally, should be tempered with some caution. There is a danger that such approaches become part of a specifically Western realist social scientific construction of sets of problems with global reach. Contrary to appearance, risk and trust are not new subjects of academic inquiry within the social sciences.[3] The consideration of issues of public acceptability became formalised between the achievement of commensurability amongst adherents of competing positions[4] and those arguing for the existence of competing rationalities.[5]

This raised wider questions about the relationship between the development of advanced societies, the concentration of complex knowledge and techniques in the hands of scientific and technical communities, and the practice of meaningful democracy. The tensions between the levels of social commitment and institutional certainty required by large-scale technological and scientific developments within discrete nation states had scarcely been engaged with in a serious manner before the implications of human intervention upon external and internal environments in relation to global issues began to be addressed. This elevated the level of debate, with serious implications for both social science as a discipline area based on sets of cognate knowledge and discursive sets of social practices, and the formulation of appropriate collective and individual responses to newly perceived threats.

In short, issues such as the threat to human life on earth arising from the use of nuclear arsenals, ecological catastrophe, and the spread of lethal viral contagions arrive ready-made in much social theory. Threats, particularly threats arising directly from human invention and activity, thus become accommodated as evidence of an abstract capacity of humans to intervene reflexively upon society. The social construction, negotiation, and struggle entered into in the formation of the threat remains an unexamined 'black box'. We will show here that neglecting the contents of this black box produces an over-inclusive view of global threats and reflexivity. In particular we argue that a historical understanding of the development of threats and risks is vital to the consideration of current risk status, risk consciousness, and risk averse behaviours. By developing this argument we go on to suggest a number of refinements to Beck's notion of risk position which avoid the simplistic association between risk consciousness and behaviour present in his original formulation.

In traversing the terrain sketched above we will offer a concise review of the major relevant themes within the work of Beck and Giddens and proceed to elaborate our argument through a consideration of HIV/AIDS, our 'devil', and environmental degradation, our 'deep green sea'. Viral contamination has become a rich metaphor used in a wide range of commentaries upon life in the late twentieth century.[6] The idea of personal contagion and planetary vulnerability have become linked within a variety of discourses.[7] Pollution and the depletion of atmospheric screening agencies act in a similar manner to HIV in that they undermine the ability of ecosystems to withstand attacks which they are normally immunised against. Acid rain, for example, reduces the ability of trees to withstand a range of pests. Friends of the Earth (FOE) directly link such environmental concerns and HIV/AIDS in campaigning material which urges 'us' to save the tropical rainforests as this will slow harmful climate change and preserve the source of potential 'cures for cancer, heart disease and AIDS.'[8] Aside from the organic richness of this metaphor we have a number of explicitly social reasons for selecting this material.

Our concerns here centre on the relationship between activist discourses linking HIV/AIDS and environmental awareness, and expert discourses which seek to establish regulatory regimes and practices capable of intervening to minimise the consequences of such global threats. In particular, we will question the extent to which the dominant discourses generated by regulatory agencies rely, in both cases, on imagery of pollution, death and decay, brought about by lack of individual discipline. This emphasis tends to produce models of control emphasising individual discipline and action to change significant aspects of personal life. Regulatory regimes literally implore us to 'think global act local' whether this be in relation to 'safe' sexual practices, energy use within our own homes or the disposal of our domestic refuse. In following the environmental movement's catchy slogans, attention is diverted away from other possible courses of action based on a range of intermediate collectivities.

The collectivities we have in mind here are capable of an

enormous range of expressions, from new social movements, located categorically within the sphere of civil society, to local and regional government tiers, to the state at a national level. Beyond this level lies the postulated 'world society'[9] where an increasing array of international organisations abrogate increasing amounts of policy related power. Recent literature emphasising globalisation has, we believe, made it easy to underestimate the continued importance of intermediate collectivities whether these be within civil society or the state.[10] We would emphasise that we regard these collectivities as constituted through the operation and interaction of a wide range of processes which can simultaneously produce significant continuities and radical innovations within the social fabric of society.[11]

Modernity, Reflexivity and Risk

Beck and Giddens developed their work independently of one another, though essential similarities in their arguments can be seen to arise from a common preoccupation with the institutional forms of modernity and their capacity reflexively to accommodate radical change. Radical change is seen by both writers as arising through individual lifestyle politics giving rise to new social movement activities. In this way, the institutional dynamics and capacities of modernity contribute to a form of reflexivity constituted by knowledge claims *and* sets of social practices.[12] In essence, individuals have no choice but to confront a range of known, and unknown, risks associated with daily practices and activities.

Beck in particular argues that 'risk' lies across traditional boundaries such as those between theory and practice, value and fact, and across the borders of specialist fields.[13] In the view of both authors risk/trust relations become a central theme around which individual and collective narratives are organised in high modernity.

In this formulation then, there is no absolute rejection of metanarratives, but rather a reflexive accommodation to the ever present discursive formation of previously unperceived risks. The specificity of these risks becomes a seamless web which binds together individuals in a variety of 'risk positions' within the totality of globalised threats to collective existence.[14] Risk positions become formalised when they become known and Beck speaks of them as breaking through a protective shield of taboos to 'be born scientifically in scientized civilisation'.[15] The 'paradigm' case of such hazards for Beck 'is the gene altering effects of radioactivity', which cannot be detected directly by any of the human senses but abandons its victims to 'the judgements, mistakes and controversies of experts', leaving those affected subject to terrible psychological stress.[16]

For Beck particularly the pervasive existential presence of risk position, where consciousness determines being, is the key element in the creation of new identities and new forms of citizens' initiatives.[17] Beck's paradigm case thus has much in common with the HI virus which is equally invisible to the senses, and a potential threat to the entire corpus of the sexually active population so long as disputes over identification of the virus and transmission pathways continue.

Beck's formulation subordinates the designation of risk status to scientific authority in a particularly stark manner, a tendency also present in the work of Giddens. Beck asserts that in order to break the taboos of regulatory institutions 'the victims themselves' must 'make use of all the methods and means of scientific analysis in order to succeed with their claims'.[18] Social groups with the necessary cultural capital and freedom from immediate economic constraints thus become the bearers of the necessary reflexive insights.[19]

When confronted by the conflicting rationality claims of such groups science and other key institutional forms of modernity are portrayed as having 'squandered until further notice their historic reputation for rationality...until they have learned self-critically and practically to accept the consequences for this'.[20] In a revealing passage Beck thus argues that the necessary realignment of fields of expert knowledge becomes 'the cardinal problem of systems theory and organization'.[21] Similarly, Giddens considers that the reflexive appropriation of knowledge becomes 'integral to system reproduction'.[22] Such concerns with systems theory and system reproduction belie an incipient functionalism[23] in the work of both authors which leaves bodies of expertise already established within the system beyond the boundaries of reflexive challenge mounted by the victims of modernity.

Beck's discussion of reflexivity within science further substantiates this observation. Here the transformative agency is the 'discipline of the critical application of science to itself'.[24] Expert conflict in the public realm between representatives of competing scientific factions creates situations where the appearance of competence becomes crucial.[25]

What is evident here is a faith, on the behalf of both writers, that in the late twentieth century there can be an application of scientific scepticism to the canons of institutionalised scientific inquiry. Internal scientific disputes over boundaries and problem definition, as well as appropriate methodology, are argued to combine with the public relativisation of scientific claims to produce a societal reappraisal of the scientific enterprise. Within this the veil of objectivity 'is systematically researched away in reflexive scientization'.[26] For Beck at least then the 'critique of risks is not a normative critique of values', and he goes further in asserting that the scientific determination of risk does not 'assert moral standards openly, but in the form of quantitative, theoretical and causal implicit morality'.[27]

In Beck's formulation the implicit morality mentioned represents another black box. In our view even the narrow questioning of scientifically determined standards and values *is* a moral challenge to the institutional integrity and practices of 'high modernity'. Scientific risk assessment is rarely a matter of pure science but also involves political and economic determination. To question numerical pollution limits derived from the institutional repertoire of modernity is thus to question not only the hallowed status of science but also the status of other key institutions and values of society such as democracy. To challenge one value element is thus to challenge the whole edifice of scientific, technical and social regulation. Once scientific standards become subject to legitimation stripping, the whole interlocking edifice of 'high modernity' is placed at risk.

Beck's analysis suggests that the institutional structure of modernity can survive such a radical unpacking of its regimes of legitimation. For this to occur some version of Habermas's ideal speech situation has to be possible for the opposing social forces to communicate. The standard institutional response to critics of 'acceptable limits' and 'existing best practices' continues to be an assault on their credibility via appeal to other central values. An important consequence of this for reflexivity is that dissenters tend to be marginalised and ascribed oppositional identities on the basis of a range of social, cultural, political and moral categories. In our view this insulates the institutional forms of modernity from significant sources of reflexivity.

The Devil

In this section we examine further the 'implicit' nature of morality in relation to science. Here we follow cultural and historic analyses of science which have emphasised the way moral evaluations are embedded in scientific accounts of the natural world.[28] The ambiguities involved in definitions of 'risk' in relation to HIV epidemics indicate the problems inherent in the assumption that a critique of risks can be separated from a critique of values. It is significant that the group first touched by the epidemic in the West, gay men, were already marginalised. The basis of gay identity is behaviour which has historically been defined as deviant by medical science. As Weeks points out, a disease came to symbolise 'the perils of living outside the norm. It came to represent the fruits of permissiveness.'[29] The stigmata of the diseases associated with the syndrome added to pre-existing stigma. It was a set of diseases with a 'medico-moral history'[30] that shaped institutional responses. Those affected could be dismissed as already morally tainted, resulting in the portrayal of AIDS as the result of moral slackness.[31]

The outcome of the way the first observations of the virus elided identification of 'risk' with the identification of difference was to focus scientific research and publication on 'lifestyle' as a risk factor.[32] The consequences of conceptualising risk in terms of 'risk groups' rather than 'risk behaviours' have been analysed by several commentators.[33] The definitional process not only isolated 'risk' within these groups, but transformed these groups into the 'risk' which had to be controlled in order to protect wider society. This led to cultural boundaries between normal and deviant or marginal identities being exacerbated, and fused measures for control of HIV with moral evaluations of difference. As the spread of the disease touched on not only those of 'deviant' lifestyle such as gay men, IV drug-users and sex-workers, but the poor and ethnic minorities, then 'culture' came to be used in a similar way, as a fixed boundary that both contained the risk group and also the key to why they were being particularly affected by the virus.[34]

As Leap points out, AIDS has become a signifier, entering into the definition of, amongst other things, social structure.[35] The new signifier is integrated into existing processes of definition, in which individuals, groups and dominant society are all participating. The way in which individuals bind together in risk positions, the creation of new identities, does not happen in an historical vacuum: the historical processes of moral definitions within which science is bound up contributes to the determinacy that shapes new formations.

The neglect of the moral dimension has serious consequences for the way both Giddens and Beck conceptualise social space. Giddens develops Durkheim's insights that development of logical conformity was a necessary first step to moral conformity.[36] However, by focusing on the way an increasingly coherent conceptualisation of time and space combines with innovatory communication technology to render geographically wide areas of social space uniform, Giddens neglects the way the same process can also formalise and multiply cultural and social boundaries. As the potential for surveillance increases, the density of information concerning society is enhanced, and the way this information is ordered creates discontinuities in the social fabric.[37] Bauman has emphasised the importance of the increasing power of modern society to organise and mobilise a moral order on the basis of 'rationality'. In his analysis an increasingly bureaucratic culture prompts us to view society as an object of administration, as a collection of so many problems to be solved.[38] It is within this dynamic definitional context, where moral boundaries can be erected to distance and marginalise difference, that social movements are formed. Social movement identity is thus

constituted by both internal and external processes of definition and selection.

Treichler has accepted that basic scientific research on
immunology, virology and epidemiology were able, because of
progress in the last 20 years, to make advances in knowing
HIV. But she also points out, following Simon Watney, that
investigations of the last two decades provide a crucial foundation for the analysis of AIDS in the human sciences as well.[39]
Such a foundation prepares us to analyse AIDS in relation to
questions of language, representation, the mobilisation of
cultural narratives, ideology, social and intellectual differences
and hierarchies, binary divisions, interpretation, and contests
for meaning.[40] It could be argued that this aspect has provided
an important dynamic in both constituting and contesting 'risk
positions'.

The gay community has mounted an impressive vocal
challenge shaping perceptions of risk in relation to HIV/AIDS.
This challenge has resituated scientific knowledge concerning
the virus, by rendering explicit the forces that have tied
knowledge of viral behaviour to economic, political and
symbolic marginalisation. The critical contextualisation of
scientific formulations of risk has enabled the gay movement to
mobilise definitions of risk that are meaningful and useful to
members of this collectivity without stigmatising actions
integral to their identity. This process of self-definition has
been crucial in gaining support and resources for appropriate
care and research.

It is, however, important to note that while the gay
movement has provided a set of coherent challenges organising
individual and collective narratives, other groups which have
been disproportionately affected by the HIV epidemic have not.
As social researchers have pointed out, the categories of
definition which policy makers and epidemiology work with,
such as 'Hispanic', 'African-American', 'Prostitutes', or 'drug
users' often bear little relationship to people's own self-
identification,[41] or the significant local community groupings
within which understandings of the virus and responses to it
develop.[42] Neither did approaches which visualised 'lifestyle' as
a risk factor encompass the economic and political relations that
structured these groups' position vis-a-vis wider society.[43] As

Quimby points out, the generic structural inequalities that created poverty, lack of access to education, health-care and basic needs shape everyday experiences within which the risk of HIV infection can have a low priority.[44] The determinants of risk position can overlap with factors inhibiting the mobilisation of challenging identity formation. Conceptualising society as an undifferentiated space, within which individuals can take a number of 'risk-positions' regardless of pre-existing boundaries organised through economic, political, social and moral categories, overlooks important historical forces that contribute to the structuring of responses to risk. This insight from this brief consideration of HIV/AIDS draws attention to the need for a historical analysis of social forces shaping contemporary concerns frequently presented as issues of risk perception. The need for such an approach becomes pronounced in a consideration of Beck and Giddens' formulation of the role of new social movements as agencies of reflexive modernisation.

For both Beck and Giddens, new social movements become the bearers of reflexively gained knowledge claims which are reflected in a range of legitimation stripping activities directed towards key institutions of modernity. For the reflexive modernisation of modernity to be an achievable social project several conditions must be met. First, it is crucial that the combined knowledge claims, and the social forms of representation evolved around new social movements, are 'heard' and responded to within the institutions subject to their reflexive intervention. This would constitute a minimal condition for reflexive modernity to become attainable. For a reflexive modernity to be fully realised, however, a second criterion must be fulfilled. This would require recognition that the ultimately moral messages that the victims of modernity bear must also be 'heard'. It will be our argument that there needs to be much greater attention given to the interaction between social movement and institutional actors in both of these spheres. It is far from clear that Beck's analysis permits this task as he asserts that such interactions must be on scientific terms.[45]

This moral realm is of vital importance because reflexivity is not solely a matter of knowledge claims. As Beck recognises, supplying social movement activists with information will not make their protests go away. Such deficit models of public understanding of science and scientific issues are the subject of a sustained critique elsewhere.[46] What is at stake here is the limitation of the reflexive loop to include only those willing and capable of intervening from within the discourse of science. This denies the possibility that various publics evaluate the practices of institutional actors by other means derived from moral categories. Far from being peripheral to definitional debates, negotiation of legitimacy often takes place on moral, rather than 'rational' or 'factual' grounds. Critical reflexivity arises from the application of a range of moral perceptions. These include perceptions of justice in dealings, the appearance of trustworthiness on the behalf of the representatives of institutions, and the application of locally generated knowledges to expert discourses.[47]

Explicitly moral evaluations also evoke a range of other cultural registers which provide grounds for reflexive contestation. Culturally specific notions of natural beauty and wilderness experienced in childhood can, for example, lead to opposition to nuclear developments in adulthood.[48] Nor can such responses be dismissed as mere NIMBYism, as they constitute the logical development of a personal narrative which prioritises specific sites of resistance in relation to wider knowledge-based perceptions of issues. The point of significance here is that it is the transgression of the remembered childhood wilderness as a cultural and symbolic token, and identification with others sharing this aesthetic appreciation, which initiates the reflexive intervention, rather than knowledge claims specific to the present. Such personal narratives can also be mobilised in order to justify and legitimate decisions taken by those responsible for regulation within the institutions of modernity.[49]

In summary, we believe the construction of personal narratives, the self-identification that permits individuals to form significant shared associations within which they can take a meaningful 'risk position', are constituted through a much wider base than scientific formulation of risk.

Identity and Social Movement

In this section we want to explore the relationship between processes of identification and the formation of 'new' social movements. The importance of elaborating these concerns arises from the tendency for much social theory to postulate social movement activity as an important new dimension of socially organised conflict within high modernity.[50] Despite this, the means through which social movements constitute themselves, the processes by which social movements prioritise and select objects of opposition, the ways in which discourses of challenge and critique are formed, and a host of other issues of central importance, remain seriously under-researched.[51] An important consequence of this for the work of both Beck and Giddens is that the constitution of the social movements they refer to is never specified.

We have already criticised Beck's work for the tendency to prioritise scientific knowledge as the basis for social movement formation at the expense of more moral sensibilities. Giddens' work on the breakdown of trust relations as part of the process of social movement formation emphasises a wider set of relations apparently escaping the scientific foundationalism of Beck. The formulations of trust and faith offered by Giddens in relation to these constitutive practices of social movements are, however, problematic as a consequence of their psychological rigidity. The role of faith and trust in the constitution of self-identity for Giddens is determined by the initial negotiation of relationships with significant others during infancy.[52] Giddens thus argues for a link between the kind of trust relations developed within infancy and adult relations with the risk society. The connection is so problematic that it is worth quoting the relevant piece of text in full:

> Basic trust is a screening-off device in relation to risks and dangers in the surrounding settings of action and interaction. It is the main emotional support of a defensive carapace or *protective cocoon* which all normal individuals carry around with them as the means whereby they are able to get on with the affairs of day to day life.[53]

Though Giddens chooses to emphasise cocoon, the more telling term is carapace—a hard exogenous shell. In our view there are fundamental problems in constituting emotional processes of trust negotiation between infant and parent as the foundation of adult relations with expert systems and risk society. In Giddens' account the contours of this carapace effectively define the capacity for individual trust relations in general, trust in institutions, and the limits of individuals' ability to sustain their own narrative in relation to the social environment.[54]

Whilst sharing Giddens' arguments about the continual negotiation and maintenance of self-identity through a process of individual reflexivity, we would wish to prioritise a number of other significant mediating factors of a more social nature in determining trust relations between adults and the institutions of modernity. Such trust relations do not only occur on a day-to-day basis. The institutions encountered by denizens of the risk society have institutional histories and cultures. Institutions such as the nuclear enterprise may still be organisationally imbued with the ethos of a past era within which they could treat the public with contempt and arrogance. The modern protestor's relationship with her parents is only one possible mediating factor on this objective social relationship which determines social distance in a crucial manner within ascribed sets of power relations.

Equally it would seem from empirical observation that life-cycle characteristics are at least as important in citizen/expert system confrontations than any unfolding psychological framing factor. Individual leaps to scepticism can coincide with fundamental changes in personal identity mediated through change in occupational status, sexual orientation, career status and a range of other destabilising events. Rather than being the product of individual capacity for emotional security, bounded by experience in infancy, trust relations should be conceived of as predominantly social relations through which collective power is exercised and contested. There is then room to discuss life cycles of individuals and institutions in terms of their articulation of faith and trust relations. It is in the articulation of these social relationships that social movements are formed around specific issues.

A further feature of the work of Beck and Giddens that has serious implications for their arguments is the manner in which the strong case for reflexivity, that is, the threat of nuclear accident, ionizing radiation, or nuclear holocaust, arrives within their sociological discourse pre-formed.[55] In arguing for trust relation as a theoretical category the social and cultural organisation of power within specific institutions of high modernity constitutes another black box, particularly within Giddens' work. This is particularly pronounced in the discussion of 'portals of access' where 'face work' occurs and where expert discourse is presented as being particularly vulnerable.[56]

Beck is more sophisticated here in some respects, and emphasises the way in which engagement in legitimation-stripping activities brings social movement actors into contact with a multi-faceted 'bureaucracy of knowledge', with Kafkaesque 'long corridors, waiting benches, responsible, semi-responsible, and incomprehensible shoulder-shruggers and poseurs'.[57]

This gives a sense of the immense power relations embodied in the institutional fora through which scientific and expert challenges to the machinations of high modernity *must* be mounted to have legitimacy *within* the terms laid down by its overarching discourse of high science. In the case of Beck the evil which is to be overcome is the centrality of positivist reductionist science with its demands for causal proof of the dangers of modernisation risks. Despite recognition of the labyrinthine nature of the beast, little attention is given to the processes by which his limited reflexive modernisation of modernity could come about.

Whilst Beck argues that the consequences of modernisation risks can only be 'forced on the sciences...by way of public recognition', and that these disputes are based not on 'intrascientific' concerns but 'overall social definitions and relationships', the ultimate 'agents of rupture are the disciplines of the critical application of science to itself'.[58] Leaving the resolution of reflexive crisis in the hands of the 'ultimate agents of rupture' is unlikely to constitute any resolution at all. Applying the reflexivity of science to science would, we believe, result in business as usual, and afterwards, to paraphrase Beck's

70

formulation of his original problem, the two sides would *still* be talking past each other.

Without a consideration of the social and cultural nature of the *institutions* of science, the associated regulatory bodies, including the relevant political offices, *and* the relationships between them and a diverse range of constituent publics, the whole process would merely set the scene for a further round of new, revealed risk locations which would struggle for recognition. It is our view that an essential part of the contestation of high modernity through social movement activity is precisely a struggle for the establishment of a number of morally credible trajectories of future development. For such trajectories to be meaningful, the social and cultural *negotiation* of a range of futures which are collectively worth striving for is required. Commitment to cultural negotiation would embrace the idea of a diversity of radical movements, none of which seeks to impose a particular 'truth' or moral order on humanity in the name of its own version of liberty.

The Deep Green Sea

Initiatives for the regulation of global environmental change provide a particularly rich source of material through which to illustrate some of the ways in which activist, academic and political initiatives in the environmental arena fall short of this kind of negotiation. If HIV/AIDS is our 'devil', a threat posed in terms of well established categories of social demonology, then the environment constitutes the all encompassing green sea. The environment serves the dual symbolic role of provider and potential destroyer of human effort. The transcendence of environmental constraints through social and technical innovation has been one of the hallmarks of high modernity, where domination of the natural world has been taken for granted. Despite a wave of environmental concern as recently as the 1970s, the rapid rise of environmental issues which took place from 1987 onwards has come to be regarded by many as a 'new' phenomenon. Though less well known than the history of sexuality, environmental concerns can be traced at least as far back into history.[59]

The 1980s' wave of environmental concern was distinctive in that for the first time the rise in profile involved prominent world leaders and international organisations. Involvement was a response to the prominence achieved by notable works such as *Our Common Future*[60] described by some commentators as 'The landmark 1987 report on common challenges'.[61] Brundtland captured the attention of many heads of government, including the British prime minister Margaret Thatcher, and coincided with increasing international concern over global climate change. The elevation of environmental concerns in the international agenda culminated in the 'Earth Summit' held under the auspices of the United Nations in Rio de Janeiro during June 1992.

For some, the prospect of world leaders appropriating the discourse on the future of the environment raised the spectre of Andre Gorz's sentiments that 'Ecology is like universal suffrage' in that the ruling elites denounce it as unthinkable subversion until they are forced to embrace it in the face of rising popular pressure. At this point 'what was unthinkable yesterday becomes taken for granted today, and fundamentally nothing changes.'[62] The fact that the Summit was sponsored by the United Nations Committee on Environment and Development heightened such suspicions in the minds of those who regard 'environment' and 'development' as mutually contradictory terms.

The mechanics of the summit were centred around the enunciation of an 'Earth Charter' which would establish principles which should guide human environment interactions into the next century. The Charter was to be accompanied by a programme of action known as 'Agenda 21'. Long before the summit, national coalitions of environmental and ecological activists were lobbying national governments in the North on how they should respond to Agenda 21.[63] Fears that such fringe messages would go unheard continued to mount and increasingly focused on the right of Non Governmental Organisations (NGOs) to have full rights of representation within the summit. This pressure was partially successful with 1,400 NGOs, predominantly 'sophisticated and well funded North American ones', gaining accreditation to the official summit. Fifteen of these were integrated within national delegations.[64] The final compromise reached was for there to be a parallel NGO summit which would produce independent statements on 'Agenda 21' alongside the main 'summit'.

Before the summit convened it was clear that there was a pre-formed activist agenda which could be seen to rank nation states in terms of their environmental political correctness. Key in this respect was allegiance to preserving biodiversity. Concern with biodiversity was tied to a wide range of other issues, prime amongst which was deforestation, a key activity leading to species destruction in tropical rainforests. In the run-up to the summit key rhetorical devices began to construct a discourse which maximised the pressure on world leaders to act in these apparently decisive areas.

The rhetorical devices relied heavily upon collectivising 'global' images, evoking 'common problems' requiring co-operation in the achievement of 'common' solutions. There was thus a focus on a collective present containing a series of collective issues requiring collective action through the endorsement of Agenda 21. As with earlier Global initiatives, such as the Intergovernmental Panel on Climate Change (IPCC), the portrayal of such an easily won consensus on what was to be achieved and how to set about the process proved false.

The second focus of rhetorical construction was centred around a series of issues which raised issues of inter-generational justice. The centre piece here was the obligation to leave an earth worth inheriting by future generations. In its purest moral form arguments about the central value of biodiversity are frequently couched in these terms. The diverse bounty of nature is to be valued in and of itself irrespective of any material benefit which may accrue to humankind. Such rich-ness is seen as providing a psychological or spiritual benefit to human subjects and is typically associated with 'Deep Ecologists'.[65]

There is a marked symmetry between these rhetorical devices and the formalisation of 'risk', trust, identity and reflexive social action considered in the early part of this chapter. This symmetry is at its strongest in relation to the globalising assumptions attributed to environmental processes where an unspecified 'we' share a 'common' fate. The Rio summit shattered any illusion about the possibility of an easily shared global agenda. Particular issues such as biodiversity revealed just how fractured prospects for such a shared agenda were. Biodiversity, whilst constituting a category of environmental concern around which it is relatively easy to demonstrate widespread concern, proved to be a term bearing very different sets of social meanings for conflicting sets of actors.

When tied to deforestation some heads of government baldly asserted their right to log their forests, pointing to the fact that the developed North had already done so, extinguishing whole species in the process. Why should there be a dual standard? US President George Bush attended the summit, and defended the American decision not to sign the biodiversity treaty on the grounds that it was tantamount to signing a blank cheque to the future. The resultant furore led to speculation that environment and development issues would create tensions on a scale similar to the recently ended Cold War, whilst others regarded the summit as a source of considerable opportunities for the US.[66]

The Ecologist described the summit as a victory for the World Bank, the US and the 'free market environmentalism' of the transnational corporations. Environmental groups which had found direct representation as part of government delegations were regarded as successfully co-opted to an UNCED initiative which had 'condemned itself to irrelevance' before it had even started. Against the array of 'vested interests' represented, *The Ecologist* emphasised the 'moral economies' of local people faced with daily struggles for survival against environmental degradation. *The Ecologist* asserted these communities' right to 'reject UNCED's rhetoric of a world where all humanity is united by a common interest in survival', and declared the urgent need to reinstate their communities as sources of social and political authority.[67]

What the Earth Summit revealed was that academic and activist attempts to portray as ascendant a series of globalising discourses are premature. Much more attention needs to be directed towards understanding the environment as a site where a number of competing and conflicting sets of interests meet and intersect, producing complex articulations of interests and meanings. Such conflicts appear set to become significant means by which the hegemony of Northern interests will become challenged through some key institutions of modernity.

The Earth Summit established the Sustainable Development Commission as a new organ within the UN as part of the Economic and Social Council.[68] Since the Earth Summit the Non-aligned Movement has begun to consolidate around demands for autonomously determined, environmentally sound development packages. The Non-aligned Movement thus will become the source of a range of country specific environment and development demands upon the global organs of modernity. Such demands will increasingly challenge the global reach of institutions used to dictating the terms of development packages.

These attempts to establish meaningful expressions of collective autonomy have parallels in relation to HIV/AIDS. For example, the deployment of expertise and resources to counteract the epidemic in the developing nations has been dominated by Western financial and bio-medical concerns. At a global level, the decisions that have been made have frequently bypassed governmental agencies, channelling funds through global NGOs, raising complex issues of accountability and questioning the possibility of co-operative diversity. The complex interplay of significant relations of risk and trust that are involved takes place on multiple sites, between individuals, local communities, self-identified movements and wider society, and internationally between nations and global institutions. The diverse conflicts of interest at every level are not easily resolved. This factor is compounded by the range of culturally specific interpretations affecting perceptions of the virus and appropriate risk behaviour.[69]

In these senses *difference* and social *diversity* are far more important than ideas about a 'global risk society'. Before this term can serve any useful purposes whatsoever it requires further elaboration and refinement. The Earth Summit, and the case of HIV/AIDS, suggest the following terms as means of refining Beck's conception of 'risk position'. First, it is vital to think about risk positions in terms of distance from the point of contamination/degradation. Second, it is vital also to perceive risk position in terms of distance from the portals of access described by Giddens. In both these terms distance is to be understood as a relation which situates the individual vis-á-vis a particular process of environmental threat within the context of a particular site. This need not be a relation of spatial distance but could be a matter of gender, age, occupational status, etc.

This kind of differentiation requires a more sophisticated interpretation of 'risk positions'. Even taking Beck's prime example of ionising radiation such terms offer a better under-standing by being able to accommodate the differentiated human response to ionising radiation. Here age and gender are key distancing mechanisms with radio-sensitivity being highest in the womb and lowest in old age. Similarly in the case of HIV infection, individuals' ability to distance themselves from threat can be dependent upon their power to demand that a condom be used for penetrative sex.[70] This is thus a more nuanced relationship than that argued by Beck where risk 'knows none of the distinctions which our world has constructed'.[71]

Distance from portals of access is also ascribed through a wide range of social categories. Here characteristics demarcat-ing boundaries of inclusion and exclusion can be subsumed under the heading of cultural capital. Without the necessary cultural resources participation is foreclosed, and attempted participation becomes subject to sanctions. Contestation at this level can also be aimed at undermining the legitimacy of the organisational forms of high modernity. Such legitimation stripping is frequently based upon a moral agenda which denies the ability of such fora adequately to represent democratic process, ensure justice, or a rational outcome. Such positions are frequently derived from the moral prioritisation of other means and other ends.

Conclusions

In this chapter we have argued that inclusionary theorising within the social sciences orientated around notions of globalisation and an unspecified 'we' are unhelpful in framing approaches towards specific problem domains. This argument has been elaborated in terms of problem domains within advanced industrialised societies and domains which span the North/South divide. In both cases we would argue that inclusionary theorising acts, perhaps unintentionally, as a trojan horse which smuggles implicit and explicit Northern interests into the heart of debates where pluralistic acceptance, or at least recognition, of diversity are crucially important.

Risk and trust relations are, we believe, important dimensions of social scientific endeavour required to understand and locate the human condition in the late twentieth century. Present formulations, as we have shown here, lack the analytical flexibility and sophistication to accommodate the diversity of actually existing risk locations generated by the advance of high modernity. By approaching this problematic through the categories of distance from the points of absorption/degradation and distance from the portals of access relevant to a particular site of action, we believe that substantive progress can be made in relation to these areas of study.

In relation to HIV/AIDS, when the distance between a subject and the point of contamination is effectively zero the process of 'scientisation of science' becomes a luxury. The finitude made apparent by such a position calls into question many of the ethical and moral issues associated with standards of clinical practice developed within medical science. It remains a moot point whether or not environmental degradation has begun to assume a similar position for certain groups.

What is clear is that the pathways for socially organised conflicts to occur outlined by both Beck and Giddens do not allow the full range of collective reflexivity to be accommodated. Awareness of risk positions as scientised discourse in the countries of the North takes place in parallel with a reflexive moral agenda. This questions the justice in dealings and equity of risk distributions within advanced societies. These processes of prioritisation are shadowed by other moral economies from the South which seek a different range of justice in dealings. Attempts to incorporate these concerns by postulating a 'globalised risk society' and the reversal of environmental degradation via the adoption of 'new lifestyle patterns'[72] are profoundly problematic in this respect. The scientisation of risk not only forecloses the moral concerns of social movement actors in the North, it also prioritises a discourse which is global in its foundationalist claims.

Both the substantive formulations considered here thus prioritise means of taming the juggernaut of modernity which represent means of increasing the functional domination of the North's capitalist interests. The environment will continue to be a site of high pressure marketing and commodification for consumption by those able to adopt the 'new lifestyle patterns' on offer. Meanwhile the global social science discourse will risk continuing, by other means, the imperialism of previous ages.

We remain convinced that the limitation of expressions of collective reflexivity to the 'scientisation of science' will satisfy neither the moral aspirations of the North nor the South. As Shiva, notes 'The old order does not change through environmental discussions. It gets more entrenched.' The ability of the North to promulgate a discourse of 'globalisation' gives the North 'global reach' akin to the 'administrative reach' attributed to the nation state by Giddens.[73] This discourse makes the North the globalised local, prioritising international fora as the arenas where conceptualisation of problems and thus knowledge-power resides. In this sense Shiva argues that the global 'only exists in offices of the World Bank and IMF and the headquarters of multinational corporations'. For her 'Global Ecology at this level becomes the moralization of immorality': empty of ethics and concepts of solidarity, it is nothing more than 'universal bullying.'[74]

(4)

Ordering the City
Public Spaces and Political Participation

Judith Squires

> The diverse and different populations of cities must
> be seen as active political entities constituted
> through...encounters and confrontations, and urbanity
> must be a consequence of the bargaining and
> negotiation this makes necessary. For this we need
> 'tougher' notions of public space.
>
> Kevin Robins[1]

There is an increasingly prevalent concern with the creation of
new public spaces in our cities. It is not only cultural critics, but
also planners and property developers who are now showing a
renewed interest in the nature and quality of urban life. There
is a new consensual belief in 'public space'—the idea that a city
should create some sort of communal space for shared activity.[2]
There is also a renewed articulation, amongst social and political theorists, of the importance of the revival of the public
sphere. This renewed focus on the public sphere is manifest, in
various forms, within several distinct political perspectives of
current vogue. The communitarian political theorists, drawing
on a civic republican tradition, emphasise the public as the site
of a political community held together by a substantive idea of
the common good. This public sphere is constituted by a
cohesive community with shared values and commitments and
is therefore characterised by consensus and commonality. In
direct contrast, postmodern political theory, drawing on the
Derridean notion of difference and Lacanian notion of the

79

Other, views the public as a site of diversity, plurality and contestation. Situated somewhere between these two perspectives is a form of 'radical pluralism' which is characterised by the desire both to acknowledge plurality and celebrate the potential of difference, and to insist upon the need for a shared 'grammar of conduct', a common commitment—not to substantive ends—but to procedural mechanisms and political (as opposed to moral) values.[3]

Given this parallel concern with a rejuvenated public sphere within both political theory (in various guises) and current urban theory and policy, I am interested to explore whether the practical developments in the city realise the aspirations of any of these theoretical perspectives. I shall also reflect upon the extent to which the actual developments in the city provide insights into the adequacy, or otherwise, of the various theoretical perspectives outlined. In short, I want to explore what is to be learnt from the attempt to map the theoretical discourses of the democratic public sphere onto the practical attempt of urban planners and postmodern architects to revive our public spaces.

As Habermas used the method of immanent critique to compare the concept of the public sphere with its limited and distorted historical embodiments,[4] so I shall attempt to compare the rhetoric which abounds about the importance of the public sphere with the reality of the public spaces which are being created within our cities.

Joy in the City: Simultaneity, Contradiction and Spectacle

> This order is all composed of movement and change and although it is life, not art, we may fancifully call it the art form of the city and liken it to a dance.
> Jane Jacobs[5]

The seduction of the city was the subject of many of the key writings of modernity: the public spaces of the city as a space of pleasure, ecstasy and desire. The city as endless possibility. A confusion of happenings which one can never quite see, under-stand, order, because they occur simultaneously.

This vision of the city celebrates spectacle and revels in expression in its most theatrical forms. The concern with fashion, presentation of self, 'the look', it is argued, mobilises spectacle and display to celebrate cultural differentiation. Indeed, as Sennett has noted, the modern meaning of the public jelled around the same times as the body as mannequin took form.[6] Clothes to be worn in public became ostentatious and expressive; a symbol of social interaction. The public spaces created by city life, this argument goes, allow for a form of social interaction which rests on spectacle and performance, and hence enable a process of becoming and identifying.

For, as situated selves our being is relational, it is con-structed through engagement with others, it exists not within us, but between us. As we meet, clash, interfuse, so we become. And, as Arendt has classically stated, 'action needs for its full appearance the shining brightness we once called glory, and which is possible only in the public realm.'[7] The visual, the gestural, the sensual are all important modes of self-definition, of acting in the world. The communication of the city is then much more rich than simple discourse, it also about spectacle: the unconscious bodily aspect of utterance—rhythm, tone, gesture.

This urban consciousness was celebrated by the *flaneurs* of the mid-nineteenth century who relished the kaleidoscope of urban public life; who rejected the 'official' city, preferring the marginal. It was not the grandeur and pomp of the city that they relished, but the fragmented, ambiguous disorder of the city.[8] Here was the beginning of an urban consciousness, articulated most famously by Baudelaire: 'The life of our city is rich in poetic and marvellous subjects....The pageant of fashio-nable life and the thousands of floating existences which drift about in the underworld of a great city.'[9] A life, he argued, which grasps the ephemeral, the fugitive, the contingent. The city as desire: the public as performance.

Fear in the City: Order, Uniformity and Exclusion

> With cities it is as with dreams: everything imagin-
> able can be dreamed, but even the most unexpected
> dream...conceals a desire, or its reverse, a fear. Cities,
> like dreams, are made of desire and fears, even if the
> thread of their discourse is secret, their rules are
> absurd, their perspective deceitful, and everything
> conceals something else.
>
> Italo Calvino[10]

But there is also the city as fear: being both utterly alone and always surrounded, facing its perils, without stable limits. The public as a hostile, aggressive and threatening experience lacking the intimacy and security of the 'haven of privacy'. This is a vision of the public more often articulated by those lacking power within the public: to be found more readily in the writing of women than men. The female *flaneur*, Janet Wolff has noted, is significantly absent from the literature of modernity.[11]

Though Marshall Berman claims[12] that the celebration of urban vitality, diversity and fullness of life is one of the oldest themes in modern culture, to focus on this celebration without an accompanying recognition that such celebration was experienced only by some, and at the expense of others, is to further marginalise the voices of the powerless. The exclusion from, or marginalisation, sequestration and policing of some from the public is as long-standing (though less vocal) an experience. Those who celebrate the excitement and vitality of the public spaces of the city are no doubt those who enjoy the privilege of being able to withdraw from them, to return to the security of the private realm—the 'haven in a heartless world'.

Desire and fear. It is the tension between these two that has generated debate about the city and its public spaces ever since its development. The city has been the site of a perpetual struggle between twin visions of simultaneity and spectacle on the one hand and uniformity and exclusion on the other. If many nineteenth-century writers celebrated the former, we have also been presented throughout history with visions of the perfect ordered city, a city that would solve all the problems of people. A city based on order and security, and assuming the power of exclusion.

LITTLE TOWN OF NO MAYHEM
This, our little town, is surrounded by beauty; at first sight the town might be thought beautiful (or elegant, a sad second). But it isn't. Garden walls of houses fronting on the park, topped with iron spikes and barbed wire, but interrupted and thus made purposeless by pretty little gates: that says it all. This town doesn't want to know you, or me, or anything but what is already here, in the neat flower beds, in nice plastic bags in the shops. Nor will it want us to know it. The place is crawling with taboos. You can smell them. Everyone is bent over under the weight of 'em. Little rouged lavender-watered town.

Tod McEwan[13]

There is no mayhem in this life, this space; none of the motion and turbulence that makes the city so appealing.

This is the antithesis of city life: the small town idyll of utopians and town planners alike. Think of Milton Keynes and Cumbernauld; think of these and the appeal of the city intensifies. But think also of New Lanark, Port Sunlight and Saltaire; model towns built as the product of utopian vision, a desire to impose order and control, a fear of the chaos and excess of cities. There is no space to initiate, to act, to spark off new beginnings. Neither is there acceptance of plurality, heterogeneity and difference. Garden-cities, newtowns and urban utopias can all be seen as attempts at creating perfect cities, localised community feeling. They were, essentially, the small town within a city; an embodiment in stone of a political order. Town planning, like utopian writing, aimed to offer a permanent solution to the flux and flow of the city.

It is perhaps an irony, then, that the original 'Utopia' as envisaged by Thomas More embodied not a firm conviction in the possibility or desirability of such an ordered city, but a sense of ambivalence.[14] The first and second books of *Utopia* represent between them these twin visions of the city: the poverty, excess and iniquity of the existing cities: the restraint, order and uniformity of nowhere land. In this, More provides a clear articulation of the paradoxical possibilities of the city: neither vision, in isolation, we are left to infer, is truly desirable.

In cities which are inevitably diverse and complex, cohesion can only be achieved at the cost of a false sense of unity. The communities which are a product of such a project devalue complexity, difference and contradiction: unity and order are achieved through the repression of all difference, and the exclusion of those who cannot conform. For actual people are complex, difficult and plural; they are not easily planned for; they are likely to reject, to graffiti and trash one's utopian vision made concrete.

My point is that unless we recognise, and accept, that it is precisely the variety of opportunity, the profusion of pleasure, the flux and flow of the city that makes it exciting and desirable, we will not be able to create and maintain cities which articulate and fulfil genuine desires. Yet, unless we also acknowledge the power relations within such spaces which serve to police and marginalise many within the public spheres, or to exclude and deny others altogether from within its remit, we are in danger of presenting a falsely 'utopian' vision of the public. In the words of Elizabeth Wilson:

> We will never solve the problems of living in cities until we welcome and maximise the freedom and autonomy they offer and make these available to all classes and groups.[15]

Postmodern Cities: Strategies for Urban Renaissance

A renewed vision of the city is becoming an increasingly prevalent part of our contemporary political rhetoric. And whilst political theorists and cultural critics analyse, postmodern architects and planners build.

The key to the rejuvenation of the city, we are being told, lies in the recreation of its public spaces and the corresponding revival of sense of community. Public spaces, it is all too frequently claimed, will facilitate the development of political participation and bring about a sense of communal belonging.

These arguments tend to be based on the assumption that we are living in a period of great spatial upheaval, of globalisation, of increasingly complex communication networks: in a period of 'time-space compression'.[16] It is also argued that these developments work to disrupt local communities and disturb location-based identities. The forces of globalisation, of movement, speed, mobility and flexibility are argued to disrupt our sense of place, of stability, community. In this context there also develop strategies to recreate precisely these things which are being swept away: to revive our grounded sense of place. These strategies are often manifest in the form of creating public spaces: physical embodiments of a grounded sense of belonging. Theories of postmodernity do in this respect fall into two categories: those which analyse the tendency towards techno-organicism and globalisation, and those which engage in the possibilities of recreating the lost sense of community and locality. These discourses almost without exception refer either to the loss of public spaces, or the attempts to recreate them, or both.

Hence discussions of postmodernity and the city tend to focus on (a) the uses of technology to promote decentralisation, the development of communication networks, tele-shopping, on-line access to councils; or (b) the rejection of the universalising forces of modernity and its resulting abstraction and anomie, and the nostalgic longing for history, locality, and particularity. These two, quite distinct understandings of what postmodernism is in relation to the city might be labelled techno-organicism[17] and rosy romanticism respectively. Whilst the former focuses on the forces at work to eradicate public spaces, the latter focuses on the attempts to recreate them. Neither, however, manifests the vision of a renewed public sphere which could convincingly claim to realise the possibility of democratic political participation.

Techno-Organicism

The city is being restructured, it is argued, by networks of transport and communications which serve to create an urban region that resembles a centreless web. The move from Fordist to post-Fordist society, from industrial to post-industrial, from organised to disorganised capitalism, necessitates different forms of social relationships: relationships become stretched out over space and compressed in time.

Manuel Castells, describing what he sees to be the advent of the 'informational city', identifies 'the historical emergence of the space flows, superseding the meaning of the spaces of places.'[18] Paul Virilio calls this 'techno-organic' postmodern city, the 'overexposed city': 'In the place of a discrete boundary in space, demarcating distinct spaces, one sees spaces co-joined by semi-permeable membranes, exposed to flows of information in particular ways.'[19] Baudrillard talks of the delirium and vertigo in the face of such images and flows.[20] This postmodern city has no public spaces at all—no face-to-face interaction. Communication becomes exchanges mediated by telephone wires and computer cables. Space is not recreated for public interaction, it is compressed through global exchange networks.

These aspects of postmodernity can be seen not only in Los Angeles and Tokyo, but also in edge cities. During the last 20 years more than 200 'edge cities' have developed in the USA. These edge cities are new towns, but new towns which are not the product of the vision of politicians or planners, but of unregulated market forces; of speculation; of the interstate freeway network; of the American yearning to leave the city and to find somewhere to park. Edge cities are cities without an under-class, for the under-class has been left in the abandoned zones of the old inner cities.

The dimensions of these edge cities are unknown, for distances are judged in terms of minutes rather than miles and the boundaries are therefore fluid. Their names are also uncertain. 'Refusing to accept they are a community', comments John Lichfield, 'edge cities frequently have no generally accepted name. Sometimes, they are known by the name of the shopping mall at their centre.'[21] Other times they are known by numbers of the two interstate freeways which intersect nearby: identity defined in terms of the shopping mall or the motorway. 'It is an attempt to generate a sense of community, of commitment to the common good, of common purpose to shape the future which is the antithesis of what edge cities represent. Edge cities are the symbol of the unplanned, or under-planned.'[22]

But does this absence of a sense of community matter? One of the inhabitants of an edge city responds thus:

> As much as there are many advantages to living the way we do—great homes, pleasant surroundings, jobs nearby—there is something missing. We are less involved in other people and more and more involved in ourselves....People compensate by making their own communities, of people living in places like this hundreds of miles apart, connected by airlines and the interstate and faxes and telephones.[23]

The disorientation and vertigo that these developments manifest in turn generate a desire to find 'new localisms'[24]. This desire is much discussed in the literature of the postmodern city. Harvey argues that this desire is a reactionary search for stability;[25] Jameson is less critical and calls for a cultural mapping to reorient ourselves.[26] Kevin Robins argues: 'The driving imperative is to salvage centred, bounded and coherent identities—placed identities for placeless times.'[27]

However, these discourses can imply that there was a sense of locality, of community, of belonging, and that these have been lost. In other words these narratives make sense of the experiences of those who have fled the inner cities for the edge cities and now desire to recreate something which they feel is lacking. They do not address the experiences of those left in the inner city ghettos. For these people retain a very strong sense of locality: they are unlikely to feel disorientated by the flux and flow of communication networks, or of time-space compression. For, as Massey notes: 'Much of life for many people, even in the heart of the first world, still consists of waiting in a bus-shelter with your shopping for a bus that never comes.'[28] The reality of the urban experience is probably not as glamorous, disoriented, flexible, as many of these techno-organicist theories would imply.

Rosy Romanticism

Heaven, we are reliably informed, is a place where nothing ever happens. It is a place where everything you've ever wanted is under the same roof and within easy reach. It has perfect weather, there is always parking space, and no one ever has any problems. It's blissful and bland in the way that only paradise can be. I think heaven must be like a shopping centre.[29]

Certain 'postmodern' building and planning strategies focus upon difference and particularity, upon recovering a lost sense of territorial identity, a lost sense of community. The resurrection of a differentiated way of life against, what is characterised as first a modernist push towards uniformity and standardisation and then a post-Fordist drive towards globalisation.

It is argued that the local dimension has been 'for too long neglected by an overcentralised, dominating and exclusive modernist culture'.[30] And, in recognition of this fact, postmodern planning and architecture 'seeks to restore identity to local cultures swamped hitherto by the austere universalism of modernist aesthetics.'[31] The key to reviving cities is seen, from this perspective, in a return to human scale and the recreation of community. The building of new enclosures which will protect us, physically through spatial definition, from the flux and flow of the urban experience.

A paradigm shift is thus argued to be taking place in the way we think about cities, from the Fordist to the post-Fordist city—from drab monotonous uniformity to cosmopolitan diversity, choice and vitality, from anomie to community. Franco Bianchini argues that we are now able to revitalise local public spaces and a politics of identity.[32] David Harvey argues that postmodernism 'abandons the modernist search for inner meaning in the midst of present turmoil and asserts a broader base for the eternal in a constructed vision of historical continuity and collective memory'.[33]

Many such attempts to revive the city are steeped in a concern with 'community'. Even the British Arts Council argue in their document entitled 'An Urban Renaissance',[34] that the 1960s 'have come to symbolise the alienating force of modernism: urban renewal resulted in concrete tower blocks on a vast, inhuman scale, destroying established communities in the process'.[35] Now, in the 1990s, the time has come to get it right. 'To succeed', they claim, 'redevelopment must consist of more than bricks and mortar. It must rebuild communities.'[36]

These arguments then, go something like this: the logic of modernism was centred around efficiency, functionalism and impersonality—it eroded a sense of place. Whereas 'postmodern space aims to be historically specific, rooted in cultural, often vernacular style conventions.'[37] This space, it is argued, is a forum for spectacle and display and, as such, a positive force in urban life, creating the possibility of a playful popular democratic impulse.[38] The extent to which this postmodern vision does imply a revival of democracy is, however, questionable. For it is not a pluralism of lifestyles that reign in this postmodern vision of the reconstructed public spaces, for these public spaces are, in practice, to be found in the shopping centre. To quote Ron McCarthy, the London shopping centre entrepreneur:

> The traditional mall no longer has a competitive edge. As north American experience shows, the retail environment must provide more than just shopping. It must be a dynamic celebratory space.[39]

New 'urban romanticism' or new 'localisms' seek a cohesive city life, one which avoids real conflicts and fails to confront real diversity; and does so through physical enclosure and exclusion. As such, these urban strategies can be viewed as the practical embodiment of the communitarian political vision. It is a localism and particularity achieved through the power to exclude. It is the creation of a public space emphasising art, culture and consumption. Spaces for consuming which are insulated from the poor and other 'deviants'. This kind of postmodern urban strategy involves the simulation of the public spaces of old city centres, and their conversion from centres of commerce and industry to places of spectacle and heritage. Their sense of style and place is usually borrowed from the places they have replaced. They assume usage by cohesive communities and require the exclusion of disruptive 'others'. Trouble is not something you get in shopping malls with their high-tech methods of surveillance. In the words of one American mall's marketing director:

We can maintain much greater sensitivity over what happens here, than they can in the old urban downtown. If someone is behaving here in a way we don't like, a way which might disturb our other customers, this is private property, we can invite them to leave. We can stop them coming back.[40]

Thus, contrary to those who argue that postmodern cities are about reviving public spaces, I would argue that we are actually witnessing strategies for the creation of 'new enclosures'. The creation of physical and spatial barriers around those who have the power—economic, social and cultural—to isolate themselves from the undesirable manifestations of urban life. This is not about reviving a democratic impulse; creating spaces in which we can act, interact and achieve; bringing us together in all our diversity in order that we can experience and appreciate difference. Nor is it about the revival of a sense of community in an inclusive, participatory sense. It is about the flight from unmediated encounters with others who challenge our sense of security. And this clearly is an option that is only open to the few.

Neither the technological globalisation nor the reconstructed localism of these 'postmodern cities' imply, to me at least, the development of the sort of public sphere that would create a more democratic society. The notion that reimagining the city thus is also to recreate the conditions for democratic discourse is flawed. As the neo-classical façades of postmodern architecture will do little to engage with the real crisis of the cities, so the easy invocation of 'commodity' will do little to confront the realities of pluralist, multicultural society.[41]

Urban crisis, as Elizabeth Wilson has argued, is not simply a matter of architectural style, nor primarily a crisis of consciousness. It is the economic restructuring of cities that has brought about change.

The urban crisis is not then, symptomatic of a loss of meaning in the world, but on the contrary, has identifiable causes and effects which can be explained in economic and political terms.[42]

The issue then, becomes: do we want to create a sense of place and of belonging, and sense of community and place-bound politics? And if so, what economic, political and social structures would allow us to do so? Must a place-based politics aspire towards cohesion and stability and thus necessitate exclusion and surveillance? Or could a place-based politics, located in a public sphere, actually realise the celebration of difference that is discussed so frequently in these postmodern times?

Critiquing the Cohesive Community: Contestation in Public Spaces

Someone who has theorised 'the public' more explicitly than most is Hannah Arendt. The public sphere is given primacy of place within Arendt's vision of the political: it is here that we act, and to act is to realise the political. The public sphere is here depicted as a 'space of appearances', a place in which we can initiate, and be seen to do so; to spark off new beginnings which will ripple through space and time in a sea of narratives, securing for us an immortality which is impossible to achieve through the everyday cyclical processes of work and labour. This space is always contingent, never institutional and static; it exists when people come together in action; it disappears when they retreat to the shadowy world of the private arena.[43]

It is here that people distinguish themselves, reveal their unique identities; but to do so they must share a common world, exist within shared structures of human artifice. Thus the public sphere both relates and separates us: it 'gathers us together and yet prevents our falling over each other'. This common world requires permanence and durability, and the space of appearances, transience and potentiality. Both are required for a democratic political vision. To act in the public sphere is to engage in political participation, which is to establish relations of solidarity and civic friendship. It is not to generate a sense of intimacy or community—these are the proper manifestation of the particularity of the private sphere. To quote d'Entreves:

for Arendt the danger of trying to recapture a sense of

> intimacy and warmth, of authenticity and communal
> feelings, is that one loses the public values of
> impartiality, civic friendship and solidarity.[44]

Or in the words of Cannovan, one acts in the public sphere
'coolly and objectively'.[45]

Thus the sort of 'public spaces' that are discussed in the
context of contemporary urbanity are precisely not what
Arendt had in mind when she spoke of the vital importance of
the public sphere. For these public spaces are 'social' (in the
Arendtian sense), not truly public, in nature. The modes of
activity proper to the private realm have spread their operation,
ensuring that the public space of politics becomes nothing more
than a 'pseudospace of interaction in which individuals no
longer "act" but "merely behave" as economic producers, con-
sumers and urban city dwellers.'[46]

I note Arendt's conception of the public to indicate that the
celebration of the public as a space of action, appearance and
political participation has an echo in current political theory. I
note it also because some of the critiques of Arendt's work
seem to me to be particularly relevant to the above discussion
of the nature of the public sphere in existing cities.

'The agonistic political space of the polis was only possible',
argues Benhabib,

> because large groups of human beings like women,
> slaves, labourers and non-citizen residents, and all non-
> Greeks, were excluded from it and made possible
> through their 'labour' for the daily necessities of life
> that 'leisure for politics' which the few enjoyed.[47]

Here we have it: the vision of a public sphere all too often rests
on the implicit exclusion of all those who will disrupt its
operation, or who are required to create its conditions. Is the
creation of the public sphere as envisaged by Arendt therefore
reliant on the exclusion of many for the benefit of the few? Is
it, as Benhabib asks, necessarily an elitist and anti-democratic
project 'which can hardly be reconciled with the demand for
universal political emancipation and the universal extension of
citizenship rights that have accompanied modernity?'[48]

And, if it is only under conditions of political and moral

homogeneity, with the existence of a common world, that distinction and action can occur within the public sphere, is this ideal realisable in contemporary society? If society lacks homogeneity and a shared vocabulary, are the boundaries of the public sphere too porous to survive? Thus policing the boundaries of the public, ensuring that it is not disrupted by the presence of those who do not share a common world, or those who assert the importance of the intimate, becomes vital to its continued existence. 'The struggle over what gets included in the public agenda', notes Benhabib, 'is itself a struggle for justice and freedom.'[49] The recognition of the importance of this struggle is absent not only from the work of Arendt, but also from the writings of all too many contemporary theorists of the public spaces in the city.

Iris Young, however, in her discussion of the public sphere, challenges this celebration of commonality and prioritises the issue of policing the boundaries of the public. Here we find someone who directly addresses the power relations which operate to determine who is to enter the public sphere and what issues are to be articulated within it. 'The stances of detachment and dispassion', she says, 'that supposedly produce impartiality are attained only by abstracting from the particularities of situation, feeling, affiliation, and point of view. These particularities still operate, however, in the actual context of action. Thus the ideal of impartiality generates a dichotomy between universal and particular, public and private, reason and passion.'[50]

Anxiety in the face of disorder has long been manifest in the social sciences. It results in the celebration of the harmonic, and a desire for the hermetic. More specifically (the focus of my argument here), there is a tendency in democratic theory to deny or think away social difference by appeal to an ideal of community, located in a 'soft' public sphere. The generality of this realm requires the repression and transcendence of partiality and differentiation which, as recent feminist analyses point out, involves its location in a private sphere of the family.

The assumption of homogeneity, I am arguing (not uniquely), involves excluding from the public those individuals and groups that do not fit. In Western capitalist patriarchal society this means those who don't fit the model of the rational citizen capable of transcending body and sentiment. This has two key foundations: the tendency to oppose reason and desire; and the association of these traits with specific kinds of persons. The universal citizen who inhabits this civic public tends to be the white bourgeois male. The bodily, sexual, uncertain, disorderly aspects of existence come to be identified with women, homosexuals, Blacks, Jews, Orientals...the list goes on. The battle between order and disorder within the city is, by this strategy, played out by associating disorder with certain social groups and then excluding them from the ordered, civic public.

The need to reconstruct city life is all too often addressed in terms of a dangerous myth of communal solidarity. As Richard Sennett has argued, in affluent cities people frame for themselves a belief in emotional cohesion and shared values which are forged in order that people can avoid dealing with each other. This myth of community, talk of ties that bind, makes a coherent image of community: 'purified of all that might convey a feeling of difference, let alone conflict, in who "we" are.'[51] Commonly painful experiences, unknown social situations full of possible surprise and challenge, can thus be avoided by the common consent of a 'community'. The consequences of such communities, argues Sennett, are: a loss of confrontation and exploration between individuals; the repression of deviants, which becomes necessary if people are to keep convincing themselves of their collective dignity through sameness; the polarisation between communities and escalation of violence. The sad but increasingly prevalent manifestation of this logic is to be seen most vividly in the policies of ethnic cleansing currently being enacted in Europe.

It is this insight that informs the claim of Iris Young that:

> The repoliticization of public life does not require the creation of a unified public realm in which citizens leave behind their particular group affiliations, histories, and needs to discuss a mythical 'common good'.[52]

For this ideal of community expresses an urge to unity, a longing for harmony, for consensus, for what Foucault calls the Rousseauist dream.[53] Yet the irony is that the 'logic of identity' inevitably generates dichotomy instead of unity. The urge to bring things into unity necessarily entails expelling some properties or entities—there is always a remainder. To put this in another way, the community is defined in opposition to that which is excluded from it.

So difference becomes dichotomous hierarchical opposition; the unified and the chaotic. This is an opposition which I have tried to show has been battled out within the city. Thus the creation of soft public spaces, the aspiration towards civilised cohesive communities with shared values, languages and aims, inevitably involves exclusion—and hence the creation of ghettos. The postmodern strategy of creating a sense of localism, community and public spaces fails to create strong public spaces, and certainly does not create anything like a Habermasian public space where 'access is guaranteed to all citizens'.[54] The response to the crisis of the cities which advocates the creation of decentralised, autonomous communities where people exercise local control over their lives and neighbourhoods on a human scale, reproduce the problems of exclusion that the ideal of community poses.

The urban public space should be a place accessible to anyone—therefore in entering the public one always risks encounter with those who are different. What makes urban spaces interesting, draws people out in public to them, gives people pleasure and excitement, is the diversity of activities they support: the simultaneity of action, the *frisson* of difference. This difference should be celebrated rather than assimilated into a single dominant norm of community life. In the words of Iris Young: 'city life also instantiates difference as the erotic, in the wide sense of an attraction to the other, the pleasure and excitement of being drawn out of one's secure routine to encounter the novel, strange, and surprising.'[55] The erotic attraction is precisely the obverse of community; a pleasure, not in feeling affirmed, but in encountering a subjectivity that is different.

Worries About Unassimilated Otherness

Is this to be a celebration of fragmentation, the co-presence of multiple discourses—of music, street and body language? Is this a celebration of urban tolerance for difference, an example of what Iris Young calls 'openness to unassimilated otherness'? I want to signal very real problems I perceive within this celebration. To do so I borrow a case study from David Harvey[56]—a fleeting glance at another concrete public space: a park. If the shopping centre is the answer to the romanticist postmodern dream of community, perhaps this park is the plural, playful postmodern vision of Young's politics of difference.

The park is Tompkins Square Park in New York City, as recounted by John Kifner in the *International Herald Tribune*. The groups located around the park, at the time of these articles, comprised not only 300 homeless people, but also in the words of Kifner:

> Skateboarders, basketball players, mothers with small children, radicals looking like 1960s retreads, spikey-haired punk rockers in torn black, skinheads in heavy working boots looking to beat up the radicals and punks, dreadlocked Rastafarians, heavy-metal bands, chess players, dog-walkers—all occupying their spaces in the park, along with professionals carrying their dry-cleaned suits to the renovated 'gentrified' buildings that are changing the character of the neighbourhood.[57]

It is precisely this sort of scene that makes the city in general, and New York in particular, so stimulating. It is in this sort of scene that many a cultural theorist would locate the origins of the postmodern.

If we are to follow the argument thus far, we should not aim to obliterate the differences within the park, to homogenise them into some social order, but to celebrate Young's 'unassimilated otherness'. Maybe, but if we stop a while longer at the park, we will witness the battle to evict the homeless, the violence between the punks and the skinheads, the rape of the woman walking the dog....As Harvey notes:

> The potentiality for 'openess to unassimilated otherness' breaks apart and in much the same way that the cosmopolitan and eminently civilised Beirut of the 1950s suddenly collapsed into an urban maelstrom of

warring factions and violent confrontation, so we find sociality collapsing into violence.[58]

Or, as the *New York Times* commented on the dilemma of the park:

> There are neighboured associations clamouring for the city to close the park and others just as insistent that it remain a refuge for the city's downtrodden....There is only one thing that is a consensus, that there isn't a consensus over what should be done, except that any new plan is likely to provoke more disturbances, more violence.[59]

In reality, the question was resolved by evicting everyone from the park and closing it entirely 'for rehabilitation' under a permanent guard of at least twenty police officers. This public space was militarised, semiprivatised and ultimately extinguished.

If, then, the park is taken as a microcosm for the city, for social organisation, what conclusions are we to draw about the celebration of difference? Whilst we may all agree that an urban park is a good thing in principle, how are we to respond to the fact that in practice its uses may be so conflictual that it breaks apart? The lesson would clearly seem to be that there must be a minimum of solidarity—agreement over what constitutes a public space and its proper scope of usage.

> The tolerance, the room for great differences among neighbours—differences that often go far deeper than differences in colour—which are possible and normal in intensely urban life, but which are so foreign to suburbs and pseudosuburbs, are possible and normal only when streets of great cities have built-in equipment allowing strangers to dwell in peace together on civilised but essentially dignified and reserved terms.[60]

But what is the nature of this 'built-in equipment'? Does this take us anywhere other than back to the age-old liberal debate of neutrality, the priority of the right over the good, the framework within which people can experiment and pursue their own goods? The question then becomes: what is radical about such pluralism? Has this lengthy excursion into post-modern political strategies brought us full circle back to a liberal pluralism?

I tentatively suggest that the difference lies in the acknowledgement that we need to gain a deeper understanding of the forces at work shaping the conflict in the park. Whether it be property development or drug dealing, we must contextualise the 'otherness' against a background of political-economic transformation occurring within urban life: against the operation of power-structures which generate hierarchies, oppositions and tensions. It is no use simply celebrating unassimilated otherness as though all differences are chosen with pride, are democratic in impulse and glorious in manifestation. What might conceivably make a pluralism radical is an awareness of the existence of structural oppressions and the need to act positively to overcome them.

Conclusion: Tougher Public Spaces

What we have seen are the attempts both to stress commonality at the expense of plurality and respect of differences, and the denial of any form of commonality in the name of plurality and difference. What is needed instead are 'tougher notions of public space': the geographical location for a form of commonality that respects difference. If there is to be any common good it is a 'grammar of conduct'—the rules of the space.

So the appeal of the urban public, for me at least, echoes the words of Raymond Williams:

> The modern metropolis has always evoked feelings of alienation and disorientation, but it has equally been associated with new possibilities for encounter and solidarity and there has always been a sense of the 'vitality, the variety, the liberating diversity and mobility of the city'.[61]

This ideal is one in which we match community and security with the kind of openness that can stimulate a positive sense of challenge and contestation. The political challenge is to work out whether the city can cope with diversity: that is, whether it can generate a sense of community without denying scope for positive contestation.

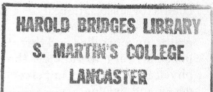

HAROLD BRIDGES LIBRARY
S. MARTIN'S COLLEGE
LANCASTER

(5)

Symbolic Antagonism, Police Paranoia, and the Possibility of Social Diversity

Sean Watson

Antagonism, Shame and Paranoia

In police discourse one can often see formally how out-groups are being discursively constructed through the creation of chains of association. For example the black man becomes discursively associated with laziness, irresponsibility, criminality, uncontrolled and threatening sexuality, and so on. In the police officers' world view the council estate is associated with physical decay. This imperceptibly slides into a vision of moral decay and degeneracy.

> Well, there's a much larger coloured population here. The crime is more prevalent and tends to be more violent.
> *Why is that? What kind of explanations do you have?*
> Well I think probably the West Indians, in particular, are perhaps more prone to using violence. I mean, generally, we have got to say that housing in this area is of quite low quality. It's not very well looked after whoever's responsibility it is and they are tightly packed on top of each other, it's like a rabbit warren.[1]

Similarly unemployment is associated with moral degeneracy, as is illicit drug use and non-standard lifestyles in general.

They would prefer to squat rather than pay rates to the local government, they try and evade taxes, they don't want to conform to society at all, prefer to go without work. Going back to our roots sort of thing, fend for themselves. So they cause us problems in that respect, they squat in any empty dwellings and also they have tended to in the past cause us problems at somewhere like Stonehenge, or somewhere they see as a free festival, say Pilton. Something that's free, something that tries to breakaway from conformity, they would want to get involved in, and of course *we're here to represent the society and safeguard morals, so we're then brought in so there's obviously friction there.* [my emphasis][2]

Often patterns of discursive association of out-groups with dirt and disease are found, whilst simultaneously dirtiness is ascribed to any form of non-standard appearance and duly interpreted as signifying inner moral degeneracy.

Yes, OK, well I mean the drunks and the hippies are around the town and they're either begging or they're, well, just throwing up on corners and things, its disgusting really. They've no respect for anything, people's property, you know. They do present a general public order problem.[3]

These kinds of discursive strategies have of course been well documented elsewhere:

I tell you something about users that bugs me. I don't know what it is exactly. You want me to be frank? OK. Well, I can't stand them; I mean I really can't stand them. Why? Because they bother me personally. They're dirty, that's what they are, filthy. They make my skin crawl.[4]

Mary Douglas considers there to be a universal tendency in human societies to respond to the transgression of social/symbolic boundaries by attributing a confusing mixture of physical and moral pollution to them:

Pollution ideas work in the life of a society at two levels, one largely instrumental, one expressive. At the first level, the more obvious one, we find people trying to influence one another's behaviour. Beliefs reinforce social pressures: all the powers of the universe are called in to guarantee an old man's dying wish, a mother's dignity, the rights of the weak and innocent. Political power is usually held precariously and primitive rulers are no exception. So we find their legitimate pretensions backed by beliefs in extraordinary powers emanating from their persons, *from the insignia of their office* or from words they can utter. Similarly the ideal order of society is guarded by dangers which threaten transgressors. These danger beliefs are as much threats which one man uses to coerce another as dangers which he himself fears to incur by his own lapses from righteousness. They are a strong language of mutual exhortation. At this level the laws of nature are dragged in to sanction the moral code: this kind of disease is caused by adultery, that by incest; this meteorological disaster is the effect of political disloyalty, that the effect of impiety. The whole universe is harnessed to men's attempts to force one another into good citizenship. Thus we find that certain moral values are upheld and certain social rules defined by beliefs in dangerous contagion, as when the glance or touch of an adulterer is held to bring illness to his neighbours or his children.[5]

What has rarely been dealt with in such analyses of the discursive construction of out-groups, and the attachment to them of beliefs about dirt and pollution, is the *affective* force with which loathing of the supposedly morally and physically polluted rears its head.[6] This paper is specifically about the nature of that affective force. In particular what are the conditions for the emergence of violent loathing towards out-groups, how are the police implicated in such violent loathing and how does this issue relate to the politics of diversity?

Post-Lacanian psychoanalytic theory suggests that the unconscious is inscribed within the symbolic systems we use to forge an identity. The unconscious is present in everything we utter and in every gesture we make. The arbitrariness, the contingency of the symbolic field is always threatening to make itself visible. We must constantly find ways of blinding ourselves to this lack of necessity, lack of substance, lack of 'being'. Systems of difference are constantly under threat and this is perhaps nowhere more obviously the case than in the context of the police identity which is forged against the background of an 'Other' which he/she comes into contact with and deals with routinely every day in the course of doing the job of being a police officer. The 'Other' of the police officer is the so-called 'criminal fraternity'. This is the major object of police discourse and the antithesis of the policing identity (so far as the officers themselves are concerned).

> The mental picture really is that there are really two communities in ──. The community that you see living on the surface, and the people that are living just beneath the surface, that element that live close by or in the criminal fraternity. Which is quite a big criminal fraternity, and you will realise that while you are doing observations on a house, for instance, you will see people coming and going, and all those people come and go and you will know they are associating in crime somewhere, whether it's a brother and sister, or whatever. They seem to stick together. They use certain pubs, certain cafes in town, there's a strong bond between them.[7]

The discursive identification of the 'criminal fraternity' is not simply a matter of cold mechanical discursive orientations but is forged in the context of a constant 'anxiety'. The 'Other' must be constantly and very clearly identified and set at a conceptual distance in order to realise the integrity of the police identity. The police officer is obviously being constantly bombarded with evidence which could threaten the deep natural and moral gap which he, necessarily, perceives to exist between himself and the criminal and he must find ways of dealing with this within the context of his moral and cognitive constructs and identity constructs. If this is not done then the threat to the police identity is very real. The final form of the solution to this ongoing crisis is of course not uniform. What might be expected, however, is that forms of association and stereotyping will be rigid and clear cut. Grey areas will be felt to be dangerous, subversive and associated with pollution or contagion. You have to be either 'for them' or 'against them'.

There are things which give policemen satisfaction, things which make them very angry, things which they loathe and which disgust them, things which they hate and detest, things which they think are 'going on' in the world (policemen have many paranoias). We must understand the discursive context within which these associations come about, but we must also understand the emotional force with which reactions appear.

What do I mean when I say that policemen are paranoid? Policemen perceive all around them objects possessed by affective forces. Objects possessed by hatred, evil intentions, evil qualities, threatening powers of chaos and destruction. This is no exaggeration: the policeman's world is composed almost entirely of threatening objects.

> It's not a black and white problem, it's a criminal fraternity problem. There is a hard core of black violent criminals there who have got no interests whatsoever in talking to the police. No criminal is interested in talking to the police and they're totally opposed to normal policing down there because it interferes with their activities, drug money, prostitution, illegal gambling and illegal drinking. It's a criminal problem but it is peculiar, they're a very vociferous and violent bunch out there, more so in my experience than the white criminal, they don't seem to bunch together in such large numbers.
>
> *How can you deal with that kind of confrontational situation as a police officer?*
>
> Personally, or what should we be doing down there?
>
> *Well, both.*
>
> Well, I feel that the only way we can deal with the problems we've got at the moment is by excising them from the community and if that means sending them to prison for a long long time, then so be it. They are not representatives of their race, the majority of coloured people obviously have got no time for them, they can't

control them, they've got no time and patience for them. I feel that they should be removed and locked away. Obviously, due legal process. The hardest part is *actually improving the jobs we get against them*, but I do feel a special stand has got to be taken and that we won't have black ghettos, we won't have infiltration of black gangs. We won't tolerate white gangs. As soon as a white gang emerges or there is a group of whites who go together to commit a certain crime then all the resources are brought to bear and the judges make an example of them. Whereas I feel that when we do successfully prosecute members of the black criminal fraternity down there then, there are far too many people still willing to make excuses for them instead of just treating them as violent criminals and that's what I feel we are going to have to do.[8]

Is the 'criminal fraternity' a paranoid formation? Is it what Zizek calls the 'Other of the Other'[9], the Other that pulls the strings of the symbolic—an imaginary 'string pulling' necessary to obliterate the real driving force of any paranoia which is the horror at the sheer blind contingency of the symbolic? It is a general over-determining object of hatred which obliterates particularities. Individuals are seen as members of this body. The qualities of them are derived from the object.[10] Notice the line in the interview about 'improving jobs against them'. The judgement is not based on experience of bad things which these people have done but on bad qualities ascribed to them. Catching them in the act of committing a crime is just a means to an end—a means of ritually purifying the social body of their presence. This is the affective pressure at the heart of the common practice of 'targeting'.[11] This is amplified by references to gangs, their tendency to group and references to the racial object. At the same time the object of the black race is effaced by this stain in it. The discourse functions simultaneously to condemn the criminal fraternity by juxtaposing it with the race of which they are not representative, but at the same time typifies the rest of the race as unable to control its unrepresentative part—it is weak, dependent on the white race to do its dirty work for it. The discourse legitimates police intervention in the community by identifying police actions with the will of the majority of the black community but then simultaneously condemns the majority by 'polluting' them. Two paranoid objects are constituted simultaneously.

Another paranoid object...

> We did have a big problem with travellers. It seems to run in a funny sort of pattern. There's the black criminal down there; then there is the abuser down there. There seems to be a lot of white and asian and black hangers on and they seem to be, the black seem to be feeding off them and they are pathetic little creatures some of them. They've got heroin habits, that's their way of life. That's the way they've fallen and ended up and they are living in pathetic conditions and they are being preyed upon by a lot of people down there, black and white, not all blacks.[12]

The presence of a black evil 'preying' on the 'fallen'.

And again...

> I find it offensive, men with men and men with children, I think there's nothing moral about that. Men with children, I think you've got to protect those children. I don't think that's a moral issue at all. Men with men in their own homes, no offence. As long as they are self-consenting adults, it's up to them. But when it comes out to the fact that, it must be 18 months to 2 years ago now, one of the city centre shops...where it happened, it's rife, and when you think there are young children using these toilets, and the parents unsuspecting send them in there. Certainly there was 11 people arrested within about 2 hours, I think that's disgusting. Whether you think it's morally wrong, but it's corrupting those children. That's about it really.[13]

We see here the classic conflation of homosexuality and child sexual abuse as an object constituting huge threat and inspiring equally powerful loathing.

Yet another threat...

Well years ago I think the problem was down at...the Docks and it's slowly moved inwards because [the docks] doesn't get a lot of ships anymore, they just moved into——[inner city predominantly Afro-Caribbean and Asian community]. Pimps are coloured men. Girls are attracted to coloured men for some reason. Their physical attributes or whatever you want to say, but I mean having weighed it up and talked to some of the girls that are actually prostitutes down there, one of them gave me a very good explanation why white girls go out with coloured blokes, which is that they are treated properly. She said to me that she lives at—— [predominantly white council estate]....A Friday night would be—he would pick her up in an old banger and take her to the local pub. He'd sit her down with a couple of his mates' girlfriends, they sit three of them in a corner chatting and he was up at the bar drinking with his mates telling dirty stories, having a go on the fruit machine, getting involved in a fight perhaps, having a game of pool. Then he'd say come on its time to go, they might go on to a night club which was very rare because he would be paralytic. He'd try a quick fondle in the back seat of the car and get his leg over and drop her off and that was it. Suddenly, along comes Mr Nice Guy who is coloured. He sits with her, he talks to her, he buys her a drink, takes her dancing, looks after her, buys her a present and that's the attraction isn't it. I mean in comparison if you were a girl would you take a bloke that gets drunk every night and has a quick fondle in the back or a coloured guy who treats you right? Of course, so the story goes, they are nice to you up to a point and then they suddenly lock the door give you a good hiding and say go and get me some money. The girls feel obliged to get them some money, so out they go. The only way they can get their money is on the game. That's how they start. It's good that, isn't it, have you ever thought of that before?[14]

Again the existence of racist discourses linking black men to crime via excessive, mysterious and deviant sexuality and a threat to white women is not a new discovery. Also the fact that it pervades police discourse may have been assumed in the past. However the function and affective force of these paranoid formations has never been adequately explained.

As I have said, police discourse is endlessly populated by these paranoid formations, these possessed objects. They are paranoid about the working classes, about the middle classes, about the criminal classes, about the rest of the criminal justice system, about youth, about the unemployed, about racial and ethnic minorities, about political activists, about travellers, hippies, squatters, drunks, drug users. They literally perceive threat emanating from just about every object in their conceptual universe—they are, I believe, almost universally paranoid (a fact which incidentally seems to cause considerable pain to policemen and their families). Let me be quite clear about what I mean. I mean that the police force as a whole is necessarily a 'paranoid formation' (in the sense which I have detailed above— that they perceive threat emanating from everywhere in their moral and cognitive universe). I have provided, in the context of this paper, only a small sample of empirical data supporting this claim. To do more than this would demand a whole book or more. For the moment I can only say that the large quantity of interview data I have amassed together with study in the field leads me to the conclusion that the quotes given above are quite typical of police accounts of 'their world'. The question is: why?

Michael Rustin has recently attempted an analysis of racism based on post-Kleinian psychoanalysis.[15] He believes that racism is a psychotic projective identification. That is, it is a projection of unwanted aspects of the self onto others. Aspects of the self which one is disgusted or frightened by are projected onto other objects, persons or groups; *aspects of the self which cannot be assimilated into the biographical narrative constituting the conscious self.* A similar theme can be found in the work of Victor Burgin.[16] Burgin is however more influenced by Lacanian themes. As such the significations of 'inner' and 'outer' which prevail in the Rustin model, are not found in Burgin. His is a concern with the *inevitable* failure of the subject to be fully constituted in the symbolic system. He presents a very interesting quote from Freud himself: 'It was incorrect to say that the perception which was repressed internally is projected outwards. The truth is rather, as we shall see, that what was abolished internally returns from without'.[17]

This is the basis for Lacan's notion of the 'return of the Real'. What is at the heart of paranoia is not repression but foreclosure.[18] There are un-symbolisable hostilities and antagonisms at the heart of the subject. This foreclosure, or inability coherently to assimilate certain elements of the symbolic structure of the subject into the narrative of the subject, results in the return of the affect associated with this foreclosure in the form of external objects possessed by threat—paranoic objects. 'The mechanism of symptom formation in paranoia requires that internal perceptions shall be replaced by external perception.'[19] What at first appears a bizarre claim (how can the external world become possessed by forces originating inside the individual?) begins to make sense only when one understands that inner/outer dichotomy is simply a symbolic construct anyway. For Lacanian theorists both are constituted in what Zizek calls the 'big Other'—that is, the symbolic system—so elements can shift from one to another quite easily.[20]

Anthony Giddens attempts to deal with similar issues in his book *Modernity and Self Identity*.[21] In the chapter called 'Existential Anxiety and Ontological Trust' he points to the fragility of the 'natural attitude' and the flood of anxiety attending its disruption (citing Garfinkel etc). This constitutive anxiety is what post Lacanian psychoanalytic theory has termed simply 'lack'. The universe is ultimately devoid of Being.[22] Being is constituted symbolically and the subject is balanced precariously on the precipice of the void endlessly searching for an impossible symbolic completion or 'closure'—the search for a totality and necessity amongst blind contingency, for a coherent historical narrative amongst discursive chaos, and crucially for a full and complete self presence amongst the incompatible fragments of the self. A sense of self presence/'Being' can only be constructed differentially/relationally—that is, in contrast to 'otherness'.[23] The notion of meaning being a product of systems of difference is of course common to the whole of the structuralist and post-structuralist traditions from De Saussure onwards. Here, however, it takes on a specific significance in that the signifier in question is the subject (in particular, for us, the police subject) and the system of signs against which it is defining itself is a system of out-groups or 'others'. Any ambiguity in the relationship between the subject and these out-groups threatens the very existence of the subject. A great deal is at stake in the maintenance of these symbolic boundaries, a great deal of anxiety is potentially implicated.

Giddens is optimistic about people's ability to live with plurality, fragmentation, hybridity, difference and so on. He admits, though, that as some people cannot deal with difference, they become paranoid in the face of diversity. His explanation as to why there are some trusting individuals and other paranoid individuals is fundamentally rooted in infantile development. This is where the individual will develop the ability or inability to trust, to bear diversity and fragmentation; to tolerate an ambiguous identity and an ambiguous symbolic environment. He paraphrases R.D. Laing in saying that the ontologically insecure individual is unable to sustain a continuous narrative of self—they constantly experience anxiety about being crushed, engulfed, obliterated or overwhelmed by external events (again similar to the phenomena being identified by Rustin and Burgin). Giddens develops this rather questionable developmental explanation of paranoid tendencies into an equally questionable typology of normal and abnormal psychic type.[24] One rather useful point emerging out of the paper however is that Giddens points out that an awful lot of attention has been given to the issue of guilt in psychoanalysis but that something which may be more important in the late twentieth century is the issue of 'shame'. Guilt is the result of the 'exposure of misdemeanours or transgressions'. 'Shame' however is the exposure of hidden traits which compromise the narrative of self-identity, a concept not unlike Rustin's unacceptable elements of the self. So 'shame' is the result of *symbolic antagonisms*.[25] 'Shame' produces anxiety—an anxiety, an 'ontological insecurity' that cannot be symbolised within the context of the subject. In other words it is 'foreclosed'. Perhaps, then, such 'shame' re-appears in the form of paranoid projections[26] or 'returns of the Real'.[27]

Let me be clear then about my theoretical moves here. Following Rustin, Burgin and others I am suggesting that symbolic antagonisms at the heart of the subject may lead to an inability to sustain a coherent self-narrative. For example one might find inconsistent moral imperatives which cannot be coherently assimilated to a single coherent narrative (something one might expect to be a problem for police officers perhaps). This produces an affect Giddens calls 'shame'. This affect is itself un-symbolisable. In other words it cannot be made meaningful to the subject and it cannot be made to 'belong' to the subject. This inability to integrate an affect into the symbolic field is what Burgin (following Lacan) refers to as 'foreclosure'.[28] 'Foreclosure' is part of the mechanics of paranoia. The affect associated with the 'foreclosure' manifests itself in the form of the appearance of dangerous and threatening qualities attached to external objects: the so called 'return of the Real'. The affect has simply become attached to objects which help to sustain the subject's solidity rather than threatening its existence. If the threat to existence is experienced it is experienced as a threat from outside rather than from within. Threats from outside can of course be dealt with much more easily than threats from within. The threat from outside simply needs to be destroyed, eliminated, purified. Thus we have a theoretical model linking symbolic antagonisms with violent behaviour towards the 'other'. The *affective loathing* directed towards the 'criminal fraternity', hippies, homosexuals, ethnic minorities, etc., is in fact a manifestation of internal antagonisms in the police subject.

Why might policemen be plagued by 'shame', and thus by paranoia, and how can we explain their vulnerability to it without resorting to the sort of developmental psychoanalytic explanations used by Giddens?

Specific symbolic antagonisms at the heart of the police subject which may be sources of 'shame' are too numerous to cover with any adequacy. The policeman sees himself as an agent of Law yet despises the rest of the criminal justice system's inadequacy; he sees himself as an agent of the community yet believes the community is composed of 'know nothings' who 'get the service they deserve'; he feels that respect for the police can only be generated by an element of fear, yet believes he polices by consent; he believes the force should be more open to the community it serves yet feels he can only trust his fellow officer. A whole series of *incommensurable world views* are offered up at different times, classical liberal, positivist, labelling theory etc; and whole series of different masters appear: the public, the community, society, the victim, the state etc.

The police subject is plagued by dislocation and shame. I would now like to examine one particularly interesting area of dislocation. I believe it to be of interest since it bears directly on the issues of the contingent nature of social reality itself and the possible limits to diversity, tolerance and hybridity therein.

The Surplus of Violence

In outlining his 'Policing Principles of the Metropolitan Police' Sir Kenneth Newman begins by referring to two axiomatic principles around which his discourse of police functionality revolves.[29] These are 'The Rule of Law' and 'The Queen's Peace'. There is a constant tension throughout between these two principles, and for good reason as I shall show. It seems that they have historically divergent and symbolically antagonistic significance. For the moment however I would like to point to what perhaps seems an obvious but nevertheless crucial tacit assumption lying 'behind' or perhaps 'within' the text of Newman's 'Principles'. He says that 'In discharging the duty of maintaining the Queen's Peace the Metropolitan Police will cooperate with others in maintaining a state of public tranquillity.'[30] There are many points of interest in this quotation. What is perhaps most fundamental to Newman's ability to make such a statement meaningfully is the assumption of the possibility and desirability of a governable public. It is both desirable and possible to maintain a state of 'public tranquillity'. It is possible through the activities of agencies (the police amongst others) designed to realise that possibility. This assumption of the possibility and desirability of regulating a populace in depth is a historically specific one. Where does it emerge historically and what sort of vision of the world does it imply?

Michel Foucault's intention in his analysis of governmentality is to demonstrate the gradual historical transition from discussion of the problem of sovereignty to discussion of the problem of the 'art of government'.[31] Two notions which rest on quite different views of the social world and of the relationship between rulers and ruled. For Machiavelli, Foucault tells us, the issue was to define the relationship between the prince and his territory, to define the strategies and calculations to effect forcible control over his territory. The prince is external to the principality, that which is 'subject' to his 'will'. The problem is to force a link through violence, tradition and treaty (with other princes), between the 'will' of the prince and his principality. The ruler's 'will' is here the principle of 'reason of the state'. The central axiom of this discourse then is of the manifest assumption of the natural subjection of a province and its populace to a transcending external 'will'. Rather more tacitly this transcendental 'will' can be found running through Newman's 'Principles'. He says that 'Where a conflict arises between the duty of the police to maintain order and their duty to enforce the law, the solution will be found in the priority which is given in the last resort to the maintenance of public order.'[32]

Rather less tacitly this 'will' is of course signified by 'The Queen's Peace'. So this transcendent imperative derives from a gradual assimilation of the logic of sovereignty and a transcendent 'will' into a discourse which superseded it. The logic of sovereignty per se has been superseded, but its traces remain as crucial elements in police discourse. The discursive contradictions between this imperative and the twin principle of 'The Rule of Law' has very real consequences in terms of the police practices tied up in these discourses. Debates over the miners' strike, the inner city riots, the prevention of terrorism, and the Wapping strike, to name but a few, have to a great extent centred around the question of whether there is a *transcendent duty* which the police must discharge which may *override their commitment to, and constraint by, the 'Rule of Law'*. This debate is, I suspect, however only the tip of an iceberg of symbolic crisis.

To return to Foucault's story for a moment—in what way can the logic of sovereignty be seen to have been superseded between the sixteenth and seventeenth centuries then? Foucault analyses an early anti-Machiavellian text, that of Guillaume de La Perrière. What is most striking about La

Perrière is that he writes not of sovereigns but of 'governors'. His definition of 'the governor' is very wide, governors of households, of souls, of provinces, of children, of convents, of religious orders, of families and so on. Whilst the sovereign is singular and external, or transcendent, forms of government are internal and immanent to the state. Government operates not over but within society.

Government is to become subject to the discourse of reason; the art of government is to become the science of government. Throughout the next 200 years, during the processes of demographic and monetary expansion, 'economy' develops as a field of reality constituted by a technology oriented towards 'the problem of population'. A technology in which a set of 'autonomous regularities' are to be 'known' via the collection of statistical data.[33] The family has a privileged position. The well developed notion of oeconomy—'the meticulous attention of the father towards his family'—is transplanted as metaphor to signify 'meticulous attention' to the quite new discursive invention of *population*. In the new articulation the family becomes the prime source of information and also a major point of intervention.

As economy becomes the field of reality within which government, is exercised and population becomes the object of economy and economics, so the end of government comes to be articulated as the 'welfare of the population'. A population is seen to have 'needs' which must be 'known' and dealt with. The development of this technology, the final transition from the structures of sovereignty to the science of government, signals the birth of political economy for Foucault. The major problem for government becomes the development of disciplinary technologies by virtue of which a population may be managed 'in depth' in order to realise the 'proper disposition of things' as dictated by the science of political economy. Governmentality is for Foucault then three things:

(1) the ensemble formed by the institutions,
procedures, analyses and reflections, the calculations
and tactics that allow the very specific albeit complex
form of power, which has as its target population, as
its principal form of knowledge political economy and

as its essential technical means apparatuses of security.

(2) the tendency which, over a long period and throughout the West, has never ceased to lead towards the pre-eminence over all others (sovereignty, discipline, etc.), of this type of power which may be termed government. Which resulted in the formation of, on the one hand, a whole series of specific state apparatuses pertaining to the government and, on the other, to the development of a whole complex of 'savoir'.

(3) the process, or rather the result of the process through which the State of Justice of the Middle Ages, which becomes the Administrative State during the 15th and 16th centuries, gradually comes to be governmentalised.[34]

Law, in this context, is not crucially important in itself, the mark of the governor is not the right to kill but knowledge of the 'disposition of things'—*law is simply a means* for achieving the correct 'disposition of things'.

I would like to suggest that there is a fundamental continuity between the imperatives of governmentality to penetrate, pacify and manage populations in depth, and the subjectivity of the individual police officer whose identity, whose whole raison d'etre, lies in the realisation of this possibility. The police officer's subjectivity somehow has to be coextensive with a general principle of governmental regulation, yet simultaneously the police officer represents symbolically only the juridical subject—the rule of law. The rule of law is however only one tool in the toolkit of governmentality. *There is a lack of fit between the symbolic principle legitimating the presence of the police officer and the governmental subject underlying it. The police officer is a fundamentally antagonistic subject.*

Newman asserts that 'the fundamental values of British society are underpinned by procedure and legal assumptions' and that 'these values emphasise a just balance between order and freedom and a marked abhorrence of unfair or arbitrary action by the State or its officials';[35] also that it is necessary to strike 'the optimum balance between the collective interests of all the citizens and the personal rights of individuals'.[36]

This is pure classical liberal rhetoric. Tacitly assumed is the existence of a social contract embodying a collective interest in 'public tranquillity', freedom from 'the fear of crime' and the protection of private property. From this perspective 'the Rule of Law', which is for Foucault part of a disciplinary technology of governance, is the embodiment of collective values expressed via the institution of parliamentary democracy. This is the way in which it derives its legitimacy so far as Newman is concerned. It is also the way in which policing derives its legitimacy. If asked about their role police officers will often state that they are 'upholders of the law'. But, as I have already shown, Newman himself is well aware of the ambiguity surrounding this issue. The status of law as simply one tool of governance becomes apparent when he explains that the priority of 'The Queens Peace' may transcend the law. Ironically then 'The Queens Peace', sovereignty, returns in the guise of a legitimation of the more general pacifying functions of policing. It legitimates the fact that in depth government disciplines, manipulates and moulds a population in a manner which is so detailed and mundane at the point of application that it is logically and practically incompatible with democratic control.

We can see the seemingly contradictory development of an institution which practises in depth surveillance and management of a population which it simultaneously articulates as its master. The police are 'public servants', policing is practised with the 'consent of the public'. Newman says:

> the British ideal is that policing should be shaped by the consent of the population. Such consent is conditional upon the observance by the police of the individual's rights and liberties. Only in this way will the respect of the public be retained and the duties and functions of the police be capable of being effectively discharged.[37]

The police are sensed as an omnipresent eye but it is the eye of the public itself watching over itself. It is embedded in the greater omnipresent technology of the state/government which finds its legitimacy again in the rhetoric of public consent and democratic procedure. However this rhetoric is supplemented by the simple sense of enormity and omnipotence which the discursive technologies, constituting the state, are able to inspire. Silver describes this process as an 'integration of the centre and the periphery'. He writes of 'the capacity of bureaucratic organisations to make the values of the centre palpable in daily life by means of detached persons operating on organisationally defined missions'.[38]

Policing is then a technology for the creation of moral consensus through 'continual pervasive moral display'. As for the 'integration of centre and periphery' however, in the post-structuralist, post-Lacanian frame there is no 'centre' other than the 'sense' of a centre and that it is precisely this 'sense' which is consensualising since it is a discourse which articulates connotations of 'wholeness' and coherence. 'The public', 'the Nation', 'the British people', 'our Society', 'our way of life': this is the currency in which policing rhetoric and governmental rhetoric in general often deals, as can be seen from the above quotes from Newman.

The conclusion we have to draw at any rate is that moral display is not the only principle at work. In fact moral display is subordinate to another principle: that of force. The ultimate principle is the preservation of the Queen's Peace. The Queen's Peace is an *attempt to signify a violence external to the rule of law*. That is why Newman says that in the event of a conflict between the two the former will prevail. The point is that the Rule of Law is premised on the threat of violence signified by Newman's commitment to the Queen's Peace yet *that very commitment can never be fully legal*—it cannot be assimilated into the discourse for which it provides a basis. The implicit violence of Newman's commitment is what Slavoj Zizek refers to as the irreducible unassimilable kernel of discourse, it is why discursive closure is impossible—or to put it another way, why symbolic antago-nism and therefore shame and paranoia are inevitable.[39] He points to the way in which all law is founded on a fun-damentally irrational moral commitment. In the end law is valid for no other reason than that it is 'the Law'. Each system of law has its origins in a fundamental violence which cannot be assimilated into the legal code itself—law cannot make itself legal. For Zizek this unassimilable kernel is always the source of a psychotic 'enjoyment':

it is not sufficient to point out how the racist's Other presents a threat to our identity. We should rather invert this proposition: the fascinating image of the Other personifies our innermost split—what is already 'in us more than ourselves'—and thus prevents us from achieving full identity with ourselves. The hatred of the Other is the hatred of our own excess of enjoyment.[40]

In the context of the analysis Giddens gives us, this dislocation must be a source of shame. If it is the source of shame then it can drive paranoid fantasies—paranoid fantasies of threatening objects, the violent repetitive elimination of which will be the source of enjoyment for the police officer. Thus Giddens's and Zizek's analyses are compatible (at least at this level). We have then (to repeat the theoretical proposition which has run through this paper) a theoretical *linkage* between a symbolic dislocation, a production of shame, a production of paranoid objects and finally the appearance of psychotic enjoyment through the repetitive elimination of the threat.

This precipitous situation leaves the police officer clinging on to the juridical subject—the Rule of Law—as the core of his identity. Police officers always talk about themselves as agents of law when you ask them what they do:

> *What image do you think this age group/part of the population should have of the police? How would you like to see them view the Police?*
>
> It's not how I think you should view the Police, it's how I think they should view the law of the land. The Police are only acting, they are only trying to ensure that most people comply with that for the safety of everybody else.[41]

To try to preserve this image the police officer is involved in a constant battle to eliminate difference and complexity and symbolic contradiction within his own subjectivity

> *You don't feel that PACE (Police And Criminal Evidence Act) has put any restrictions on your ability to do the job?*
>
> No. No, I think if anything, it's provided us with

more powers, useful ones as well. The general power of arrest for instance, great, terrific. It is really useful. To ascertain name and address. The problems we used to have with that. People just refusing to give details, having only committed perhaps a minor offence, we had hardly a leg to stand on, we were always twisting and bending the rules which isn't right, the law should provide, which it does now.[42]

This battle against complexity, contradiction and ambiguity is reflected in the level of hostility to complexity and difference within the group subjectivity—the institution as a whole. The enormous pressures for conformity within the police are well known. This produces more and more acts of foreclosure, more and more returns of the Real, more and more paranoia. The uniformed police officer, functioning as the mirror image of our juridical subjectivity, cannot tolerate difference within so he cannot tolerate difference without.

It is very interesting that Egon Bittner made much the same point about the police in fact being agents carrying the surplus violence after the pacification of modernity—a role which simply made the law just one of their tools—a means to an end.[43] Finally, he puzzled about why this conclusion had been so firmly resisted despite overwhelming evidence that policemen did very little law and order work (one arrest per month for a New York Patrolman—three convictions per year) yet on the basis of his observations they systematically used violence from day to day in the pursuit of public pacification. But of course this is a necessarily foreclosed truth. The legality of the police is a fundamental founding myth of modernity.[44] The systematic illegality, or perhaps non-legality, of much police activity which is a functional requirement of modernity cannot be seen for what it is. Equally he could not understand why they constantly went 'over the top' and seemed to derive pleasure from this, but then he did not perhaps understand the shaming effects of this self-deconstructing discourse, the consequent paranoia and how this may be related to the enjoyment of violent elimination of 'threat'.

Further attempts are made to paper over the cracks such as the mobilisation of positivism in order to portray law as tool for provision for needs of society so that the needs of society may legitimate that violent surplus.

Newman states that:

> the continuing aim of the Metropolitan Police must be to work with others to develop collaborative strategies against crime and disorder.
>
> This aim includes invoking the assistance of statutory and voluntary agencies and local authorities. Many of the apparently isolated incidents to which police are called are symptoms of more general and substantive problems with roots in a wide range of social and environmental conditions. The aim of the Metropolitan Police will, therefore, be to work with other agencies to develop what is known as a 'situational' or 'problem solving' approach to crime prevention, where, rather than merely dealing with individual acts of law breaking, careful analysis is made of the total circumstances surrounding the commission of types of crime, taking better account of wide ranging social and environmental factors, in order better to understand—and counter—the causes of those acts.[45]

He also writes of:

> co-operation with others in the *creation* and maintenance of a *way of life* in *communities* which strikes the optimum balance between the collective interests of all citizens and the personal rights of all individuals.[46]

Here we see an almost seamless articulation of the social engineering talk of positivism with the rights talk of classical theory. And again they must 'co-operate with local planners in schemes for "designing out" crime and promoting informal social controls' and also 'improve analysis and assessment of environmental factors which give rise to crime, fear of crime and neighbourhood decline'.[47]

This is not a police force dedicated to the simple repressive task of law enforcement; it is a discourse which manifestly articulates the police as a constitutive power, an agent not just of social engineering but of social 'creation'. The language is one which is so 'naturalised', so 'common sense' that it appears almost transparent until we place it back in its historico-discursive context. It is only then that the enormity of the assumptions lying behind it become apparent, and we see that those assumptions are historically specific and not 'natural', obvious, and un-problematic at all. This is especially the case when we begin to see that traces of all of the discourses I have discussed remain in co-existence delicately 'sutured' to produce an apparently seamless web of 'naturalised' rhetoric. They are not seamless, however; the dislocations remain.

The notion of 'dislocation' is an interesting one here. It operates at the heart of the work of Ernesto Laclau.[48] For him the point of dislocation between unassimilable discourses is always the point at which conditions of possibility for new formations appear. This is that place at which the subject appears (including, presumably, the paranoid subject) and at which freedom appears.[49] An optimistic politics oriented around difference, hybridity and the ensuing possibilities for human freedom and autonomy has been developing on the basis of this theoretical frame. Post-metaphysicians such as Laclau along with Rorty, Lyotard, and others, insist that freedom lies in the direction of the multiplication of 'discourses', 'vocabularies', 'Phrase regimes', etc.[50] Rorty and Laclau simply ignore the existence of affective horror associated with such discursive fragmentation and breakdown. They are interested only in the conditions of possibility for new discursive modes which it brings about. Lyotard on the other hand positively valorises the affect at the point of disintegration/fragmentation in the firm belief that the imagination is in the end comfortably capable of overcoming this experience of the sublime.[51] Yet what is the politics of contingency and diversity to do about communities which are inherently paranoid, which respond to the presence of dislocation/the sublime not by hybridising but by foreclosing, hating and purifying through violence? And what if the most deeply paranoid of all communities is a community which seems fundamental to any radical democratic polity, the community of the police? After all hybridisation requires trust and, as Giddens points out, the ability to trust is based on the creation of a protective cocoon blinding us to existential dangers (including the dangers of violence, social chaos and death). It is the police as the bearer of the violent surplus in modernity which provides a guarantee of general pacification, a guarantee which insulates us from many existential threats, a guarantee which provides us with ontological security, and which enables us to indulge in the joys of hybridity, plurality, diversity, etc. Police paranoia is inevitable both in the sense that it is an inevitable outcome of the symbolic antagonisms they bear[52] and in the sense that it is a pre-condition of their ability to do what E.C. Hughes referred to as 'good people's' 'dirty work', in his insightful analysis of the deep ambivalence underlying the pacified middle class's attitude to the social control of potentially threatening out-groups.[53] Perhaps our ontological trust, and thus our acceptance of diversity, is, paradoxically, conditional upon the paranoia of the police officer.

(6)

Bodies, Boundaries and Solidarities

A Psychoanalytical Account of Racism and Ethnic Hatred

John Bird

the message itself, one about the hidden and unseemly face of our confident, affluent, brave world, and of the dangerous game this world plays with human moral impulse, seems to be resonant with ever more widely shared concerns.[1]

Hence, emotion lies at the heart of the thinking process....My point...is to begin to take [this] thought seriously.[2]

There is, in one of the novels of the American science fiction writer Kurt Vonnegut, a character who collects news items which give bad signs of the times. Ethnic cleansing—as an idea and a practice, as a myth and/or a reality—might well be one of these bad signs, and contains within it some of the ambiguities of ethnicity. In particular, these might be community coexisting with hate, ideas of the dirtiness of otherness and the desire for cleanliness, failures to live with contingency and ambivalence.

In addition, it points to some of the major lacunae in social scientific theorising—how do we explain ethnic conflict and its ubiquity? On what foundations—if any—can we build a democratic politics of ethnic diversity, one that avoids intolerance and exclusion?

Introduction

There is a certain optimism in the politics of postmodernity which includes a commitment to the tolerance of diversity and to the realisation of that tolerance in a democratic—albeit a radical democratic—system. This optimism sits uneasily with the history of racism, and with the current re-emergence of ethnic tensions in the former USSR and Yugoslavia. The national thing, as Zizek calls it,[3] is dark and violent, filled with passion, and makes constant reference to bodily parts and states; it is part of a phenomenon that can best be termed pleasure in hatred.

What follows below has a number of themes: one associated with psychoanalytic approaches to racism and ethnicity,[4] in particular those derivable from Melanie Klein's work;[5] another derivable from Durkheim's views on solidarity and the role that emotions and sentiments play in communal life[6] and yet another located principally in Bauman's writing,[7] on the relationships between modernity and the problem of ambivalence. These themes seem to be linked through an emphasis on bodies and on boundaries and how these relate to social solidarity. The intention is, therefore, to link the more social concerns of Durkheim and Bauman with the more psychological concerns of Klein, and to see if—in respect of racism and ethnicity—the pessimism of Kurt Vonnegut's character is all we can aspire to.

Two possible end points of the arguments that will be developed are (1) that ethnicity and solidarity are *not necessarily* forces for good, although members of ethnically solidary communities often feel that is the case; and (2) that racism and ethnicity are not entirely historically contingent. Put another way, racism and ethnicity are not simply reflections of some other set of structures/interests, and the solidarity of communities—ethnic groups—carries with it problematic dealings with other communities.[8] In an important way, therefore, it is the very non-contingent nature of ethnic and racial differences which may render them so obdurate.

Ethnicity, Bodies and Passions

The Contribution of Psychoanalysis

Psychoanalytic approaches to racism are of long standing—we can mention here Dollard's work[9] at one end of the historical spectrum, and Rustin's [10] at the other. The commitment to such an analysis takes us to one of the central issues in the debate about racism—if racism is rational then psychoanalysis can have little to offer; if it is irrational then psychoanalysis may be useful.

It is the contention here—and something suggested in Rustin's work—that psychoanalytic views can fill in some spectacular lacunae in existing accounts of racial and ethnic differences. These include how we account for the *ubiquity* of race/ethnicity; for the *passions* that attach to such differences; and for the role that *bodies* play in defining these differences. The contribution that psychoanalysis can offer arises from its central concern with bodies, with how boundary drawing and maintenance are essential to selfhood, and with the centrality of emotions in thinking processes, even those which have a patina of rationality. As Young emphasises,[11] if we argue that social context is crucial in the explanation of any phenomenon, then the early development of the person in a context which is usually termed a family, will also be part of that social context and will have determinate effects.

It is particularly noticeable not only that psychoanalytic approaches to racism have had a recent resurgence but that they have focused upon that brand associated with Lacan;[12] receiving less attention have been those approaches located in the works of Klein which might on the surface—with their emphasis on splitting, bodies and hate—be the more obvious candidates.

It is not the intention here either to outline a Lacanian account of racism, or to criticise such a perspective. What is worth pointing out is the terminology of that approach: the Other, signifiers, presence/difference, the Imaginary, the mirror, Desire, lack. Like the Kleinian terminology—of splitting, hate, schizoid, depressive—there is the suggestion of otherness, of the constant effectiveness of unconscious forces.

When applied to racism there is something close to Bauman's linking of racism and modernity: '[a modernity which] demands unity and integration of the realm and security of its borders...[and therefore some] non-rectifiable differences [between people].'[13]

The imaginary, desire, splitting, the Other are about the other side of the border, about the outside of community and about structures of solidarity. As such, as will be argued below, the language here is close to the language of Durkheim.

The reference to borders and to security suggests interesting parallels: for example, for the Kleinian, the journey to maturity is, in part, a journey where we learn the difference between self and other and learn to deal with difference in a mature fashion, whilst never giving up the earliest strategies—the schizoid position, in which the other is always the depository of hate, aggression and nastiness. For Klein, the schizoid and the depressive positions are not stages, and the potential to 'occupy' them remains throughout life. The schizoid position is the earliest and is the way that the new born child deals with hate, anxiety and aggression. For Klein, the person's earliest experiences—which precede the ability to use language—are of a fluid, fearful and unstable self, where boundaries are ill-formed. The self is not formed early and is not formed easily. The schizoid position is an attempt to stabilise a self, an identity in a world of competing and powerfully positive and negative feelings. Its essential features include the division of aspects of the world into good and bad ones and the expelling of the bad into particular objects and the good into others. The bad objects can be treated badly, even though the fear that they will retaliate is never far away. What is involved is splitting, especially of the mother, into a loved and a hated part, parts which are irreconcilable. The child thus avoids dealing with the central features of the depressive position—that all people have good and bad parts, and that my hate and aggression *do not*—in any simple and unrestrained fashion—have the power to destroy others. Therefore, in the schizoid position we love what makes us feel good and hate what frustrates us—the hate and love are projected on to a carer; in the depressive position we hate the hating self and attempt to repair and protect what we have/can damage, whilst being anxious that we cannot make this reparation. In another language, the schizoid position might be characterised as one in which we split away differences, and the depressive position as one in which we come to terms with differences.

As Rustin indicates, there is a similarity between what the racist does and what the individual does in the schizoid position; what are involved are processes of projection and projective identification. These processes include projection into and attacks upon others or parts of others, the desire to take over and control others, with psychic consequences which involve splitting, a feeling of being in pieces, a feeling the self is depleted, depersonalisation and anxiety. Hate, fear and aggression are dumped on others, and then we fear that these states will come back to attack us; the language here is noticeably military and political—states, attack, aggression— and is close to that of the Bauman quotation above: unity, border security and irreconcilable differences.

Now the weakness of the Rustinian and of many other psychoanalytical accounts lies in their difficulties in explaining the conditions under which, in this case, the schizoid position, which is the archetype of racism, arises. What we are given in Rustin and others is an *isomorphism* (a similarity of structure) between the schizoid position—which, it must be emphasised, has little to do with schizoid states or with schizophrenia—and racism, and nothing that approaches a causal link. We could, of course, be satisfied with this, and not seek such a causal link. One reason we should be on our guard here is the universality asserted by Klein for the schizoid position. If this position is universal then anyone is, under the requisite conditions, likely to become racist, regardless of their colour. If this were the case it would require a rethinking of the theoretical position that seeks to relate racism to what the powerful do to the powerless, and the empirical position that only certain groups seem, consistently, to suffer the effects of racism.

What Rustin *does* give us is an account of the emotional charge of racism—his linking of racism to Sartre's characterisation of anti-semitism as a passion, and an explanation of why racism is both common and has a common empirical content— bodies, blood, dirt, sex. What is missing is a lack of specificity about (a) when racism will emerge, and (b) what can be done about it. The implications for remedies for racism are, in fact, pessimistic: training and education do not work because racism is about emotion and passion and not about reason; inducing guilt does not work because that merely feeds the strong passions that are already there. There is little exploration of what does work and little drawing on one possible Kleinian process—reparation—that might relate to remedies for race hatred. It is worth mentioning here the brief and rather strange application of reparation to colonised societies in Klein's own work.[14]

If we accept that racism and ethnic tension are closely associated with boundaries and difference then we can understand some of the tensions inherent in times of boundary changes as, for example, in the former Yugoslavia. The redrawing of boundaries—the creation of new imaginary communities—actually involves people passing across and between past borders; involves what was once inside being outside; what was once 'us' becoming 'the other'. It may very well be that one of the conditions for racism and ethnic tension is the redrawing of boundaries, a redrawing which tests and put under stress the coming to terms with difference which is, in our contention, the essential feature of the depressive position. There are, here, close parallels between what Klein is saying about the construction of the self, what Douglas[15] and Bauman[16] are saying about ambivalence and anomaly, and what Durkheim says about community and solidarity.

The Contribution of Durkheim

There has been considerable debate—in one view, brought to a close by Mestrovic's study[17]—over the extent to which Durkheim's sociology is on the side of reason or on the side of the passions. It is the contention here, and no attempt will be made to assess the implications of this for Durkheim's methodology of the social sciences, that he presents an approach to solidarity which is (a) potentially pessimistic, and (b) which gives considerable weight to emotions, sentiments and passions.

This concern with emotions and sentiments is found most

clearly in sections of the *Elementary Forms*[18] and in the later parts of *Primitive Classification*.[19] In part, the reference to sentiments points to their dangerous capacities: 'Under the influence of collective enthusiasm they are sometimes seized by a positive delirium which compels them to actions in which they do not recognise themselves.'[20]

In other references, sentiments are seen as generated by participation in social groups, sentiments which are for good, and would, moreover, not have arisen without the social group (for example, in *Elementary Forms*). In *Primitive Classification*, sentiments are what account for the *use*, by members of society, of the classificatory systems which society provides:

> From the fact that the external form of the classification was furnished by society, it does not necessarily follow that the way in which the framework was used is due to reasons of the same origin....There are sentimental affinities between things as between individuals....The differences and resemblances which determine the fashion in which they [things/people] are grouped are more affective than intellectual...it is this emotional value of notions which plays the preponderant part in the manner in which ideas are connected or separated. It is the dominant characteristic in classification.[21]

If we assume that the analysis of the role of emotions and sentiments in what Durkheim calls elementary/'primitive' forms give us some insight into *all* systems of classification and beliefs, then this may be the route to a Durkheimian approach to communal/ethnic conflict. The Durkheimian idea that 'primitive forms' give us a clear insight into the bases of more 'developed forms' is—in one interpretation—evolutionist. In another possible interpretation, however, it is similar to the Kleinian notion of positions, in which the earlier are never given up and are always likely to return.

Thus, mechanical solidarity which, for Durkheim, gives a central role to sentiments and to the suppression of difference, is always a potential within social systems, rather than being something which is abandoned. As indicated in the above quotation, affectivity rather than the intellect is central; central in the way that it is central for Klein in the development of the person, and for Sartre in the development of anti-Semitism.[22] It is intriguing that Klein, Durkheim and Sartre all give a central role to passion in their fields of study.

Let us therefore sketch a version of the mechanical/organic distinction which says something about ethnic difference. There is much agreement over the essentials of Durkheim's approach to solidarity and the division of labour; mechanical solidarity exemplifies traditional, non-industrial societies, and organic solidarity is characteristic of the modern world. Uniformity, collectivity, sameness, repressive law, a single religion, concreteness of conception, on the one hand; differentiation, individuality, divergence of belief, restitutive law, and abstractness of conception on the other.

As typifications of societies these two have received considerable—and probably justified—criticism. They are seen to be empirically dubious and the mechanism of the passage from one type of solidarity to the other is seen as unduly mechanistic. More important for the argument here is whether there *is* a passage from one to the other, and the role that religion plays. On the first, it seems more empirically convincing to emphasise the coexistence of types of solidarity; a background of organic solidarity with pockets of mechanical solidarity. The whole dynamics of ethnic difference then becomes the possibility of mechanically solidary communities coexisting with each other. This could be differently stated: the issue is the *creation* of mechanical communities as a consequence of the emergence of the modern world, as safe havens from that world. When, for example, Richards[23] argues that racism is based on an intolerance of the psychic fluidity demanded by the modern world, we could add that the problem is also how social fluidity is treated in the modern world. The purging of ambivalence and the extermination of the ambiguous to which Bauman refers[24] is the very kernel of the psychic processes of the schizoid position and one of the social correlates of mechanical solidarity.

The passage from mechanical to organic solidarity also has implications for religion. In mechanical solidarity there is one strong belief held by the whole community which takes on a religious character—references to the sacred, to emotions, to inclusion. With organic solidarity, there is a weakening of the *conscience collective* which has little power to sway people, and is replaced by a religion of the individual with a universalised morality. Now, of course, the strong beliefs held by a whole community which take on the character of religions are very like beliefs about ethnicity and culture. It is precisely emotion, inclusion/exclusion, and sacredness which are the features of ethnic identity and which make that identity so intolerant of otherness.

Racism, Ethnicity and Ambivalence

We might characterise the debate about modernity (and, of course, post-modernity) as one between optimists and pessimists:[25] on the one hand, Giddens with his views on the possibility of the transformation of intimacy and the resultant transformation of the whole social world;[26] on the other Bauman, with his perspectives on the holocaust and the endless purging of ambiguity characteristic of modernity.[27] Giddens's optimism is evident in the following:

> We have no need to wait around for a sociopolitical revolution to further programmes of emancipation....Revolutionary processes are already well under way in the infrastructure of personal life. The transformation in intimacy presses for psychic as well as social change and such change, going 'from the bottom up', could potentially ramify through other, more public, institutions.[28]

The medium for this transformation is an ideal pure relationship, based upon the principle of autonomy, and the limitation of the power of the strong. What we have is a radical politics of emancipation through radical democracy.

Bauman's pessimism seems to follow from a view that boundary building and maintaining are essential to social existence and that the problem with modernity is that boundaries are abolished/reduced:

> Modernity brought the levelling of differences—at

least their outward appearance, of the very stuff of which symbolic distances between segregated groups are made. With such differences missing, it is not enough to muse philosophically over the wisdom of reality as it was....Differences had to be created now, or retained against the awesome eroding power of social and legal equality and cross-cultural exchange.[29]

It is on this basis that racism is seen as a modern product:

Modernity made racism possible. It created a demand for racism; an era that declared achievement to be the only measure of human worth needed a theory of ascription to redeem boundary-drawing and boundary-guarding concerns under new conditions which made boundary-crossing easier than ever before.[30]

The technologies of the modern world and their bureaucracies facilitate this boundary-drawing and maintaining, which is further enhanced by developments in morality and ethics; a process by which some social actions—dealing with enemies, with outsiders, with the other—are removed from the realm of moral concern, a process which Bauman terms adiaphorisation.

Now the major problem here is the reference to the need for boundary drawing and the moral effects of being on the wrong side of the boundary, which Bauman sometimes argues is systemic: 'Indeed, the adiaphorisation of human action seems to be a necessary constitutive act of any supra-individual, social totality.'[31]

We should recognise that boundary drawing and maintaining are central themes also for Durkheim and for Klein. For Durkheim, the issue with organic solidarity is how a social totality is possible when individuals are differentiated and divided and have—as it were—constantly to work across boundaries. The answer is probably a weak one—legal reparation for wrong; the cult of the individual coexisting with a universal morality; and ideas of humanity-as-a-whole. This is a weak answer because there is always an outside to humanity-as-a-whole; such dichotomies are exercises in power in which *outside* and *other* coexist. The situation is no more easily dealt with when we recognise that organic solidarity and mechanical solidarity may coexist, for that coexistence—the recrudescence of mechanical communities—is itself a response to confusion and ambiguity about boundaries.

The Kleinian perspective—as outlined above—may provide some insights into the anxiety about ambiguity and some vision of what 'living at peace with ambivalence may look like'.[32] There are four key elements of this Kleinian perspective: embodiment; relationships between the schizoid position and boundary formation; links between the depressive position and ambiguity; and finally the role that reparation can play in living with others.

Embodiment

It is fundamental to Klein that earliest experience is focused on the body and bodily states. This is clear in the schizoid position where there are only part objects which are not persons but anatomical parts, and are split into ideal and persecutory aspects.[33] It is to these bodily parts that profoundly strong feelings—negative and positive—are attached. It is, in addition, the body which is the original container and the original basis for boundary-formation. It is no accident therefore that Douglas[34] points to the role of the body in saying things about the unities and division of the social world, and stresses the central role of pollution and purity. It is also no surprise—when we keep in mind the role of the skin as container for the body[35]—that we find Fanon referring to the process of epidermalisation in racism.[36] Hinshelwood—citing work by Bick and Meltzer—indicates the central significance of skin in the earliest establishment of identity. Skin is seen as the original boundary/container, but one with holes from which things— real and fantasised—leak in and out. This suggests an anxiety over leaking and fluidity, and some interesting parallels with fears of immigration derived from travel through water and air, elements which are, themselves, permeable.

This stress on embodiment suggests the possibility of a biological metaphorics of racial and ethnic hatred which has roots deep in the psychogenesis of the individual and the development of his or her identity. In addition, it is likely that, to the extent that ethnic and racial differences are based upon passions, they derive their content from earliest experiences.

Boundaries and the Schizoid Position

It is important to remember that the schizoid position is never given up. It is also important that the means of stabilisation requires a drawing of strict boundaries and an intolerance of ambiguity that is, for Bauman, the essential feature of modernity. The stranger/outsider for him play the role that the bad object and its introjects play for Klein. Both are outside but forever dangerous; both are both socially and ethically outside. In a sense, therefore, the schizoid position and modernity are of a piece; in neither can difference be tolerated without plunging those who are different into a moral and political vacuum. The consequent adiaphorisation legitimates our dealings with those who are different, including expulsion, exclusion and destruction.

The Depressive Position and Coming to Terms with Ambiguity

The crucial difference between the schizoid and the depressive position for us relates to ambiguity; in essence, the depressive position is a combination of three things—a realisation that others are persons and not bodily parts; a recognition that others contain both good and bad behaviour/motives; and a realisation that we can make reparation for having thought and acted otherwise in fantasy and in reality. Splitting into good and bad objects is increasingly a thing of the past; instead we come to terms with the indeterminateness and ambiguity of people/things. As Hanna Segal puts it:

> [in the move from paranoid/schizoid to depressive position] splitting and projection, with resulting persecution and idealization, give way to realistic discrimination and a capacity for love and realistic concern with mature object relations which allow for interdependence and acknowledgement of ambivalence.[37]

As such, we could see the depressive position as equivalent to postmodernity which asserts the fluidity and plurality of identities, a fluidity which—despite the maturity associated with the depressive position—may continue to presage a resort to schizoid mechanisms.

Reparation and Living with Different Others

If reparation for past hates and loathings is not simply a strategy for the infant's dealing with its carers, then it may also be a route to some tolerance of difference. What is important about this notion is that it places the responsibility for reparation on the loather and hater, rather than on the hated/loathed/excluded. In addition, it seems to be more 'realistic' and rational than loathing and hating which are, as Sartre realised, passions. As Alford summarises:

> The morality of reparation is other-directed, as well as other-regarding. We do not love and care for others *in order* to achieve depressive integration. Rather it is *because* we have achieved this level of integration, and hence this level of consolidation of the self, that we may direct our care and concern towards others.[38]

This idea of reparation takes us right back to discussions of pessimism and optimism. If, as Alford and Bauman argue, instrumental reason fails by condemning whole groups to nullity and, in the extreme, physical extermination, then reparative reason—the ethical correlate of the depressive position—may be a more ethical and mature way of doing things. However, there is no guarantee that instrumental reason or schizoid mechanisms can be avoided. Indeed, for Bauman, the postmodern condition is no guarantee at all of tolerance of ambiguity, and may yield a form of tolerance in selfishness:

> The postmodern condition has split society into the happy seduced and the unhappy oppressed halves—with postmodern mentality celebrated by the first half of the division while adding to the misery of the second. The first half may abandon itself to the carefree celebration only because it has satisfied itself that the misery of the second half is their rightful *choice*, or at least a legitimate part of the world's exhilarating diversity....And thus drawing the line between the inside and the outside seems to have lost nothing of its

genocidal potency. If anything, this potency has grown, as no missionary proselytizing prospects salvage the outsiders from total and final condemnation.[39]

There is an echo here of Cornell West's view of race and postmodernity:

> The ragged edges of the Real, of *Necessity*, not being able to eat, not having shelter, not having health care, all this is something that one cannot not know. The black condition acknowledges that. It is so much more acutely felt because this is a society where a lot of people live a Teflon existence, where a lot of people have no sense of the ragged edges of necessity, of what it means to be impinged upon by structures of oppression.[40]

The essential issue here is that the contingency of postmodernity gives no guarantee that other ways of life will either be tolerated or even engaged with; indeed, the very contingency of other ways—despite being based on oppression and misery—provides a reason for leaving them alone, for being indifferent, for engaging only at the level of the newspaper colour supplement. There seems to be a choice here: between the acceptance of differences and dissensions, but an acceptance which does not end up as self-satisfied and distancing; and a resort to forms of community sometimes called 'neo-tribes', communities which, for Bauman at least, inflame, attract and produce ardent loyalties, but which—unlike mechanically solidary communities, and very like the individual's resort to schizoid mechanisms—are temporary and bound to fail in that they generate false hopes.[41] The former—requiring, in Bauman's words 'nerves of steel'[42]—may seem distant from the realities of the former Yugoslavia, but is the wager that we may have to make.

It is interesting here to note that three of the politics which Bauman sees as appropriate to the postmodern world[43] are, from the point of the view of the argument developed here, problematic and redolent of schizoid mechanisms. Tribal politics which inflames with false promises, the politics of desire which imbues symbols with strong emotive power, and the politics of fear which gives centrality to the body and body management, and which involves concern over damage to the body (both individual and politic) are all—from a Kleinian perspective—deeply reminiscent of the schizoid position. In this politics which Maffesoli calls neo-tribalism there is a coming together of people for no other reason than that everything we do 'should bathe in the affectual ambience...with [consequent] disengagement and irresponsibility.'[44] This affective ambience is Durkheim's sacred reborn in the postmodern world.

Conclusion

I side with Bauman's relative pessimism concerning ethnic differences, and against the optimism of Giddens, and have used and adapted some Kleinian ideas as a way to do this; the depressive position and the politics of reparation may be desirable but they are difficult to develop and manage in practice. It is, indeed, difficult to work out what a reparative politics of ethnicity would involve and that has not been the aim of this chapter. I also side with those—including many psychoanalytic thinkers—who place limits on contingency and on the possibilities of difference. It is the non-contingency of elements within racial and ethnic hatred that provides for the dangers of the 'national thing' referred to by Zizek, and the pleasure in hatred which is so much a feature of the former USSR and Yugoslavia.

That there is, in racism and ethnic hatred, a representational pleasure in hating relates, in part, to Zizek's idea that racism and ethnicism are about fears that our pleasures have been stolen and usurped by the Other.[45] We take pleasure in hating those who are not only the repositories of our projection but also because those projections have been associated with issues that are about pleasure/ambivalence—sexuality for example. That theft has occurred across a boundary—ethnic and/or racial—and from across that boundary return, largely in fantasy, fears of uncontrolled pleasure/desire/ambivalence.

(7)

New Foundations

Contingency, Indeterminacy and Black Translocality

Chetan Bhatt

Religion is the general theory of this world, its
encyclopaedic compendium, its logic in popular
form, its spiritual point d'honneur, its enthusiasm, its
moral sanction, its solemn complement and its
universal basis of consolation and justification. It is
the fantastic realisation of the human essence since
the human essence has not acquired any true
reality.

Karl Marx, Introduction to
*A Contribution to the Critique of
Hegel's Philosophy of Right*

Traitors beware! Lord Ram is awake! Victory to Lord
Ram! Victory to Bharat Mataji! Any Hindu whose
blood does not boil has water in his veins! The
Ayodhya temple is just the first step! Mathura and
Benares are next!

Hindu *kar sevak* chant

Introduction: Living in the Obsolete

In September 1992, an article in the 'Living' column of the
British *Independent* newspaper described a day trip by a coach
party of Asian Muslim women from Dudley, a post-industrial
working-class town in the Midlands, to Church Stretton, a
village in Long Mynd, 'a beautiful Shropshire valley with a

stream, steep green slopes, countryside redolent of A.E.
Housman, English pastoral poetry and patriotic platitudes
about our green and pleasant land'.[1] This Asian interference in
the imaginary of pastoral Englishness was registered by two
middle-aged white women who arrived and placed their deck-
chairs with their backs to the picnickers but 'could not resist
turning around frequently to stare blatantly at the unexpected
company'.

The disruption of the peaceful, graceful semiology of the
English countryside caused by this insertion of 'Asian alienness'
is important not simply because it demonstrates a rudimentary
incompatibility between the immanent Englishness of British
nationalism and the black presence but because it discloses
important ambiguities about the 'modern' or 'postmodern'
identities implied in that presence. Many of those Asian
Muslim women came to the Midlands as partners of industrial
foundry and steel workers from rural (peasant) Kashmir,
themselves displaced to Britain in the 1950s as a result of a
wholly modernist enterprise: a major dam-building project
undertaken by the British government. Similar unprecedented
movements of black colonial labour from Asia, the Caribbean
and Africa to European colonist countries resulted in a unique
presence, the 'rational' economic exploitation of which formed
a key feature of the modernisation of post-war and postcolonial
Europe. The intrusion of those Asian women into the rustic
symbolism of the English countryside signals a modern presence which instantly agitates the archaic components of
'Englishness'. But while the participation of Asian women in
the uncertain pleasures and burdens of the English countryside
is a product of the machinations of modernity, its discursive
presentation in the article—Indian adornments nestling in the
English clover, samosa crumbs among Albion's red roses—
alerts us to the novel relations fashionably identified with
postmodern discourse.

Those 'postmodern' relations of race and ethnicity have
been frequently articulated within the instinctive rhetoric of
'difference' and 'diversity'—so that the juxtaposition of 'Asian
alienness' and 'English heritage' appears simultaneously
aberrant but, in a cynical way, also no longer surprising.
Postmodernity thus apparently creates the space for, or the

promise of, multicultural and other identities,[2] with an extreme emphasis on marking out the self-proclaimed or imposed differences between groups rather than identifying their progressive commonalities.

However, in contemporary Europe, the acknowledgement of 'difference' and 'diversity' has not required postmodern social and political theory or left-wing celebrations of 'radical difference'. A deluge of right-wing and far-right political movements, networks and cultural associations have consciously made it their business to acknowledge 'difference': the step from an agitated backward-looking glance to physical attacks, racist murders and outright pogroms has become exceedingly short.

In this way, race remains a critical signifier in shaping the lives and experiences of those Asian women. However, their identities, and those identities claimed by black constituencies in Britain over the last decade, are themselves indeterminate within an historical narrative of colonialism, migration and diaspora. The Asian women's trip was jointly organised by the One World organisation and the Dudley Community Relations Council. Merely those names invoke prominent contemporary ambivalences. The aspiration to a common planetary identity grates against the selectivity and parochialism exemplified by 'community', just as the troubled concern with relations between groups exposes as fraudulent the universalist assurances of modernism (though the celebrated 'universalising' efforts of modernity and the universal thought of the Enlightenment have entailed the entirely partisan histories of slavery, indentured labour, colonial domination and imperial exploitation).

Many of those women's previous land of settlement, Kashmir, is itself a highly contested site of political and military struggle. Kashmir's special place in the colonial dissection of the Indian subcontinent now leaves it riven with open militarised confrontations along the axes of national liberation struggle, self-determination, centre versus state Indian politics, Pakistani and Indian nationalism and Hindu-Muslim 'communalism', the latter heightened following the destruction of the 'Babri masjid' (mosque) in Ayodhya in 1992 and the subsequent Hindu onslaught on Muslim communities throughout India.

The ambivalences in identity continue to multiply: those Asian women live in the same Muslim communities which were instrumental in political protests against Salman Rushdie's *The Satanic Verses* during the late 1980s, protests almost universally viewed as regressive ('backward') or pre-modern ('medieval') in discursive content, if not form. These assignations do not correspond, however, with the immense non-contiguous political mobilisation of Muslim nation-states and transnational communities during the 'Rushdie affair', nor indeed, with the political form and character of contemporary radical Islamic nation-states.

We thus see, in this example, a matrix of identifications—global and intensely localised, modernist and apparently 'un'-modern, race-related as well as race-transgressive. It should be emphasised, then, that these identifications travel beyond the parameters of 'race', 'class' and 'community' within which the struggles of black[3] people have traditionally been articulated. The intricacy of the diverse local and translocal strands within which the identities of British black communities are negotiated draws attention to important transformations in contemporary black political agency which are not easily accommodated within the local epistemologies of 'race' or 'ethnicity', 'black liberation' or 'multiculturalism', even as the latter now constitute precisely the terrain of 'difference' or 'diversity' which has been appropriated and frequently celebrated within the rubric of postmodern theory.

Space Race: Black Translocality and Political Agency

One important feature of much contemporary black political agency is a transcendence of those elder languages of race and ethnic relations or at the very least their drastic reinscription into novel translocal political idiolects which attempt to subside 'race'. Conversely, and again this generally constitutes a political formation far removed from multiculturalism, 'race' is detached from its social composition as a relation and reappropriated as an exclusive property of a 'racial' group, which is then transacted in the local, national and international political hypermarket: 'racial difference' becomes something not to transcend or annihilate but to appropriate and enhance. A core aspect of this appropriation is *the political articulation of the mythic*, a reinvention of antiquity in the contemporary within which the cultural movements of Afrocentricity, among other political formations, reside. A modernist application of the methods of archaeology and anthropology is important for these formations.

These two tendencies in black political and cultural agency are transgressive of earlier black political formations and neither is intrinsically progressive or non-progressive. Significantly, these tendencies have chosen (or have no choice but) to negotiate the other cultural and political diagrams drawn by contemporary movements around gender, sexuality and ecology, and, crucially, transnational politics. This constitutes an important variation from previous black political agency in the West which often converged primarily around demands of the nation-state, whether through citizenship, civil rights, equality, antidiscrimination and access to welfare services, or more passionately for 'liberation' (but still within the bounds of the Western nation-state). There was also a fractal supersimilarity in these struggles in Europe and the USA, regardless of the particular national location. That has now been superseded by radical disjunctions between different black movements and a reconstitution of the political and social composition of those black populations. This is not to say that those former struggles for equality are even remotely approaching 'completion', nor is it to suspend consideration of previous international political efforts which focused on solidarity with anti-colonial or anti-apartheid movements and subsequently against American and Western geoimperial hegemony. Indeed, it is precisely the major shifts in the meanings and manifestations of the latter that dominate and determine important components of black political agency.

Central to contemporary black political agency is a pivotal and radically irresolvable encounter with the political economy of location, itself signifying a concern with the spatial-political dynamics inherent in globalisation. It is not the process of migration, cultural change and social adjustment conscientiously highlighted through social anthropological forays into the early black communities that is being referred to here, but rather the recent, innovative changes in the political structures and trajectories of those communities. The most significant of these changes is a symbolic transcendence of British nationhood and national belonging in preference for completely unprecedented cultural, political and economic patterns of transnational association. Paul Gilroy has pointed this out:

> [In Britain] non-European traditional elements, mediated by the histories of Afro-America and the Caribbean, have contributed to the formation of new and distinct black cultures amidst the decadent peculiarities of the Welsh, Irish, Scots and English. These non-European elements must be noted and their distinctive resonance must be accounted for. Some derive from the immediate history of Empire and colonisation in Africa, the Caribbean and the Indian sub-continent....Others create material for the processes of cultural syncretism from extended and still-evolving relationships between the black populations of the over-developed world and their siblings in racial subordination elsewhere.[4]

These activities represent a cultural and political concern beyond the single social body composed of the nation-state and its civil society, echoing the (Gödelian) limitations discovered by contemporary sociologies of their object of study, a defined and bounded social. Diasporic re-identification among people of African descent is one aspect of this change and indeed comprises a contested terrain for the epistemology and ownership of 'race' itself. The manufacture of *umma* (the community of Muslims) during the mobilisation of British Muslim communities under Middle-Eastern hegemony during the Rushdie affair and during the West's war against Iraq is an example of anti-diasporic identification between spatially non-contiguous communities. The activism of many British, European, Canadian and American Hindu organisations and temples in support of the Vishwa Hindu Parishad[5] (VHP) and the Bharatiya Janata Party[6] (BJP), both offshoots of the fascist Rashtriya Swayamsevak Sangh[7] (RSS), during their destruction of the 'Babri masjid' in Ayodhya, Uttar Pradesh, and their attempts to rebuild a temple at the imagined birthplace of the mythic god Rama constitutes a further example.

The acute attentiveness to contemporary non-Western realities by black agents located in the West and their selective affinity to novel transnational symbols caution against the study of British black communities without a comprehension of contemporary social formations of Asia, Africa, the Middle East, the Caribbean and the USA to which British black agents have intricate political and *spatial* affiliations. It should also signal the deficiency of tendencies which have sought to delineate an uncomplicated continuity between anti-colonial traditions and black struggles against racism.[8] Many of those contemporary non-Western movements are severe departures from the taxonomy or the 'practice' of anti-imperialism, even as American geopolitical and military hegemony becomes more entrenched. Some of these religious movements constitute desacralised political agency and political ritual whose character and novelty are barely captured by the notation 'fundamentalism' or 'neo-religion' or 'neo-ethnicity' or their preliminary designation as 'postmodern' phenomena.[9]

These religious and ethnic absolutist movements frequently contain an essential comprehension of 'the West' which astutely focuses as much on the organisation of cultural, political and gender relations in the West as it does on economic, military and geopolitical domination by the latter. Consequently, the 'novel' reassessment of Western culture highlights a distinguishing feature of contemporary discourse and methodology: a Manichaean conflict over the designation of any discourse as essentially Western or essentially anti-Western. This is as much a preoccupation with the spatial conditions of discursive production as it is with the manifest non-Western 'purity' or Western 'impurity' of a discourse and its subject-identities:

> Call us primitive, call us fundamentalists, call us super-stitious barbarians, call us what you like, but your book only serves to define what has gone wrong with Western civilisation—it has lost all sense of distinction between the sacred and the profane....Rushdie 'the Islamic scholar, the man who studied Islam at

144

university' has to brag his Islamic credentials, so that he can convincingly vend his Islamic wares in the West, which has not yet laid the ghost of the crusades to rest...tell your British champions and advisors that India shall not permit 'literary colonialism'.[10]

The interrogation of discourse regarding its Western or non-Western spatial and temporal affiliations refers us to the different, prior process of national liberation and post-independence nation-formation from which contemporary absolutist movements frequently take their discursive content. However, they are not limited any more to this nationalist repertoire and can construct and rehearse different transnational or post-national discursive abstractions (for example, an essential Pan-Islamism, a Western Afrocentricity or an Indian *Hindutva*[11]) which can function both as oppositional devices against the West and can attempt to perform internal political unification or manage dissent and resistance. Nationalism, as a disciplinary ideology, thus merges—and in many cases conflicts—with these other transnational abstractions.

However, the perpetually incomplete quest for discursive purity is by no means restricted to non-Western discourses. It is a general global phenomenon of equal relevance to discursive production originating in the West. Its manifestations in the West refer us instantly to murderous neonationalism in Eastern Europe and resurgence of racism and neofascism in Western Europe, in the context of structural economic, military and political domination of the Third World. But it is also at the core of recent battles within British and American nationalism where the preoccupation with the politics of identity—especially around race, the family and sexuality—has been of equal importance to the new right, the religious right and the new social movements, particularly in the institutions of cultural reproduction, leading to *national-popular* disputes around 'political correctness' and 'loony leftism'. Within the progressive social movements, this has become moored in simulated debates on the virtues of antiessentialism[12] or the celebration of 'difference'. This illustrates the contemporary obsession with 'difference' on both left and right.

Much contemporary black agency in the West demonstrates this *new* will to archaeological and anthropological authenticity but the latter has frequently been mistaken for an eternal tradition or an unmutated ethnicity. This flaw traverses radical, liberal and conservative political traditions. It has, for example, been necessary for some on the black left to erect the legendary anti-colonial, anti-racist black agent against the assemblage of ethnic polyphony invented by executive multiculturalism. This tendency, usually associated with the Institute of Race Relations but going far beyond it, observes ethnicity as a methodology that, in its focus on culture, custom and tradition, fails to deal with the power inherent in institutional racism. But it also views ethnicity as a powerful strategy of the state to deflate black working-class struggles.[13] While the Marxist bombast against municipal ethnobabble is indisputably entertaining and functional, this tendency has persisted in its silence when its 'anti-racist, black' agent has embraced the new, highly reactionary ethnic formations which manifested themselves in Britain prior to, during and since the 'Rushdie affair' and whose primary political targets have been black women, black progressives and the black left. In turn, the legendary anti-racist black agent has itself been ravaged by those who wish to reassert an ethnic singularity or selectiveness, often based on the most fanciful historical or national parameters.[14]

Folklores in Cyberspace, the Mythic Modern

These representations of black political agency do not facilitate understanding of the novelty of, or the desire for, manifold archaeological fictions which constitute a return to traditions which have never existed and an appropriation of ethnicities which have never been. That denotes far more complicated contemporary phenomena which it is unlikely that we will be able to understand in their entirety but which—in their Western or non-Western, religious or ethnic manifestations—it is tempting to bracket and isolate as radically new global phenomena which have engaged from their inception with the modern discourses of nationalism, secularism, communism and democracy.

This is best illustrated by a brief comparison of radical Islamic and Hindu movements, and in particular the Muslim Brotherhood (MB) in Egypt and the Rashtriya Swayamsevak Sangh (RSS) in India. Both these organisations were formed in the 1920s as (semi-)secret societies and by the early 1990s they, or their various offshoots, were the main opposition forces against the ruling party in their respective nation-states. The MB and the RSS came to oppose four broad tendencies: nationalist-secular or socialist anti-colonial movements (such as Arab or Indian nationalist movements, as represented by Nasser and Nehru), traditional religious organisations (quietist Islam or passively devotional Hinduism), reformist overhauls of traditional religion which were apparently to be compatible with the post-colonial nation-state (such as non-violent Gandhian Hinduism or a reformist Islam), and socialist, communist and democratic movements and women's rights.

There are striking parallels in the histories of the MB and the RSS in their respective nations, from their alleged involvement in political assassinations (Nathuram Godse, Gandhi's assassin, was a former RSS member), their subsequent banning, their anticommunist roles, their gelatinous relationship with the state or ruling party, their period of increasing mass activity in the 1950s and 1960s, and their astonishing, deep and committed emphasis on the complete reorganisation of civil society and the creation of new disciplined 'persons' rather than a simple concern with (or in the case of the early RSS, even an interest in) the seizure of state or political power. Central to their respective ideologies was a concern with religious or 'racial' purity,[15] individual responsibility and an active conception of collective social, welfare and political action. The significance of dogged, resolute political labour in civil society should not be missed. It represents a new political philosophy in its own right and has, at best, baffled progressive opposition to 'fundamentalism' since it has been customary for the left to place its political emphasis on statist solutions: how can civil society—the proletariat, the peasants, the masses, the electorate—possibly be an enemy?[16]

The 1960s were an important period in the popular formation of new political-religious movements and ideologies. The

best example is the impact of the social and political thought of
Ruhollah Khomeini in Iran. He outlined a novel system of
'Islamic government' (*hokumat-e-Islami*), which had at its head, as
of right, the learned and 'knowledgeable' clerical elite (*velayat-e-
faqih*) and which involved the reformulation and encoding of
shari'a into the heart of the new Islamic state and civil society.
Central to this project was the reconstruction of Muslim
identity afresh in direct opposition to Western imperialism and
the 'Westoxication' which had previously corrupted it. Khomei-
nism is based on a significant epistemological break with earlier
forms of Islamic political thought. It is definitively not a simple
example of the teachings of the Qu'ran in practice, but a
political ideology deeply influenced from its inception by questions about the organisation of the nation-state and its relation
to the citizen and civil society, the organisation of the administrative, representative and legislative apparatuses of the state,
the political and economic relation between the Islamic nation-
state and the superpowers ('imperialism'), the construction of a
military complex, the complete reorganisation of 'civil society'
and of economics, and the reformation and encoding of a
'philosophy of life' into the materiality of the Islamic state.
Similarly, the Islamic state itself is not a Western bourgeois
democratic or exceptional capitalist institution onto which
medieval Islamic rhetoric has been hastily grafted: it is a
thoroughly modern and novel political formation based to a
greater or lesser degree on absolutist, theocratic and formally
anti-democratic principles of government.

The Hindu revivalist VHP was also formed in the 1960s by
the RSS and was responsible for the campaign to demolish the
'Babri masjid' in Ayodhya in the early 1990s. The RSS had, in
the 1950s, formed the Jan Sangh, a political party that was a
prominent member of the Janata coalition government in 1977.
The collapse of the coalition led to the formation in 1980 of the
Hindu chauvinist, anti-Muslim Bharatiya Janata Party (BJP),
the main opposition party in India today and closely allied to the
RSS-influenced 'family' (*sangh parivar*) of Hindu welfare,
cultural, social, economic and political organisations.

These Hindu and Islamic movements are best described as
'neofoundational' or 'neotraditional'. They are not 'fundamentalist' movements: the sacred text is important for its

semiotic and symbolic value and these movements are careful to create a considerable distance from its actual moral and ethical content and evade its manifest contradictions. Textual exegesis has usually been the preserve of orthodoxy (*the* 'fundamentalists') or reformers. Similarly, the neofoundational movements have little conception or political development of what constitutes 'the good society', the 'good life' or good relations between people, or indeed a clear (or any) conception of what is 'evil'. The latter is manifestly indeterminate and intangible and this constitutes those movements' considerable political danger. Both neotraditional Hindu and Islamic movements venerate martyrdom. 'Evil' is importantly distanced from moral considerations of violence to, and the death of, the human body.

These movements are manifestly contemporary urban phenomena: the urban environment and the city structure the differences in communities that these movements celebrate. They are also embedded in new modes of electronic communication and rely on the cyberspatial[17] relations of new technology (video, audiocassette, TV and satellite) and print technology for their impact. The significance of Khomeini's *fatwa* against Salman Rushdie is precisely related to the fact that it could not have been issued, or had a commensurable meaning, in a premodern Muslim village. Similarly, the BJP's and VHP's genocidal 'freedom ride' through India assumed the condition of cyberspatiality for its influence. That movement to demolish the 'Babri masjid' was mobilised by religious deities (primarily Rama) that only 'exist' in mythic time (anywhere from before 3102 BC to over 2 million years ago in Hindu mythology) and whose historical personalities have not been established. The Rama cult only manifested itself as a major devotional movement in the latter half of the eighteenth century and began to focus from the latter half of the last century on an incident—the alleged demolishing of an earlier Hindu temple at the alleged 'birthplace' of Rama by Moghuls— for which there is no historical evidence, despite copious Persian, Indian and Chinese documentation of the period, and which, interestingly, makes its first textual appearance in the colonial documents of the British after 1870.[18]

At the core of Hindu revivalist growth is the importance of

deploying and recreating historically unbounded and unreach-able *myth*. Myth is made irrelevant to realist and historical interpretations and is accounted for as a matter of faith and devotion. The latter is determined to be entirely legitimate in a modern social formation and is considered inseparable from the modern body politic. Importantly, modernity and the mythic are deemed not just compatible but essential for each other. Myth does not simply serve allegorical purposes but often constitutes the reality of political action: Hindu *kar sevaks* (religious volunteers) who destroyed the 'Babri masjid' believed they were working for, and under the guidance of, Rama, the true God, the only manifestation of *Brahman*.[19] However, the erasure of realist or materialist historiography in favour of adherence to the legitimacy of myth and devotion also creates a hermeneutic, revisionist framework for the invention of new contemporary histories about the period of Moghul and British rule, the liberation movement and Partition, and about con-temporary Muslim communities. These recombinant aspects constitute a novel 'tradition' and ethnicity in which the diverse sects, traditions and philosophies of Hinduism are constrained by the new highly disciplinary articulation of one cult god, Rama, and one utopia, *Ramrajya*,[20] which will arise once the 'poison ivy'—Muslims, Christians, 'pseudosecularists' and Hindu 'traitors'—are 'expelled' from India and 'Hindu rule' is established. The spatial disturbance around the modern post-colonial nation is also present in some Hindu revivalist claims that 'Mahabharat'[21] should cover not only the present geogra-phical boundaries of India but should include Pakistan, Bangladesh, Kashmir, Sri Lanka, Nepal, Bhutan, Tibet, all of Burma and sizeable chunks of Thailand, Laos and China, all of which were apparently part of a mythical 'Hindu empire'. The manifest importance of bodily, civic, national and translocal purity as well as myth, the marking and celebration of absolute difference from 'others', the revenge against 'history' and an indeterminate national or translocal space is definitive of the proto-fascistic movements in India.

The Western Races

The related movement to neotradition among some British black communities has often involved a careful supersession of 'race' and 'place' that demonstrates the limits to understanding contemporary black political agency simply through the parameters of race, ethnicity, racism, nationalism and class. The self-positioning of black subjectivities in relation to extranational frontiers is highly politicised and appears to work against the parochial identification around 'race, class and community' to which black agents are discursively confined. However, the symbolic transcendence of racialised spaces is frequently ambivalent and unstable. The following, an extract from a letter by the Bradford Council of Mosques to the (then) prime minister Margaret Thatcher, illustrates this:

> The Muslims of Bradford and all over the world are shocked to hear about the Novel called 'SATANIC VERSES' in which the writer Salman Rushdie has attacked our beloved Prophet Mohammed (PBUH) and his wives using a dirty language which [no] Muslim can tolerate....[We] Muslims will never allow or ignore such rubbish words used by a person who is either mad or thinks he is ruling the whole world in which there are Millions of Muslims. We [were] very much distressed when we came to know about the author living in Great Britain and the publishers too. As citizens of this great country, we have expressed our very ill feelings about such [a] harmful novel and its publishers and state that the novel should be banned [immediately].[22]

The letter instantly invokes a global, extranational Muslim identity (a contemporary *umma*) which at once displaces 'racial' or ethnic identification with Asians and supersedes affiliation to British nationhood. However, a claim to the latter is subsequently asserted in a manner which again displaces explicit racial identification by ignoring the racialisation of British greatness. But finally, 'race' is obliquely implanted by the need at all to stake a claim to British citizenship. This spatial fluctuation, or contemporary indeterminacy of positionality, defines an important virtual political space occupied by Britain's black communities in which sketches of existential location can be buried in the single social space ('community', 'society' or 'nation'), but can also overlap or surpass it.

Consider, to recompose an example used by Doreen Massey,[23] the multiple transposed zones of location embedded in the life of any urban street in London. An 'Indian' restaurant here, run by a Bangladeshi family whose relatives may have been recent flood victims in Bangladesh, an East African Asian newsagency there, part of a national chain run by a family of refugees from Uganda, descendants of Indian indentured labourers, whose immediate fortunes are bonded into the recession of the British economy and the actions of the German Bundesbank, and whose children are spoken to by African-American expressive culture. Overhead, a plane carries (if she is lucky) a Somali woman, who has lived in border refugee camps for several years, and who may seek housing in Camden, the housing officer perhaps being the son of a Jamaican woman who arrived in Britain in the 1950s to work on the buses. In another street, a heterosexual black man visits an AIDS project, staffed by gay men who were inspired to establish the project through the political activism of American groups.

The collision of spatiality in each of these events generally has the West as its locus—this is the 'power geometry' of time-space compression which Massey addresses. However, the asymptotic relations of power that globalisation entails are also subject to agency, however limited, by those disciplined into spatially organised domination. It was thus by transcending nation, and hence their organisation into the geometry of the latter as a subjected 'race', that British Muslims acquired their symbolic power, however temporary it may have been. Their rearticulation of their spatial relations (the allegiance to global Islamic movements rather than the local nation) was precisely at the root of the British government's notice to British Muslims to 'behave British' or leave.

The contours in the symbolic maps of location may be latent to the agents who negotiate them, or they can become animated and dynamic. The spatial and temporal borders which condense in the 'racial' tensions in the United States between African-Americans and the new arrivals, South-East Asian refugees and immigrants, literally unearthed through Amer-

ican neo-imperial adventures in Korea, Vietnam and Kampu-
chea, illustrate this. The hegemonic discourse of 'race'
embodied in the post-civil rights and post-black power movements cannot encompass these new maps of location and
positionality, negotiated through an entirely different contemporary geoimperialist relation.[24] Korean immigrants and
refugees in the USA inhabit a novel political and economic
relation to 'race' and place which displaces and may
fundamentally conflict with reconstructions of African-Amer-
icanism inspired by 'diaspora'.

'Diaspora' can entail both an 'ownership' of 'race' and
attempts at its transcendence. 'Race', within the discourse of,
say, right-wing black nationalism, can lose its meaning as a
political relation and is reified as a permanent property held by
a 'racial' group. In this tautological circuit other groups, with
the exception of whites and Jews, are displaced from the
national racial equation. Conversely, within liberal, conservative or radical American political discourse, 'race' is frequently
conferred onto African-Americans so that 'race', and indeed the
appropriateness of racialisation itself, becomes an attribute that
is uniquely identified with African-Americans. This is
frequently contested by black Americans—the Thomas-Hill
hearings epitomised this war of position, with Anita Hill's
testimonies frequently constituting the resolute, though
frequently unheard, counterpoints to the overbearing and
aggressive racialisations of the incidents.[25]

This tension in the West between the discursive enclosure
of African-diasporic peoples within the boundaries of race, and
their labour in reinscribing or overcoming this, also has consequences for the racialisation or otherwise of other non-white
populations. It is here that new forms of identification arise
which perpetually hint racial signification but simultaneously
rescind it. The ineffability of 'race' as a self-evident signifier for
the formation of South-East Asian communities in the USA is
one such example, and its relation to hegemonic conceptions of
race was illustrated during the height of the riots in Los
Angeles following the Rodney King verdict. *Newsweek*
reproduced a photograph of a Korean-American shopkeeper
standing in an aggressive posture on the rooftop of his store
with a machine gun during the height of the riots. The

shopkeeper was wearing a T-shirt emblazoned with a large picture of Malcolm X and the slogan 'BY ANY MEANS NECESSARY'.[26]

Here the preeminent motif of African-American liberation was appropriated, in post-civil rights, post-black power fashion, and used objectionably against black Americans, articulating them as a 'race' and, by seizing the slogan for Koreans, simultaneously displacing themselves outside of a particular construction of 'race' but still hinting at an elusive, indeterminate and subtle racial affiliation. This is not to say that 'race formation'[27] as it is currently understood will not transpire for Korean-Americans, but that its discursive content or form cannot be determined by existing civil rights, black power, affirmative action, equal opportunity or multiculturalist configurations of 'race'. Korean-American 'race formation' is likely to be as configured by political and economic relations with Latinos and blacks as it is with whites or the state, or by the discursive formation of Asians as possessing an inherent 'alienness' which is not shared by other communities.

In Britain, similar matters arise. Frequently, this has been assumed to be the disengagement of many Asians from the collective discourse of 'black'. However, this is less important than the unique relation or otherwise to 'race' in the different contemporary relations demonstrated by the black refugee experience of displacement, rebellion, civil war, dictatorship and genocide, and subsequently neoracist atrocities within the 'refuge' itself. Refugee politics can itself be highly fractured and indeterminate within left-right boundaries or 'ethnic' allegiance. It is unclear how post-colonial antiracism, or indeed race formation in Britain of Asian and Caribbean peoples, can accommodate these new contingent arrangements unless the latter are merely reduced to some variant of an antiracist or black nationalist project. That reductionist process—the abbreviation of any racial discourse into the grammar of racism-antiracism—is a dominant tendency in much oppositional black nationalist or antiracist labour. However, the refugee experience is exophoric to this discourse and its relation to black liberation is far from understood *even though* refugees may bear the brunt of racial discrimination, poverty, border controls and racial violence in Europe. The formation of original refugee identities, which are not uncomplicatedly or evenly 'racial' is occurring in relation to a multinational Europe, rather than a single nation-state. This, as well as the complex trajectories and alliances of refugee politics are not easily comprehensible within the discourses of race, immigration and class exploitation. Similarly, the neo-nazi pogroms against refugee hostels in east Germany do not differentiate between, for example, African and Romanian refugees. Serbian genocidal 'ethnic cleansing' in Bosnia-Hercegovina is aimed at white Muslims. Polish theocratic antisemitism is aimed at a Jewish community which now barely exists in Poland. Romany, Sinti, Albanian, southern Italian, Czech/Slovak, Hungarian, and a multitude of white communities have become the primary targets of new ethnic movements. It becomes difficult then to inscribe the latter white communities within the already overburdened discourse of 'race' and 'racism' unless either that 'race' is released from its post-colonial baggage, in which case we are then speaking of entirely new subjectivities, or that unreconstructed 'race' becomes a subset of an altogether new epistemology.

Regulating the Body: Discipline, Dissent and Differentiation

The transcendence of the local in contemporary black political agency has its obverse—the political management of local black communities and, hence, identities. This sets up an important dynamic between the realisation of translocal political ambition and the limits of the local political economy of community. This important dialectic between translocality and local territorialism has been an important feature of modernism and an important attribute of postmodernism. In black political agency, its articulation has primarily been around the politics of community, family and, frequently, nation. The regulation of that space has become a decisive battleground between absolutist and progressive black political tendencies.

Interior to these conflicts is a fundamental contemplation of space and body—the territories of the private and public, the organisation of family and domicility, the reproduction of gender and the supervision of sexuality. The habitual displacement of these issues, except by black feminist and a few other interventions, as irrelevant or subordinate to the confrontation with racism and fascism should not remove attention from their central place in the composition of contemporary black political agency. Just a cursory examination of the content of the blasphemies in *The Satanic Verses* which instigated the global protests emphasises that they were insulting precisely because they were in the vicinity of the body and its pleasures. The passages unambiguously evoked prostitution, sexual licentiousness, immodesty, sodomy and sexual perversion: the insults hurled at the prophet and his wives were sexual indignities. This was the 'dirtiness' referred to by the Bradford Council of Mosques (page 151).

A manifest concern with the public and private territories of the body preoccupies black Caribbean, American and Asian absolutist tendencies, just as the priapic obsession with sexuality, gender and the family has configured the political interventions of the new right and Christian right over the last decade. These tendencies claim their legitimation by declaring a return to the purity of tradition or ethnic essence. However, this cannot be taken as evident, nor should it simply be constructed as 'regressive' because its aims are frequently to reorganise those territories in novel directions, to recreate gender and sexual diagrams of family and community that have never existed. The critiques of the West contained in novel varieties of Afro-Asian nationalism involve a prominent apprehension of sexual 'debauchery' contained in the West or as practised by whites—a profoundly interesting reversal of colonial discourse which placed black colonised populations at the core of uncivilised sexual depravity. These critiques often contain elaborate and comprehensive reconstructions of the gendered body, its sexualities and its social territories. These are communicated beyond their absolutist borders and can make significant political impact:

ASIANS IN ROW OVER ANTI-AIDS CAMPAIGN
The Health Education Authority is spending thousands of pounds on an anti-Aids campaign aimed at the Asian community....Leaders of the Asian community are protesting that the wrong conclusions will be drawn from

the advertisements....[Headteacher Shreela Flather said] 'I find this campaign very worrying. Why target the Asians? It does not take into account the intrinsic morality of the group. I would have thought they are the least vulnerable group....We can't keep an eye on [youngsters] all the time but the girls are under strict control. This campaign seeks to undermine Asians'. The advertisements show photographs of Asian families as well as obviously well-heeled young people.[28]

A powerful but metonymic construction of sexuality makes its presence felt here in the manufacture of essential Asian family morality. While it would be a relatively simple matter to point out a millennium of Indian carnal, concupiscent art to those Asian community leaders who fear wrong conclusions about their culture, this would not disrupt the core rearticulation of body, family and community taking place here. The desire to make the Asian body uninhabitable by unspoken sexualities, to cleanse it of aberrant sexual content is performed both by the depiction of sturdy, impregnable Asian family life in the poster itself and by the invention of moral communities by the protestors. However, both these are respectively undermined by the need at all to have the education campaign or by the admission of impulsive sexuality in the need to exercise strict control over the activities of young women and the acknowledgement of limits to surveillance. This identification of sexuality and its regulation with the female gender is a central structuring theme in absolutist discourse. Women constitute both the 'tradition' that is to be preserved and the transgressive sexuality that is to be repressed.

In this illustration, the absolutist spaces which the Asian body must inhabit or traverse are 'family' and 'community'. But these are unstable, dangerously contingent spaces where the meanings of locality, privacy and gender have not been settled. Monological constructions of 'community' and 'family' are subjected to other transgressive Asian formations that have been unable to create visible spaces in public culture in the manner that African-Caribbean and African-American youth cultures have. These include the complex articulation of pleasure through progressive syncretic cultural styles in Asian nationalist Indi-pop, hip-hop, rap, ragga and some reformative *bhangra*, Asian women's ascension in community and cultural politics, the growth of Asian lesbian and gay groups, the development of Asian youth spaces in daytime and nighttime disco, utilised unconventionally by Asian young women as much as men, the production of irreverent Asian youth media and the staunch celebration of 'sexual emancipation':

ASIAN STRIP SHOW ANGER
Ban this filth say Muslim protestors....Showing two scantily-clad Asian girls in provocative poses, the posters promise punters a feast of 'mujara bhangra followed by a topless striptease with a two-girl duo'....The girls encouraged the leering audience to fondle and dance with them, and later they performed their striptease as well as simulated lesbian acts.[29]

These cultural spaces do not have an elementary concern with anything approaching anti-racism but are informed by the organisation of pleasure times and spaces against the obdurate, but constantly reorganised conventions of community probity. Qumar Ashraf and Zarina Ramzan, the young Muslim women who organised and performed the striptease in Southall, elicited the wrath of *young* Muslim men not simply for daring to unclothe, but because of their sceptical reappropriation of the symbols of their oppression. Their performance not only invoked Muslim courtesan traditions, constituted through the pastiche of the film *Pakeezah*, but involved the brazen display of Islamic religious adornments during the striptease. But, most significantly, the women were uncompromising in their autonomy and for this they received numerous enraged calls, death threats and organised pickets of their shows. The women responded unequivocally:

We have a right to act as we choose. In our culture, the men are allowed to drink, smoke and have mistresses, but a woman can have her legs broken if she is seen talking to a man.

The sexual and cultural politics of this incident are highly complex and transgress feminism and anti-racism just as they transgress Islam. The appeal to freedom from patriarchal religious 'fundamentalism' to engage in activities—the sexual display and objectification of women for the benefit of men—which feminism has traditionally protested against creates a space which, even if carefully constructed as an autonomous right of women, still refuses to conform easily with feminism, even as the two women powerfully valorise their rights over their bodies through its language. But, in illustrating the need for active, indeed activist, policing of the female body, and by extension policing of women's control over their sexuality, the incident signifies the incompleteness of 'family' and 'community'. The increasingly obsessive absolutist interventions into these territories of gender, sexuality and family symbolise a rarely debated crisis in the latter, a crisis in which the economic and social realities of Asian family life and their toll on women continue to aggravate the fantasy of the cheerful, secure Asian extended family.

However, absolutist interventions into these spaces can have contingent, highly contradictory outcomes. Asian feminists have pointed out how the demand for separate schools for Muslim girls (but, revealingly, not with anything approaching the same vociferousness for boys), the wearing of headscarves and modest clothing and the regulation and control of women's private and public spaces betray a fundamental concern with the body. In the need to regulate the voyage of the body, the need to shield, contain, conceal and repress it, attention is paradoxically focused on it, and new resistive bodies are produced in Foucauldian fashion.

An illustration of a related process occurred during the campaign in 1987 by the London Borough of Haringey to promote 'positive images' of lesbians and gay men in primary and secondary education (again, the institutions of cultural reproduction). This campaign began in the aftermath of the local revolt against the police on Broadwater Farm estate in 1985 and the arrest of Winston Silcott, Mark Braithwaite and Engin Raghip for the murder of PC Keith Blakelock. Protests against the local authority's policy had involved white parents and various new right and right-wing bodies, including the Freedom Association, the New Patriotic Movement and a motley assortment of neofascist groups. However, it was the subsequent involvement of black nationalist organisations in these protests that contingently changed their pace and direction. The black nationalist groups included Caribbean, African and Asian organisations, Christian, Muslim, Hindu and Sikh (giving a novel voice to the idea of black unity).

While the fracturing political tendencies along the axis of sexuality and 'race' were highly complex and compounded, a basic resemblance informed all these fragments. For some black organisations, education around the validity of homosexuality was 'genocidal' and 'racist' and was destructive of the black family, while for some lesbian and gay organisations, denial of that education was 'institutional heterosexism' and black communities were essentially 'homophobic'. This clash between the discourses of black nationalism and lesbian and gay liberation should not however conceal their essential similarities and intersections. Both were selectively appropriating the discursive regimes of the other. The semantics of 'equal opportunity' utilised by lesbian and gay organisations were themselves formed through anti-racist enterprises. However, some black organisations could not concede their novel, progressive and different rearticulation around homosexuality and attempted to reprise them for nationalism. Similarly, the discourse of sexuality was not confined to lesbian and gay articulations but sincerely informed the content of black nationalist interventions. Conversely, some lesbian and gay organisations uncritically partook of black nationalist reconstructions of 'Asian' and 'African' cultures in their designations of those cultures as essentially homophobic or sexist.

One manifest consequence was the repoliticisation of black sexualities in a direction which unambiguously signalled the presence of 'new bodies'—black lesbian and gay identities. However, that production is itself highly irresolute. The assemblage it created often 'illogically' articulated the discursive content of both black nationalism and lesbian and gay liberation, but migrated beyond these and frequently manufactured its own incommensurable epistemologies of anthropological purity:

> [The] most crucial challenge facing black gay scholars is to develop an affirming and liberating philosophical understanding of homosexuality that will self-actualize

black gay genius. Such a task requires a new epistemology, a new way of 'knowing' that incorporates the views our African ancestors had about the material and metaphysical world....In some African cultures, gays were considered blessed because the Creator had endowed them with both male and female principles.[30]

The constant mutation and differentiation of identities, especially those identities formed at the microedges between social movements, reveal problems with political strategies founded on the acknowledgement and acceptance of diversity and difference. This is not simply because the political content and trajectory of identities is indeterminate and not guaranteed to be inherently or eternally progressive. 'Social difference' is continually remade and is a contingent, incomplete and aggregate process rather than a preexisting edifice. There is not, a priori, a settled series of differences which can subsequently be systematically articulated together under a hegemonic project. Indeed, the process of joint articulation of diverse identities can itself cause their further proliferation and differentiation. For example, the Greater London Council's populist strategy of voluntary sector funding during the 1980s led to a bizarre matrix multiplication of every social concern with every potential identity, each claiming its own reflective 'specificity'. A project which aimed to unite and enable populations under the hegemony of a reconstructed, plural 'London' instead created constantly multiplying clusters of often antagonistic identities. Each of these identities quite clearly acknowledged the 'difference' of their 'others' and, against those differences, staked their own exclusive claims.

Differentiation is also not exterior to an already defined group identity that knows its place in relation to other identities but is instead radically interior to and disruptive of those group identities. Indeed, a primary function of identity is precisely to manage and contain the differentiation which constantly threatens it:

Any Muslim who fails to be offended by Rushdie's book ceases on account of that fact to be Muslim. *The Satanic*

Verses has become a litmus-paper test for distinguishing faith from rejection.[31]

Such pursuits of pure identities conspicuously annihilate the idea of the latter—in this example, by the admission that there do exist Muslims who have 'failed' to be offended by *The Satanic Verses* and who subsequently have to be excluded from Muslim identity (this is also a bizarre reformation of Muslim identity which ironically places *The Satanic Verses* at its core). These disciplinary pursuits of identity are inherently unstable despite their dogmatic certainties, and they vie for hegemony with other equally dogmatic translocal identifications. The spaces that this creates can be explosive.

Before the burning of *The Satanic Verses* in Bradford that signalled the worldwide protests against Salman Rushdie, the book had been publicly burned in several northern British towns, including Blackburn, events which were virtually ignored by the media. But another event in Blackburn in July 1992 did, for a short while at least, seize the attention of media. For several nights Asian youths numbering in their thousands were in pitched communal battles against each other followed by 'an epilogue of full-blooded attack' on the Lancashire police who were attempting to separate them.[32] The youths, the overwhelming majority born in Blackburn, as British as fish and chips, were fighting each other as rival Indians and Pakistanis, after the former had accused the latter of harassing Indian women and organising the local economy of drugs, prostitution and petty crime.

This was one of the most serious intra-Asian physical conflicts which have occurred in Britain, perhaps superseded by the spate of firebombings of temples, mosques and *gurdwaras* in Britain which occurred following the destruction of the 'Babri masjid' by Hindu supporters of the VHP, RSS and BJP. We should note here that these intensely localised activities invoked translocal affiliations and constantly reworked the raw materials of 'tradition' into original methodologies. It is here that the Blackburn riots acquire a different resonance—the gang formations in those events were identified by national-diasporic identities (as Indians or Pakistanis), their 'difference' constituted not just through linguistic closures (as Gujeratis or

Punjabis) or ethnic identification but from historical grievances over differential access to the resources of the local state or entry into the local economy. However, all the participants in the riots were Muslims. Those youths who battled each other so fiercely had previously marched together under the motif and solidarity of Muslim identity. Two neotraditions collide here, condense into and give meaning to a local affair which is then itself transformed by these interventions and has translocal resonance.[33]

Conclusion: Spatial Incomprehension and Postmodern Barbarics

The compaction of real and social spaces and times[34] within which races, ethnicities, nations, and indeed all identities, are now recreated and lived has at its core a key instability which is related to the collective cognition or comprehension of what now constitutes the boundaries of a highly dynamic social space. If people shrink the world to their size, they can now also expand their world to our size, a cardinal lesson which right-wing forces have devoured. A central component of time-space compression is the speculative cyberspace, the electronic space within, through and around which new social and political relations are being originated, and which, in its relation to politics, generates symbols for global reception and consumption. The American Christian Right lives not just in Colorado but beams its message across Africa, Asia and Latin America, just as the symbolic motorised chariot of the VHP, and its inspirational religious folklores, the *Ramayana* and the *Mahabharat*, were broadcast on TV to every village in India. In the fluctuating velocities of social time-space compression, parochial localities meet parochial localities—is this global universalism?

These spaces are, however, embedded and recreated within the ubiquitous paradigms of capitalist accumulation which, despite the existence of globalised, apparently anti-systemic movements,[35] do not appear to be opposed beyond the local resistances of superexploited labour in the Third World. Previous anti-imperialist certainties about the configurations that political resistance to capitalist exploitation and geoimperial Western domination will take have been overshadowed by the experience of authoritarian, ethnic, religious and undemocratic oppositional movements in the last three decades. These movements share an obsession with bodily, civic, national and translocal purity and a political agency dominated by revenge against the impurities of history. They combine the Enlightenment narratives of emancipation and purity. The latter is fortified by a political narrative of the mythic in which complex social formations and histories acquire simple, intelligible, causally-reasoned elaboration against which appeals to realist history or real, actually existing conditions, appear to have little progressive mobilising power.

There is no essential faith to be had either in the mechanisms of cultural syncretism or hybridity, since, if the arguments presented above are followed, neotradition is precisely a manifestation of this hybrid process and the latter has no inherent progressive guarantees. Indeed, the process of hybridity is itself central to the creation of new essentialisms in ethnicity, religious, race, gender and sexual politics. However, some of the resultant transgressive social interstices do create insecurities for the absolutisms which surround them, and that is perhaps their only certainty.

PART 3

The Politics of Solidarity

(8)

Why do Empty Signifiers Matter to Politics?

Ernesto Laclau

The Social Production of 'Empty Signifiers'

An empty signifier is, strictly speaking, a signifier without a signified. This definition is also, however, the enunciation of a problem. For how would it be possible that a signifier is not attached to any signified and remains, however, an integral part of a system of signification? An empty signifier would be a sequence of sounds, and if the latter are deprived of any signifying function the term 'signifier' itself would become excessive. The only possibility for a stream of sounds being detached from any particular signified while still remaining a signifier is if, through the subversion of the sign which the possibility of an empty signifier involves, something is achieved which is internal to signification as such. What is this possibility?

Some pseudo-answers can be discarded quite quickly. One would be to argue that the same signifier can be attached to different signifieds in different contexts (as a result of the arbitrariness of the sign). But it is clear that in that case the signifier would not be *empty* but *equivocal*: in each context the function of signification would be fully realised. A second possibility is that the signifier is not *equivocal* but *ambiguous*: that either an overdetermination or an underdetermination of signifieds prevents from fully fixing it. Yet this floating of the signifier still does not make of it an empty one. Although the floating takes us one step towards the proper answer to our problem, the terms of the latter are still avoided. We do not

167

have to deal with an excess or deficiency of signification, but with the precise theoretical possibility of something which points, from within the process of signification, to the discursive presence of its own limits.

An empty signifier can, consequently, only emerge if there is a structural impossibility in signification as such, and if this impossibility can only signify itself as an interruption (subversion, distortion, etc.) of the structure of the sign. That is, that the limits of signification can only announce themselves as the impossibility of realising what is within those limits—if the limits could be signified in a direct way, they would be internal to signification and, *ergo*, would not be limits at all.

An initial and purely formal consideration can help to clarify the point. We know, from Saussure, that language (and, by extension, all signifying systems) is a system of differences, that linguistic identities—values—are purely relational and that, as a result, the *totality* of language is involved in each single act of signification. Now, in that case, it is clear that the totality is essentially required—if the differences did not constitute a system, no signification at all would be possible. The problem, however, is that the very possibility of signification is the system, and the very possibility of the system is the possibility of its limits. We can say, with Hegel, that to think of the limits of something is the same as thinking of what is beyond those limits. But if what we are talking about are the limits of a *signifying system*, it is clear that those limits cannot be themselves signified, but have to *show* themselves as the *interruption* or *breakdown* of the process of signification. Thus, we are left with the paradoxical situation that what constitutes the condition of possibility of a signifying system—its limits—is also what constitutes its condition of impossibility—a blockage of the continuous expansion of the process of signification.

A first and capital consequence of this is that true limits can never be neutral limits but presuppose an exclusion. A neutral limit would be one which is essentially continuous with what is at its two sides, and the two sides are simply different from each other. As a signifying totality is, however, precisely a system of differences, this means that both are part of the same system and that the limits between the two cannot be the limits of the system. In the case of an exclusion we have, instead, authentic limits, because the actualisation of what is beyond the limit of exclusion would involve the impossibility of what is this side of the limit. True limits are always antagonistic. But the operation of the logic of exclusionary limits has a series of necessary effects which spread to both sides of the limits and which will lead us straight into the emergence of empty signifiers.

(1) A first effect of the exclusionary limit is that it introduces an essential ambivalence within the system of differences constituted by those limits. On the one hand, each element of the system has an identity only as far as it is different from the others. Difference = identity. On the other hand, however, all these differences are equivalent to each other as far as all of them belong to this side of the frontier of exclusion. But, in that case, the identity of each element is constitutively split: on the one hand each difference expresses itself *as* difference; on the other hand, each of them *cancels* itself as such by entering into a relation of equivalence with all the other differences of the system. And, given that there is only system as far as there is radical exclusion, this split or ambivalence is constitutive of all systemic identity. It is only insofar as there is a radical impossibility of a system as pure presence, beyond all exclusions, that actual *systems* (in the plural) can exist. Now, if the systematicity of the system is a direct result of the exclusionary limit, it is only that exclusion that grounds the system as such. This point is essential because it results from it that the system cannot have a positive ground and that, as a result, it cannot signify itself in terms of any positive signified. Let us suppose for a moment that the systematic ensemble was the result of all its elements sharing a positive feature (e.g. that they all belonged to a regional category). In that case that positive feature would be different from other differential positive features, and they would all appeal to a deeper systematic ensemble within which their differences would be thought of as differences. But a system constituted through radical exclusion interrupts this play of the differential logic: as what is excluded from the system, far from being something positive, is the simple principle of positivity—pure

Being. This already announces the possibility of an empty signifier—i.e., a signifier of the pure cancellation of all difference.

(2) The condition, of course, for this operation to be possible is that what is beyond the frontier of exclusion is reduced to pure negativity—i.e., to the pure threat that that beyond poses to the system (constituting it that way). If the exclusionary dimension was eliminated, or even weakened, what would happen is that the differential character of the 'beyond' would impose itself and, as a result, the limits of the system would be blurred. Only if the beyond becomes the signifier of pure threat, of pure negativity, of the simply excluded, can there be limits and system (i.e., an objective order). But in order to be the signifiers of the excluded (or, simply, of exclusion), the various excluded categories have to cancel their differences through the formation of a chain of equivalences of that which the system demonises in order to signify itself. Again, we see here the possibility of an empty signifier announcing itself through this logic in which differences collapse into equivalential chains.

(3) But, we could ask ourselves, why does this pure being or systematicity of the system, or—its reverse—the pure negativity of the excluded require the production of empty signifiers in order to signify itself? The answer is that as we are trying to signify the limits of signification—the Real, if you want, in the Lacanian sense—there is no direct way of doing so except through the subversion of the process of signification itself. We know, through psychoanalysis, how what is not directly representable—the unconscious—can only find as a means of representation the subversion of the signifying process. Each signifier constitutes a sign by attaching itself to a particular signified, inscribing itself as a difference within the signifying process. But if what we are trying to signify is not a difference but on the contrary a radical exclusion which is the ground and condition of all differences, in that case no production of *one more* difference can do the trick. As, however, all the means of representation are differential in nature, it is only if the differential nature of the signifying units is subverted, only if the

signifiers empty themselves of their attachment to particular signifieds and assume the role of representing the pure being of the system—or, rather, the system as pure Being—that such a signification is possible. What is the ontological ground of such a subversion, what makes it possible? The answer is: the split of each unit of signification that the system has to construct as the undecidable locus in which both the logic of difference and the logic of equivalence operate. It is only by privileging the dimension of equivalence to the point that its differential nature is almost entirely obliterated—that is, emptying it of its differential nature—that the system can signify itself as a totality.

Two points have to be stressed here. The first is that the being or systematicity of the system which is represented through the empty signifiers is not a being which has not been *actually* realised, but one which is constitutively unreachable, for whatever systematic effects would exist there will be the result, as we have seen, of the unstable compromise between equivalence and difference. That is, that we are faced with a constitutive lack, with an impossible object which, as in Kant, shows itself through the impossibility of its adequate representation. Here we can give a full answer to our initial question: there can be empty signifiers within the field of signification because any system of signification is structured around an empty place resulting from the impossibility of producing an object which, however, is required by the systematicity of the system. So, we are not dealing with an impossibility without location, as in the case of a logical contradiction, but with a *positive* impossibility, with a *real* one to which the x of the empty signifier points.

However, if this impossible object lacks the means of its adequate or direct representation, this can only mean that the signifier which is emptied in order to assume the representing function will always be constitutively inadequate. What, in that case, does determine that one signifier rather than the other assumes in different circumstances that signifying function? Here we have to move to the main theme of this essay: the relation between empty signifiers and politics.

Hegemony

Let me go back to an example that we discussed in detail in *Hegemony and Socialist Strategy*:[1] the constitution, according to Rosa Luxemburg, of the unity of the working class through an overdetermination of partial struggles over a long period of time. Her basic argument is that the unity of the class is not determined by any a priori consideration about the priority of either the political struggle or the economic struggle but by the accumulated effects of the internal split of all partial mobilisations. In relation to our subject, her argument amounts to approximately the following: in a climate of extreme repression any mobilisation for a partial objective will be perceived not only as related to the concrete demand or objectives of that struggle but also as an act of opposition against the system. This last fact is what establishes the link between a variety of concrete or partial struggles and mobilisations—all of them are seen as related to each other, not because their *concrete* objectives are intrinsically related, but because they are all seen as equivalent in confrontation with the repressive regime. It is not, consequently, something positive that all of them share which establishes their unity, but something negative: their opposition to a common enemy. Luxemburg's argument is that a revolutionary mass identity is established through the overdetermination, over a whole historical period, of a plurality of separate struggles. These traditions fused, at the revolutionary moment, in a ruptural point.

Let us try to apply to this sequence our previous categories. The meaning (the signified) of all concrete struggle appears, right from the beginning, internally divided. The concrete aim of the struggle is not only that aim in its concreteness; it also signifies opposition to the system. The first signified establishes the differential character of that demand or mobilisation vis-à-vis all other demands or mobilisations. The second signified establishes the equivalence of all these demands in their common opposition to the system. As we can see, any concrete struggle is dominated by this contradictory movement that at the same time asserts and abolishes its own singularity. The function of representing the system as a totality depends, consequently, on the possibility of the equivalential function neatly prevailing over the differential one; but this possibility is simply the result of every single struggle being always already, originally, penetrated by this constitutive ambiguity.

It is important to observe that, as we have already established, if the function of the differential signifiers is to renounce their differential identity in order to represent the purely equivalential identity of a communitarian space as such, they cannot construct this equivalential identity as something belonging to a differential order. For instance: we can represent the Tsarist regime as a repressive order by enumerating the differential kinds of oppressions that it imposes on various sections of the population as much as we want; but such enumeration will not give us the specificity of the repressive moment, that which constitutes—in its negation—what is peculiar to a repressive relation between entities. Because in such a relation each instance of the repressive power counts as pure bearer of the negation of the identity of the repressed sector. Now if the differential identity of the repressive action is in that way 'distanced' from itself by having itself transformed into the mere incarnating body of the negation of the being of another entity, it is clear that between this negation and the body through which it expresses itself there is no necessary relation—nothing predetermines that one particular body should be the one predestined to incarnate negation as such.

It is precisely this which makes the relation of equivalence possible: different particular struggles are so many bodies which can indifferently incarnate the opposition of all of them to the repressive power. This involves a double movement. On the one hand, the more the chain of equivalences is extended, the less each concrete struggle will be able to remain closed in a differential self—in something which separates it from all other differential identities through a difference which is exclusively its own. On the contrary, as the equivalential relation shows that these differential identities are simply indifferent bodies incarnating something equally present in all of them, the longer the chain of equivalences is, the less concrete this 'something equally present' will be. At the limit it will be pure communitarian being independent of all concrete manifestation. And, on the other hand, that which is beyond the exclusion delimiting the communitarian space—the repressive power—will counter less as the instrument of particular differential repressions and will express pure anti-community, pure evil and negation. The community created by this equivalential expansion will be, thus, the pure idea of a communitarian fullness which is absent—as a result of the presence of the repressive power.

But at this point the second movement starts. This pure equivalential function representing an absent fullness which shows itself through the collapse of all differential identities is something which cannot have a signifier of its own—for in that case the 'beyond all differences' would be one more difference and not the result of the equivalential collapse of all differential identities. Precisely because the community as such is not a purely differential space of an objective identity but an absent fullness, it cannot have any form of representation of its own, and has to borrow the latter from some entity constituted within the equivalential space—in the same way as gold is a particular use value which assumes, as well, the function of representing value in general. This emptying of a particular signifier of its particular, differential signified is, as we saw, what makes possible the emergence of 'empty' signifiers as the signifiers of a lack, of an absent totality. But this leads us straight into the question with which we closed the previous section: if all differential struggles—in our example—are equally capable of expressing, beyond their differential identity, the absent fullness of the community; if the equivalential function makes all differential positions similarly indifferent to this equivalential representation, if none is pre-determined *per se* to fulfil this role; what does determine that one of them rather than the other incarnates, at particular periods of time, this universal function?

The answer is: the unevenness of the social. For if the equivalential logic tends to do away with the relevance of all differential location, this is only a tendential movement which is always resisted by the logic of difference which is essentially non-equalitarian. (It comes as no surprise that Hobbes's model of a state of nature, which tries to depict a realm in which the full operation of the logic of equivalence makes the community impossible, has to presuppose an original and essential equality between men.) Not any position in society, not any struggle is equally capable of transforming its own contents in a nodal point that becomes an empty signifier. Now, is this not to return to a rather traditional conception of the historical affectivity of social forces, one which asserts that the unevenness of structural locations determines which one of them is going to be the source of totalising effects? No, it is not, because these uneven structural locations, some of which represent points of high concentration of power, are themselves the result of processes in which logics of difference and logics of equivalence overdetermine each other. It is not a question of denying the historical effectivity of the logic of differential structural locations but, rather, of denying to them, as a whole, the character of an infrastructure which would determine, out of itself, the laws of movement of society.

If this is correct, it is impossible to determine at the level of the mere analysis of the *form* difference/equivalence which particular difference is going to become the locus of equivalential effects—this requires the study of a particular conjuncture, precisely because the presence of equivalential effects is always necessary, but the relation equivalence/difference is not intrinsically linked to any particular differential content. This relation by which a particular content becomes the signifier of the absent communitarian fullness is exactly what we call a *hegemonic relationship*. The presence of empty signifiers—in the sense that we have defined them—is the very condition of hegemony. This can be easily seen if we address a very well-known difficulty which has a recurring stumbling block in most theorisations of hegemony—Gramsci's included. A class or group is considered to be hegemonic when it is not closed in a narrow corporatist perspective but presents itself as realising the broader aims either of emancipating, or ensuring order, for wider masses of the population. But this faces us with a difficulty if we do not determine precisely what these terms *'broader* aims', *'wider* masses' refer to. There are two possibilities: first, that society is an addition of discrete groups, each tending to their particular aims and in constant collision with each other. In that case 'broader' and 'wider' could only mean the precarious equilibrium of a negotiated agreement between groups, all of which would retain their conflicting aims and identity. But 'hegemony' clearly refers to a stronger type of communitarian unity than such an agreement evokes. Second, that society has some kind of pre-established essence, so that the 'broader' and 'vaster' has a content of its own, independent of the will of the particular groups, and that 'hegemony' would mean the realisation of such an essence. But this would not only do away with the dimension of contingency which has always been associated with the hegemonic operation, but would also be incompatible with the consensual character of 'hegemony': the hegemonic order would be the *imposition* of a pre-given organisational principle and not something emerging from the political interaction between groups. Now, if we consider the matter from the point of view of the social production of empty signifiers, this problem vanishes. For in that case the hegemonic operation would be the presentation of the particularity of a group as the incarnation of that empty signifier which refers to the communitarian order as an absence, an unfulfilled reality.

How does this mechanism operate? Let us consider the extreme situation of a radical disorganisation of the social fabric. In such conditions—which are not far away from Hobbes's state of nature—people need *an* order, and the actual content of it becomes a secondary consideration. 'Order' as such has no content, because it only exists in the various forms in which it is actually realised, but in a situation of radical disorder 'order' is present as that which is absent; it becomes an empty signifier, as the signifier of that absence. In this sense, various political forces can compete in their effort to present their particular objectives as those which carry out the filling of that lack. To hegemonise something is exactly to carry out this filling function. (We have spoken about 'order', but obviously 'unity', 'liberation', 'revolution', etc., belong to the same order of things. Any term which in a certain political context becomes the signifier of the lack plays the same role. Politics is possible because the constitutive impossibility of society can only represent itself through the production of empty signifiers.)

This explains also why any hegemony is always unstable and penetrated by a constitutive ambiguity. Let us suppose that a workers' mobilisation succeeds in presenting its own objectives as the signifier of 'liberation' in general. (This, as we have seen, is possible because the workers' mobilisation, taking place under a repressive regime, is also seen as an anti-system struggle.) In one sense this is a hegemonic victory, because the objectives of a particular group are identified with society at large. But, in another sense, this is a dangerous victory. If 'workers' struggle' becomes the signifier of liberation as such, it also becomes the surface of inscription through which *all* liberating struggles will be expressed, so that the chain of equivalences which are unified around this signifier tend to empty it, and to blur its connection with the actual content with which it was originally associated. Thus, as a result of its very success, the hegemonic operation tends to break its links with the force which was its original promoter and beneficiary.

Hegemony and Democracy

Let us conclude with some reflections on the relation between empty signifiers, hegemony and democracy.

Consider for a moment the role of social signifiers in the emergence of modern political thought—I am essentially thinking of the work of Hobbes. Hobbes, as we have seen, presented the state of nature as the radically opposite of an ordered society, as a situation only defined in negative terms. But, as a result of that description, the order of the ruler has to be accepted not because of any intrinsic virtue that it can have, but just because it is *an* order, and the only alternative is radical disorder. The condition, however, of the coherence of this scheme is the postulate of the equality of the power of individuals in the state of nature—if the individuals were uneven in terms of power, order could be guaranteed through sheer domination. So, power is eliminated twice: in the state of nature, as all individuals equally share in it, and in the Commonwealth, as it is entirely concentrated in the hands of the ruler. (A power which is total or a power which is equally distributed among all members of the community is no power at all.) So, while Hobbes implicitly perceives the split between the empty signifier 'order as such' and the actual order imposed by the ruler, as he reduces—through the covenant—the first to

177

the second, he cannot think of any kind of dialectical or hegemonic game between the two.

What happens if, on the contrary, we reintroduce power within this picture—i.e., if we accept the unevenness of power in social relations? In that case, civil society will be partially structured and partially unstructured and, as a result, the total concentration of power in the hands of the ruler ceases to be a logical requirement. But in that case the credentials of the ruler to claim total power are much less obvious. If partial order exists in society, the legitimacy of the identification of the empty signifier of order with the will of the ruler will have the further requirement that the content of this will does not clash with something the society *already* is. As society changes over time this process of identification will be always precarious and reversible and, as the identification is no longer automatic, different hegemonic projects or wills will try to hegemonise the empty signifiers of the absent community. The recognition of the constitutive nature of this gap and its political institutionalisation is the starting point of modern democracy.

(9)

Towards the Politics of a Lesser Evil

Jean-François Lyotard's Reworking of the Kantian Sublime

Peter Jowers

In this chapter I examine the role the sublime plays in Jean-François Lyotard's recent writings. I gradually work towards an understanding of this central though elusive term which plays such a huge part in his thought. I am particularly interested in the way in which he uses a reworking of Kant's work on aesthetics to confront the issues of how to make reasonable judgements under conditions of difference and heterogeneity common to the postmodern condition. He rereads Kant through the prism of a very distinctive theory of language which he develops to avoid the pitfalls of a subject centred metaphysics. He uses sublimity as a form of negative critique, to reveal how various forms of political closure work. His insistence upon the sublime is an assertion of the singularity of intense feeling in the face of power. I then show how he uses the insights drawn from his fascination with visual arts to flesh out his discussion of sublimity which he then applies to the ethical and political domain.

Lyotard has written a body of work in which there is oscillation between accessible though coolly analytical prose and initially almost impenetrable, quasi-lyric writing. This we could call the sublime text. Lyotard admits to the Protean, heterogeneous quality of his work. He has 'always been attracted by formalism'. Yet he simultaneously asserts that 'as for "the traditional forms of philosophy", I know of none'.[1]

Lyotard once described his experiences growing up in war-torn Paris, of destitution, of wearing yellow stars in sympathy with Jewish friends, of their subsequent deportation, of French racism, of tanks in the streets, of seeing decapitated bodies, his brushes with the police during his activities in support of the Algerian struggle, his involvement in the events of 1968 and so on. He explicitly aimed to draw out the difference between European and American experience.[2] His writing displays a moral urgency, a constant awareness of the contingent fragility of civility and the so easy possibility of an upsurge in political terror. This accounts for the oscillations between the coolly analytical or public side of his works and the turbulent sublimity of the other. Carroll has written that in Lyotard's work 'the analytical and the affective seem to be locked in a struggle he makes no attempt to resolve'.[3]

Linking the Aesthetic and Political

Numerous commentators argue that modernity has wrought upon humankind the destruction of traditional, deeply sedimented or embedded, social relations and reconstituted them as modern ones. This process, that Lyotard once called 'derealisation', shatters agreements as to what constitutes reality. He writes, 'Modernity...cannot exist without a shattering of belief and without discovery of the "lack of reality" of reality, together with the invention of other realities.'[4]

This 'lack of reality' is a phrase, he notes, akin to that of *nihilism* but he wishes to link it to the 'Kantian theme of the sublime'.[5] A lack of reality is a form of 'ontological dislocation'. Associated with it is an *intensification of feeling*.[6] Here is hinted the key linkage we need if we are to understand the role aesthetic themes play in the works under scrutiny.

If, as David Harvey suggests, capitalism oscillates between short periods of profound upheaval when it is restructured in bursts of 'space and time compression', and longer periods of operating within such renewed infrastructures, then a precarious, quasi-ontological stability alternates with dislocation. In dislocated periods something akin to an intensification of feeling occurs widely. The social becomes sublime.[7] The ensuing discussion explores the links between these three terms, *sublimity, intensity* and *feeling*.

The settled ontologies linked to communal ways of life or *ethoi* of traditional societies gave rise to agreed ethico-political norms which could be used to legitimate judgements between conflicting parties. Justice could be pursued through litigation before legitimated tribunals. Modernity stripped local ontologies, formerly taken as universal, of their legitimacy. Lyotard views modernity as a condition where such attempts at legitimation must be made, otherwise terror ensues; but such attempts are contingent. They are created by the exercise of specific power for certain ends at a particular time and place. They *necessarily* create injustices in that some parties are wronged by any system or tribunal which dispenses justice. This is the *differend* which occurs when there are no universal rules. Lyotard seeks to find not the political good but the politics of 'the lesser evil'.[8]

Modernity *was* a condition of ontological heterogeneity and incommensurability but one in which various large ontological systems, the grand narratives, vied for supremacy. If Lyotard's thesis of exhaustion with and incredulity towards such surrogate systems is apposite, then no longer can there be any universal criteria by which to ground judgement. We are made sensitive to differences, and hopefully, as 'postmoderns', reinforce our ability to tolerate the incommensurable.[9]

Such sensitivity necessitates 'the invention of other realities'. This is linked to an intensification of feeling. Aesthetic discourse within modernity becomes explicable. The rise of Romanticism can be understood. The failure of modernist attempts at legitimation has ushered in a further intensification of interest in the aesthetic. This interest is accompanied by a keen sense of the dangers of a too ready reconciliation between aesthetics and politics. Experiences of the horrors of aestheticised politics are all too common in the twentieth century. Rather, attention to the aesthetic stems from its specific modes of discovery. It is a discursive field which has reflectively sought to understand *invention* or creative capacities as responses to feelings. Conditions of dislocation and heterogeneity do not allow clear cognitive judgement. We have to go on hunches and aesthetic modes sensitise us to injustices silenced by the clamour of accepted patterns of litigation.

Lyotard's focus on the *sublime* has been seminal in rediscovering this long neglected facet of aesthetics. Aesthetic discourse developed from Boileau's rediscovery of Longinius, through the work of Addison, Baumgarten to the work of Burke and Kant.[10] In Kant it explicitly became the focal point of a wider attempt to provide systematic criteria for critical judgement in general. Lyotard's *The Differend* is a detailed reworking of Kantian insights to accommodate both the linguistic and post-metaphysical turns within contemporary philosophy. Lyotard demonstrates how the questions Kant posed, and his proposed solutions, provide hints for contemporary judgement faced with heterogeneity.

Lyotard has been at the forefront of investigations into the aesthetic. A more general renewal of interest in the aesthetic has occurred for several reasons.

First, if the thesis central to 'our' postmodern condition, that of discursive heterogeneity, is acknowledged, this raises the issues of incommensurability and translation between discourses.

Second, this is very closely analogous to a cluster of problems Kant was struggling with when seeking to integrate freedom and necessity.[11] He was enquiring into the conditions whereby heterogeneous, allomorphic types of human experience could be properly linked. His problem was that of finding criteria for making appropriate judgements. Central to this question was enquiry into how the process of linkage, of finding bridges or *passages* between heterogeneity, works. By this I mean how well-founded judgements in one area could be used as analogies and in other ways in more problematical areas.

Third, Kant stressed the importance of certain intensifications of feeling as indicating an opening onto the need for judgement. These he noted were most prevalent in the area of ethics, politics and aesthetics. According to Lyotard, these are akin to those experienced through ontological dislocation. The sublime takes various *modalities*, but common to it is the experience of *intensification* of feeling. Hence it is analysed by Kant and then used as a indicator of and model for passages or analogies upon which to make judgements in the areas of ethics and politics.

Fourth, such dislocation stimulates the need to stabilise a

'world' but this can only be achieved through *new* linkages. Indeed, the productive imagination is at work in all knowledge according to Kant. It is analysed in relation to aesthetic judgement most explicitly.

Fifth, such linkages necessitate creativity and invention, akin to the aesthetic act. New vocabularies are needed as well as the links between them.

Sixth, *analogies*, what can be called 'as...if' types of argument, are central to this process of finding bridges between heterogeneous discourses or phrase regimes.[12] These are not strictly logical. Hence Lyotard's contention, 'Its [postmodern knowledge's] principle is not the expert's homology, but the inventor's *paralogy*.'[13] Analogies are either good or bad. They are engendered by *imagination*. They cannot be created by the application of methodological or logical rules. Hence their aesthetic quality. Good analogies must be invented.[14] Analogies are a narrower set of *parataxes*, or types of 'modern' conjunctions.[15]

Seventh, though paralogy carries semantic traces of mistaken or illogical thought, such claims are legitimate only if one set of rules, a specific set of axiomatic logic, is hegemonic for all thought. Postmodern thought is necessarily more inclusive. It accepts both the fact of competing rules of thought and the need both at times to respect and, at others, disturb the boundaries between them. One set of rules are the conditions of possibility for one set of presentations of a world. Paralogy— Lyotard's work takes this form—seeks to disturb existing discourses by supplementing them with aesthetic invention.[16]

Eighth, the urge to create analogies and new rules of linkage stems from a range of ethical and political demands which a politics of difference opens up. Anything does not go, urgent decisions have to be taken and creativity is at a premium. Recent interest in *hybridity* stems from this realisation.

Lyotard explores the links between intensity, sublimity, creativity and justice. Understanding this guides the reader towards 'the inventor's paralogy' and away from the 'expert's homology'.

Clearing the Ground: Post-metaphysics and Language

To sustain my argument a clearer picture of the distinction between the beautiful and the sublime is needed. Understanding Kant's use of the terms reveals the senses in which they are used by Lyotard.[17] Prior to this, Kant's foundationalism must be decisively rejected and his metaphysics of the subject replaced by a linguistic turn which decentres the subject.

Anti-foundationalism

There are *three* foundational aspects which need holding in mind when discussing Kantian aesthetics.

First, a metaphysics which seeks to take a god's-eye view of everything, seeks to systematise all knowledge, claims to discern essences beneath appearances and pretends to have unearthed reality as a whole is rejected. All knowledge is derived within contingent conditions.[18]

Second, the distinction between an identical 'reason' within all subjects and another part, 'empirical sensation and desire which is a matter of blind contingent and idiosyncratic impression' cannot be sustained. We must reject any a priori conception of subjectivity as well as any models seeking to bifurcate our personality into two parts containing a 'transcendent, dominant controller and the empirical bundle of desires and passions to be disciplined and brought to heel'.[19]

Third, moral principles, ethical discourse and political judgement are contingently determined.[20] We can write no foundational history. We live at the end of 'History'.[21] Such principles are contingent in a real sense. They are not subject to any speculatively grounded laws of history.[22] Both the a priorism of Kant's transcendental idealism and universal histories have no place in post-metaphysical thought.

Language and the Subject

Lyotard has developed his own idiolect concerning language and the subject. His assessment of Kantian aesthetic judgement cannot be understood without a brief discussion of a few of his terms. These are governed by an attempt to find way of discussing language which does not fall into unnecessary reliance upon subjectivity.

To phrase, to be in language, is to have a *stake*, that of winning. Lyotard argues that, 'to speak is to fight, in the sense of playing, and speech acts fall in the domain of a general agonistics'. Winning can be the pleasure of success won at the expense of other or *the accepted language, or connotation.*[23] His earlier use of the terms 'language-games' and 'narration' are displaced in *The Differend* by an even more minimal unit, the phrase, from which emerge the key terms, *phrase regimes* and *genres*.[24] The reasons why this analytical language is adopted are as follows.

(a) Phrases are the minimal elements of language.

(b) Phrases *must* be linked. There is no last phrase. How they are linked is contingent.[25] Narrative linkage is merely one way of joining phrases together. *Phrase-regimes* such as descriptive, prescriptive, ostensive or logical ones, are phrases of the same type. There are numerous phrase regimes. These are combined more complexly into genres. Lyotard writes that '*Genres* of discourse determine stakes, they subject different phrases from different regimens to a single *finality*.' By finality is meant ends or purposes. These are radically heterogeneous. Any phrase can be taken from one regime or genre and inscribed into another finality.[26] The term 'phrases' does not lock us into one genre or category of discourse as is the case with narrative. Typically genres might be thought of as akin to discourses. They could be a science, an established philosophy, car-repair manuals, etc. What they have in common is a known set of rules for combining phrases.

(c) Lyotard establishes that certain areas of social interaction are in search of their rules of combination or linkage. Primarily these are: aesthetic acts, politics and innovative philosophy. They are where linkages and passages are continually being sought. It is because this question is most pertinent with regard to avant-garde art that its problem of finding its own rules becomes a model when ethical and political genres are heterogeneous. When art occurs as the result of prescribed rules it betrays itself. By analogy, a politics of one hegemonic genre is that of terror.

(d) The use of 'phrase', removes a metaphysical error. Phrases do not logically imply a subject-player, someone who sits outside them waiting to play them as Wittgenstein's language game, speech act theory and narratology does. These still succumb to the metaphysics of the centred subject. Subjects are deictically constituted by phrases. There can be no sense of subjectivity except by way of phrases.

(e) The burden of his discussion of ethics and aesthetics revolves around the need for a link between feelings, which are types of *idiolect* or non-communicable quasi-phrases and those which are communicable. Sublimity is a version of this condition which can be used analogically to explain felt but not cognised responses to ethical and political situations where we do not have clear rules to guide our analysis and conduct.

(f) By deigesis Lyotard means phrases which indicate a link to a 'current spatio-temporal' origin. They are the basis of our sense of reality. Deictics such as, 'now', 'here', 'you', 'me', 'then', are designators of such reality. They indicate an extra-linguistic 'given'. Subjects are decentred because they appear in phrases as both subjects, 'I' and as objects 'you'. Subjects change from singular to plural, 'we'. Subjects in Lyotard's language are placed by phrases in either addressor or addressee instances. Though deictics present a given, it is always constituted by the phrase. As Lyotard puts it, 'this origin' is presented or co-presented with the universe of the phrase in which they are marked.[27] This applies to subjects equally.

(g) Lyotard analyses how this oscillation between subject positions helps understand ethical obligation, how being placed as a 'you' rather than an 'I' of a phrase disturbs our primary narcissism. This decentring engenders anxiety akin to that of the sublime experience.

(h) Since deictics linked to current ostension is socially

unwieldy it gives rise to names, quasi-rigid designators. Lyotard uses examples of Rome, Caesar, and indicates how infinite are the genres within which these can be inscribed. Proper names are key designators of reality and can be inserted within different phrase regimes and genres. Their use in networks creates 'worlds'. Cognition can lead to the change of a name, but ostension is not the source of 'worlds'. Cognitive regimes occur when one phrase is validated by another ostensive realm. As Lyotard succinctly puts it, 'to signify is one thing, to name another, and to show still another'.[28]

(i) Lyotard does not explicitly discuss individual subjectivity except by way of a discussion of the central term of phenomenology, 'experience'. His move is akin to Derrida's. 'The possibility of reality, including that of the subject, is fixed in networks of names "before" reality shows itself and signifies an experience'. The phrase is prior to the subject, both logically and temporally.[29]

(j) Lyotard provides a series of extraordinarily astute discussions of the numerous pathological ways in which the 'we' of collective subjects have been constituted historically through different phrase regimes. He relentlessly analyses the internal mechanisms of linkage within respective genres which have issued in such pathologies. His discussion of aesthetics and the sublime in particular can only be understood as part of a strategy of resistance to their malignancy. They have in common the attempt to link phrases according to *one* rule. They smother other existing and possible genres and thus create injustices or *differends*.

(k) Such pathological linkages—they are by no means all narratives—have in common the eradication of difference as their aim. They seek to enclose the radically different within already achieved rules of linkage, an existing 'world'. Lyotard uses the analysis of sublimity to show both how such closure works and how the emergence of difference is linked to an intensification of feeling.

(l) Lyotard returns to Kant because his analysis of judgement and struggle to understand beauty, sublimity, feeling and the signs of history indicate both the limits of pertinent linkages and their possibility. Unlike subsequent thought which systematised all knowledge, Kant acknowledged the irreducible differences of types of human knowledge, limited its pretensions to unity and simultaneously sought to find judicious judgements where possible. Understanding aesthetic judgement enables the process in general to be comprehended.

Aesthetics

Judgement

As a phrase, *judgement* carries extraordinarily dense semantic traces. It implies a process of sorting, separation, discerning, classification or discrimination and simultaneously a conjoining or setting side-by-side or comparing one thing with another or wider rule.[30] The first aspect we could call after Lyotard, its *territorialising* mode.[31] Kant sought to demarcate between appropriate types of judgements corresponding to different *faculties* of the mind. There is no matching of faculties to genres. The two primary faculties were those of *Understanding* and *Reason*. In Kant a faculty is a group of rules for forming and securing certain types of knowledge in relation to either theory or practice. Judgements were 'correct' if they did not apply the wrong rules to that which needed deciding.

Judgement applied to either descriptive knowledge, grounded in sensations and thus empirically verifiable, or to prescriptive questions of an ethical kind. Between the *descriptive* and *prescriptive* domains lay 'a great gulf...so that it was not possible to pass from the former to the latter'.[32] He wished to find what Lyotard translates as *passages* (the original is *Uebergange*) between what are heterogeneous areas of human activity.[33]

Kant wished to argue that all events can be accounted for in terms compatible with, where not directly derivable from, the laws of nature. Such accounts should be compatible with his commitment to freedom of the will. Numerous types of passage are possible. On various occasions Kant shows how *symbols* facilitate links between the good and the beautiful, how the signs of history, people's enthusiasm on hearing of the French Revolution, can be argued to be an indication of human progress, and so on.[34]

Lyotard has several purposes in turning to the aesthetic and the sublime in particular. He raises the issue of how problematic forging of pertinent rather than inappropriate linkages between heterogeneous phrase regimes is. The dangers of closed or hegemonic generic rules as the one legitimate form of passage or linkage poses the danger of a pathological collective 'we'. He maintains that the key to political resistance is faithfulness to the singular, to the point at which something new 'happens' which is not part of the world constituted by the existing interlocking network of names and finalities of existing generic rules. Asked what a teacher should do he replies, 'the pedagogic task [is]...an apprenticeship in resistance...against the academic genres of discourse to the extent that they forbid the reception of the "is it happening that...?"'[35] Elsewhere he wrote, 'Let us wage a war on totality; let us be witnesses to the unpresentable; let us activate the differences and save the honour of the name.'[36]

Singularity and sublimity are linked. Rules of judgement govern beauty; sublimity is the point where such rules have yet to be found. Rorty, happy with the rules of liberalism is content to banish sublimity to the margins of public discourse, to ironic privacy.[37] In contrast, Lyotard seeks to import the sublime moment into public discourse in order to prevent a closure according to any one passage, any linkages under the sign of a dominant hegemonic genre. Any assessment of Lyotard hinges on the extent to which it is *felt* closure threatens political difference. If it seems that chaotic multiplicity and heterogeneity prevent judicious ethical and political practice then Lyotard's invocation of the sublime as a model for disrupting discursive hegemony will seem frivolous if not dangerous.

On Aesthetic Judgement in Kant

Successful judgement gives rise to pleasure. Inability to judge adequately engenders anxiety. Finding the correct judgement results in equanimity and joy.[38] For Kant the beautiful and the sublime are two different, a priori types of feelings or responses. Kant makes the well known distinction between *determinate* and *reflective* judgements. Determinate judgements present us with little of interest to this discussion. They issue from well-founded knowledge of the type Kant thought Newton had established. Their prominence in Kant's system merely shows the prioritising of natural sciences so characteristic of metaphysical thought. Judgements are evoked when some new object or case has been discovered and decisions have to be made which will put it under the correct concept, so the particular is subsumed under the universal.

Reflective judgements occur when 'the particular is given and the universal has to be found for it', when no obvious rule determines its meaning. Reflective judgement is an art. It opens onto the domain of feelings, of anxiety and joy. Reflective judgement 'cannot borrow from experience, because its function is to establish the unity of all empirical principles under higher ones, and hence to establish the possibility of their systematic subordination'.[39] If this is the case then it must use paralogical techniques for the types of links it makes. Anxiously, reflection scans any unknown sensations, seeks to place them in the field of secure knowledge undogmatically. It seeks to discover in them something which remains constant and invariant. The work of reflection belongs to the productive imagination. The imagination *tracks* (Kant's image) through intuitions and creates forms or, in Lyotard's language, rules of linkage. Kant constantly insisted on the free play of the imagination and law—like lawlessness of aesthetic reflective judgements.

Bernstein and Lyotard are insistent that Kant realised that in some fundamental sense, reflective judgements were always prior to determinate ones. Lyotard expresses this process as when a subject is addressed by 'something...on the side of the other...which seeks to phrase itself....Sensation is *a mode of feeling*...a silence touched with emotion.' By the time it is a 'given', the sensation has entered the realm of experience, it is now a representation , not a presentation.[40] It has lost its event-like quality. The free play of the imagination reveals that knowledge has no ultimately secure foundations. Imagination weaves its patterns above the abyss. Lyotard writes, 'genres of discourse are modes of forgetting the nothingness, or of forgetting the occurrence...they fill the void between phrases.'[41]

Lyotard argues that Kant conceived of making judgements both as an art and the key to life and longevity. *Agitation* and *anxiety* are key motifs in Kant and Burke's treatment of the aesthetics. They generate action, conceptual and moral vigour and longevity. In Kant they are contrasted to the slumbers of dogmatism. Lyotard's drawing out from Kant's own text of the figures of judges, jurisdiction, health, illness, anxiety, and particularly his figure of war, sentinels, and above all the 'watchman', who, ever alert, never sleeping, watches the citadel against the invasion of dogma, is skilful deconstruction.[42]

Kant and the Beautiful

The third critique prioritises understanding and determinate judgement over aesthetic reflective judgement and within the aesthetic the beautiful over the sublime. The beautiful is most connected to understanding and public communicability.[43] At one stage Kant writes of the sublime as a mere supplement to aesthetic judgement in general, though he writes at inordinate length on it.[44] He places aesthetic reflective judgement securely under the thrall of 'truth', lest its abyssal non-foundational aspects emerge. Kant distributes the feelings the free play of the imagination engenders as it seeks passages, in a bifurcated polarity which has haunted aesthetic and Western discourse since. This is of course the distinction between the beautiful and the sublime. The feeling of beauty is linked to understanding, that of the sublime to reason.[45]

Secure knowledge—perhaps the knowledge of knowledge gained—gives rise to relief, to pleasure. Certainty, closure, public agreement, the cessation of dissension, all characterise the beautiful. Judgements of beauty are made according to forms which are held in common. Something is judged beautiful relative to its form not content. Form is evidence that the reflective judgement has managed to stabilise the sensations which drew forth the need for reflection in the first place.

Beauty's reflective judgements are linked to the tribunal of conceptual thought. Thus feelings are stabilised and controlled. Beauty's objects are primarily the freely found forms nature spontaneously takes. Such judgements face outward to the world in which are found tranquil pleasures. They can thus be used analogically as models for generating public civility and serenity.

By bringing intuitions under the rubric of the beautiful we match them to prior, exemplary objects.[46] Our reflective 'scanning' draws out similarities and dissimilarities. Given the exemplary, we can judge whether nature or a new art-work conforms to rules of *taste*, a key concept in Kant's aesthetic lexicon. By being placed in relation to already existing phrase universes, the radically 'new', what Lyotard calls 'the event' or 'occurrence', is already being forced into received generic rules. Taste is thus linked to another key concept, *sensus communis*.

Many writers have noted a hidden politics here. Eagleton notes that Kant conceives of aesthetic judgements as impersonally personal and that what he is trying to get at is a form of judgement which would eschew concepts but would be universally communicable through a fusion of feeling. It is on this basis that the famous *demand* of Kantian aesthetics is founded. Statements of the form 'If *you* put all self interest and personally contingent circumstances aside, you must agree with my judgement concerning the beauty of this X.'[47] If this demand is linked in the Kantian manner to ideas of community and universal structures of feeling via doctrines of taste then it is potentially tyrannical. Lyotard is deeply suspicious of the beautiful. Our century has suffered from too much official art, too much from art as solace.[48] Kantian taste contains a 'dream of uncoerced consensus' yet it only does so by 'mystifying and legitimating actual dominative social relations'. This helps explain the left's long felt suspicion of the aesthetic and Adorno's use of the term reconciliation.[49] It also explains Lyotard's turn to the sublime.

Kant and the Sublime

The Kantian sublime too, has as its tribunal, Reason. Aesthetic reflective judgements are shared out within the system, each wing grounded in contrary types of feeling involving different sorts of experience. Sublimity occurs when the subject cannot impose form or order on outer apprehension. Kant writes,

> The beautiful in nature is connected with the *form* of the object, which consists in having definite boundaries. The sublime...is to be found in a *formless* object, so far as in it...*boundlessness* is represented, and yet its totality is present to thought.[50]

The range of emotions engendered in the two cases is very different. The feelings of beauty are those of charm and beauty, those of the sublime a checking of vital powers and a consequent stronger outflow of them.[51] This is akin to the intensification Lyotard links to ontological dislocation noted earlier.

Kant argues that the feelings of the sublime 'deserve to be called negative pleasure'. They seem to do violence to the imagination. Lyotard writes, 'One of the essential features revealed by Kant's analysis of the sublime depends on the disaster suffered by the imagination in the sublime sentiment.'[52] The contrast between feelings of beauty and those of sublimity is one of *degrees of intensity*. Having evoked the scanning and discriminatory procedures of aesthetic reflective judgement, no end to the process can be found when confronted with the sublime. Form is missing. Anxiety, as agitated feeling, rules. The more easily form can be imposed on the unknown the more we approach the pole of beautiful feelings. Conversely, the less likely such a form is to be found, the more the threat of the abyssal, non-foundational quality of the world and the subject appears, the more awful the prospect, the bigger the shock.[53] Thus beauty is associated with tranquillity, calm, form, measure, taste and communicability. In contrast, the feelings associated with the sublime are of agitation and anxiety.[54]

Driven by intensified anxiety, by terror, the subject turns inward and in successive compensatory moves seeks solace in the powers of its inner imagination, which extends the range of reason because it grapples with Ideas. There in the Kantian system are thoughts not guaranteed by phenomenon but which are crucial to the inner logic of all judgement, particularly ethical ones. This freewheeling introspection evoked by the sublime spirals out to the edges of the imagination. We learn to revel in the freedom of our imagination and its superiority over mere nature, mere determination.[55]

Astonishment, dread, awe, melancholy, violence, anxiety, fear, terror, vibration, pain, excitement—all these terms occur in Kant's text—once reigned in the breast of the subject when faced with the sublime. When mastery via ideas is established, the hubris of its importance in relation to nature established, the disturbed subject returns, relieved, to pleasure.[56] The connection between the sublime and sublimation here, is painfully clear. He writes,

> Hence the pleasurableness arising from the cessation of an uneasiness is a *state of joy*. But this on account of the deliverance from danger...is a state of joy when conjoined with the resolve that we shall no more be exposed to the danger.[57]

The subject—by the way, always gendered as a 'him'—in trying to tie down an immensity it cannot comprehend, is forced by the desire for mastery into a series of spiralling internal moves towards contemplating the infinity of the cosmos.[58] The sublime must be comprehended as unstable. As bad vibes! Kant writes, 'This movement may be compared to a *vibration*, i.e. to a quickly alternating attraction toward and repulsion from, the same object.'[59] Unlike beauty's repose, it is an agitation *through which the subject passes*. This cannot be emphasised enough if Lyotard's treatment of the sublime is to be fully comprehended and linked to his wider writing strategies.

Whereas through beauty, subjects calmly reaffirm their place in a secure world, the sublime forces radical interrogations of it. Sublimity emerges by way of fear and anxiety and issues in joy. This joy it must be noted is only secure if the contemplation of grandeur is done in comparative security.[60] Real danger would return us either to the initial state of anxiety or to the realities of politics. Kant clearly knew that judgements of beauty were satisfying because they were public. They bind us to others, to community, to a 'we'. He explicitly equated self-sufficiency, 'separation from society' and sublimity.[61]

Lyotard on the Sublime

Lyotard's detailed exposition of the sublime has been developed out of his concern with visual art and painting in particular. Though most fully developed in this context, he constantly extends its implications outwards, so that his discoveries in the realm of art underpin his discussion of ethics and politics. The model of the avant-garde artist seeking rules for her art becomes key to his recent analysis of ethical obligation and politics. Consequently I first discuss his analysis of the sublime in contemporary art and then show very briefly how he extends it to ethics and politics.

The Aesthetic Sublime

Lyotard writes:

> And is not the purpose of painting—even when it is most withdrawn, even at its haughtiest, its most reserved or its most modest—to tame the savagery of the thing, to make it submit to the visible, and at the same time to make our gaze submit to its savagery?...We thought we knew how to see; *works of art teach us that we were blind.*

He evokes a world beyond concepts, indeed finds these masking, obscuring timbre, tone, access.[62] The conceptual reenacts a world distributed according to stabilised phrase-regimes. The sublime pushes beyond subjectivity, to the preconscious, beyond what he calls intrigue, 'to free the gaze from the grip of the present'. The experience of the sublime is beyond the conceptual, beyond the will, understanding, emotion—itself too subjective—beyond community. This place, this incision, is accessible only via intense feelings: 'Feeling, or rather sentiment is not a matter for the ego; it is matter taking on form...it exists before the act, before subjectification.'[63]

The connection with Kant's discussion is evident. Lyotard is attempting to convey and at times reenact in his writing the experience of anxiety when faced with the unknown. He seeks to separate out feelings akin to those Kant described, *and separate them from their link with reason.* Hence the recourse to the sublime rather than beauty which is always linking to community via appeals to taste. Lyotard seeks to tap into affect. By choosing a textually sublime style at times, he analogically destabilises expectations of easy comprehension and seeks to evoke anxiety in his readers.

Lyotard's texts are riddled with metaphors of movement. He explores certain aspects of the sublime by going back past Kant to Burke. He draws out Burke's treatment by evoking the figure of the creative person faced with the need to create. He uses Burke's linking of terror with privation.[64] He poses the question, *what if nothing happens?* Despite being sensitised by successive transformations of the 'new', this time, for this artist, it (the creation of a work) might never happen:

> This is the misery that the painter faces with the plastic surface, of the musician with the acoustic surface, the misery the thinker faces with the desert of thought and so on. The possibility that nothing will happen is accompanied by *anxiety.*

This may result in an intensification of feeling, its redirection towards joy if the event happens. This contradictory feeling—depression and exaltation—is the *sublime.* Sublimity in art is the bearing, pictorial or otherwise, of expressive witness to the inexpressible, it is a result of something happening. The free play of creative imagination is the moment of the event, the occurrence, before it is entrammelled in defences, justifications, interpretations and commentaries. This is the sublime at its most rigorous. The fact that something *is happening.*[65]

Burke and Kant prioritise words over the figurative. They argue that poetry can be charged with 'passionate connotations', in a way which they thought that painting, tied to representative mimesis, could not. Lyotard's interest here is that the subsequent development of painting has disproved this assertion. The arts in general, pushed forward by the aesthetics of the sublime, sought out intense effects. To do so they had consistently to give up the imitation of previous models that are merely beautiful, and try out surprising, strange and shocking combinations. The artists tried out new combinations in order to release the event. Art-lovers came to expect an intensification of their emotional capacities and only after the event their conceptual understanding of the rules of art.[66]

Art works engender questions, but only after they have first provoked or enacted the 'event'. In other words, any art work must affect its audience's feelings directly, prior to any questions they may ask of it. Feelings for Lyotard are linked to the inhuman, to the preconscious prior to its entry to society, but also prior to the language of the imagination of Lacan.[67] Interpretation, the necessary linkage of phrases, progressively closes off the event, enfolds it into the already known, into the literal, the merely beautiful of official culture as Adorno used to put it. Cessation of the sublime is when feeling and sensation return to the culture of beauty, to the haven of emotion and desire.

Lyotard thus aids understanding of the connection of the sublime to many currents of modern painting and writing which 'devote themselves to making an allusion to the unpresentable by means of visible presentations'. To which could be added, 'by means also of textual presentations'.[68] Lyotard's own oscillating style becomes explicable.

Lyotard identifies two forms of sublimity within contemporary aesthetics. The first stresses the *powerlessness* of subjects, their inability to create adequate representations as reality withdraws, shattered by the ceaseless transformations of modernity. This results in such feelings as melancholy, nostalgia, a sense of futility, etc. This issues in one strand 'within the chessboard...history of avant-gardes.' This mood, *modernism*, is governed by a memorial aesthetics, a nostalgia for presence.[69] The other mood, openly acknowledging the diremption between the presentable and the conceivable, stresses *the power of creative imagination*. Its dominant mood is jubilation which results from 'the invention of new rules of the game'. It is a *postmodernism* which 'denies itself the solace of good forms' and produces works which are not 'in principle governed by preestablished rules.' It is where the monstrous, the violation of taste, the dissonant, discordant, and above all the hybrid can find their expression. They 'have the characters of an event.' Both Lyotard's writing style and politics is summed up when he writes 'it must be clear that our business is not to supply reality but to invent illusions.'[70]

THE LESSER EVIL AND THE GREATER GOOD

The Political Sublime

A recurrent theme of *The Differend* is discussion of feelings. Lyotard seeks to alert readers to the differences which hegemonic finalities exclude. The links between feeling, the sublime and attentiveness to excluded ethical and political possibilities are very tightly wrought 'passages' within the text.

By means of tensions, agitations which appear as feelings 'something announces itself through feeling.'[71] The call of the other to which we have ethically to respond without question, a notion derived from Levinas, 'is not an event of cognition. But it is an event of feeling.'[72] Obligation appears first as 'the approach of what is not yet said as feeling'.[73] Being obliged is to be taken hostage. The subject is thrust from addressor to addressee position via feelings. But for Lyotard this relation of self and other through feeling to obligation can never be communal. That occurs when sublimity is falsely extended to a collectivity. This is the moment of its pathology. He writes 'obligation cannot engender...a particular community.'[74]

Just as Lyotard identified within modernism one mode of the sublime where avant-gardes were governed by nostalgia and melancholy, and another where jubilation in finding new linkages, new rules operate, so analogically this opposition can be found in his analysis of politics. Some take the malignant form of the cynical political use of myth. Genres carry their agonism with them. Every type of linkage is a success of one over another. Stakes are tied to genres. Conflicts result from them.

For Lyotard, politics is *not* a genre. It is where the question of linkage is at its most open, where a multiplicity of ends are at play. It is 'if you will, the state of the language, but it is not *a* language'.[75] Politics is like the moment of blankness awaiting the artist, and it is no coincidence that when it is being defined, references to Cezanne, and Joyce, etc., occur. On the face of it this beggars the imagination. What Lyotard is insisting upon is that political possibility is nested within any particular contingent set of political arrangements, constitutions, tribunals, etc. These seemingly solid institutions actually give rise to exclusions, to those who are wronged by them. Of course their contingency is continually and wilfully obscured by their beneficiaries. However solidly embedded they seem, they could have been, and will be, radically other. He writes, 'Politics always gives rise to misunderstandings because *it takes place as a genre*.'[76] Differences are repressed, forgotten by an existing legitimate authority through which judgement takes place.

Legitimation is organised around 'an empty centre'. Lyotard gives numerous examples of the different logic whereby political norms are created by various types of linking genres. In a series of incisive and brilliant analyses he shows how varied these have been and yet how they share the common characteristic of excluding the unique name, occurrence or event. Each attempts to deny contingency, the emptiness, the abyss which lies at their heart. Each attempts to create collective subjects. Some are more pathological than others. They do not all take narrative form. It is in this discovery that the material of phrases and linkage, insights garnered from his reading of Kant, push Lyotard's analysis way past that of *The Postmodern Condition* and its notion of meta-narratives. He is also capable of analysing linkages which lead to disaster, such as the reading of signs of enthusiasm at certain moments of history such as the French Revolution and the Paris Commune, as evidence of an essentialist collective subject such as humanity or the working class, who then figure as the subject of discourses of emancipation.

He identifies the following types of political genres which have sought hegemony. Mythic systems of names and linked narration are premodern genres: Christian eschatology which converts every event into a sign of God's work; speculative dialectics which converts singularity into mere moments of a dialectically predetermined result and thereby utterly effaces contingency; regressive, Nazi-like terror under which myth re-enters modernity, and, by confusing genealogy and the good, 'forgets its contingency and is able to raise superstition to the delirium of its being a necessity and a virtue'. Such genres legitimate a people outside of which no rules apply. Only one name, of all those in history, is chosen. For all else death is enough.[77] Other genres are philosophies of history 'that inspired the nineteenth and twentieth centuries' claim to assure passages over the abyss of heterogeneity or the event'.[78] Their belief in collective humanity and progress have been refuted by names and events such as Auschwitz and now Bosnia which resist inclusion into their system. Finally there are those genres such as the economic, performativity where efficiency, gain as growth, which efface questions of truth and justice in their inhuman logic.[79]

Sublimity appears politically as intense feelings. These Kant called signs of history. How we link them to wider arguments needs care. Lyotard repeatedly insists upon their immediacy, their singularity and the dangers of enclosing them, as evidence within a wider generic finality. When this occurs, contingent power seeks to establish its tribunals which will arbitrate as to the meaning of new signs of history. Feelings are singular. The sublime is a negative critical point disruptive of closed generic finality. Its very formlessness makes it resistant to power. It is destructive of clear political norms. It reveals the contingency of any particular genre. Is it any wonder that it stands accused of irresponsibility by those in power who seek to silence it in the name of the people, the revolution, taste or efficiency?

Conclusion

Responses to Lyotard hinge upon how much readers share his horror at the various forms of generic closure. If they do then his work on the sublime strikes deep chords. At the very least his doctrine of a politics of the lesser evil acknowledges, more explicitly than most current political theory, that heterogeneity will not be overcome through recourse to consensus-based arguments. Rather it indicates the profound importance of creativity and imagination when facing the current times in which we live. Understanding the aesthetic and opening ourselves to sublimity seem appropriate. It is time to effect multiple new connections and maximise political creativity in these dangerous times. Retreat into closure will intensify injustice. Lyotard's detailed reworking of Kant, his emphasis upon the role of linkages and passages, and his astute readings of generic finality and the role of feelings as indicators of the sublime, serve as important insights.

(10)

Essentialism Revisited?

Identity Politics and Late Twentieth-Century Discourses of Homosexuality

Frank Mort

The French sociologist, Pierre Bourdieu, in his study of the academy and its intellectuals, has given a particular interpretation of the idea of cultural crisis.[1] Crisis moments, Bourdieu has observed, compel participants to adopt a coherence to their arguments which is not required under more normal circumstances. Positions are staked out according to the logic of a civil war, producing clearly distinguished camps and forcing decisions on the basis of a single principle of choice, which excludes all evasions and equivocations. Bourdieu has argued that these are struggles over rival systems of classification, which are characteristic of the way in which power is dispersed in the cultural field. Such crisis moments act for Bourdieu as *developers*; stimulating knowledge and sites from which to speak in a manner paralleling the way Foucault conceives of the productivity of discourse.

Bourdieu's paradigm has principally been applied to intellectual systems in the narrow sense, yet his understanding might usefully be directed at the recent eruption of the term queer within homosexual discourse, in both Britain and North America. For notions of the 'q-word'—queer identity, queer theory, queer culture and politics—have precipitated such a notion of crisis in the Bourdieurian sense. Polarised positions and opposing camps have been staked out, distinctive and competing systems of knowledge produced, above all the umbrella term queer has been *developmental* in giving a renewed vitality and visibility to homosexuality. Of course, a linguistic change of tack cannot achieve that in itself; it is a shift in language which has been socially constituted. But around the loose signifier 'queer' has become fixed, or more sharply focused, a set of issues which have been rumbling within modern homosexual culture since its inception in the late 1960s: about the aetiology of the homosexual identity, about the meaning of sexual acts and lifestyles and about the possible dialogue between homosexual men and women. In microcosm, queerness has also condensed many of the recurrent problems which have bedevilled forms of late twentieth century identity politics associated with the new social movements. These have centred on the strategic implications of mobilising around identity formations and on the possible relationship between a politics of identity and politics as conceived in its formal, traditional sense.

Diasporas, National Cultures and Socially Constituted Identities

Much of the subsequent argument is focused on the dialogue of ideas which has taken place across the Atlantic between British, American and Canadian activists and intellectuals. This productive exchange of information and enthusiasms confirms that the history of modern sexuality can rarely be understood as a purely domestic scenario, comfortably bounded by national formations. It points to the existence of a well-established homosexual diaspora, crossing nation states and linking individuals and social constituencies, especially in the Western metropolitan centres. Yet despite the success of this supranational conversation, queer images and theory have been flitted across the Atlantic and back by very specific groups of actors, carrying with them a distinctive global vision. There is more than a hint of Baudrillard's version of hyper-reality here, where ideas and imagery are in a constant flux of symbolic exchange.[2] In response to that euphoric cosmology, some reaffirmation of social specificity is appropriate. This is necessary at two different registers: in terms of foregrounding the continuing links between national cultures and sexual systems, and at a more personal level by identifying the distinctive genres of identity—including my own—which have spoken in the queer narrative.

While national routes do not securely de-limit homosexuality, they do continue to shape its appearance and positioning. It is misguided to assume that simply because dialogues are productive and possible across national boundaries, such boundary lines have ceased to exist.[3] This was an issue which emerged very concretely in the take-up of the strategy of 'outing' (the exposure of prominent public figures thought to be homosexual) by British activists, who quickly discovered that English libel laws allowed much less room for manoeuvre than in the US. The specific contours of the American AIDS crisis, where the politics of HIV infection has collided with the more general demand for universal health provision, has registered a similar point about the impact of domestic agendas. Any account of contemporary homosexual discourse needs to be underwritten by an emphasis on the national limitations of queer usage, as well as its broader possibilities.

At a more intimate level, that of the personalised constitution of the self, the queer debate has pointed up the differential channels of access which shape sexual identities. It has frequently been pointed out that the eruption of queer into the vocabulary of homosexuality has made more visible the lines of generational and social division within the community, as well as producing new alliances. Lesbians who have been drawn to the queer ethos have expressed reservations about the term's usage, on account of its masculine frame of reference and confrontationalist stance. Nonetheless the queer agenda has held out the possibilities for a fresh dialogue between homosexual women and men. For many younger activists what is seen to be at issue is a generational split implicit in the use of the term queer, as opposed to the chronologically prior category of gay.[4] Gay politics has been cast as flabby and reformist; the product of comfortable, middle-aged men holding to a tired, 1970s sexual agenda which has now lost its way. It is queer which now signifies youth, style and vibrancy and expresses the strongest dissatisfactions with an equal rights politics of inclusion, obsessed with piecemeal gains. Queer activists have also claimed to break apart the cultural dominance of masculine ethnocentrism, opening up more spaces for ethnically plural subjectivities.[5]

Yet dissatisfaction with gayness as a category has not only been the prerogative of younger men and women. A number of older activists and intellectuals have begun to 'come out' and express their long-standing and hitherto concealed disquiet with notions of a gay identity.[6] I would announce myself as one of those older renegades. Confessionals have become almost *de rigueur* within progressive academic circles, demonstrating a supposedly more self-reflexive epistemology and acknowledging the inevitable entanglement of intellectual personas with knowledge formation.[7] Not all of such performances are necessarily productive, for they often fall back into the more regulatory practice of the confessional, avoiding questions about the status of knowledge produced by highly internalised narratives of deconstruction. But a socially constituted narrative of the self—and one that is attentive to what Edward Thompson in a quite different context once called the 'education of desire'—can make a significant contribution to the recent history of homosexuality, centred as it inevitably has been around the assertion of identities.[8]

Versions of my own story have been told many times, they are masculine narratives which have become almost iconic within British post-war cultural history. But they have rarely been rehearsed from the standpoint of sexual dissidence.[9] The history of my own unease with the idea of 'being gay' highlights yet again the unstable, multi-accented and culturally specific nature of homosexuality, long before poststructuralism made such instability intellectually respectable. As a northern English, lower middle-class grammar school boy, an adolescent in the late 1960s and early 1970s, gayness sat very uneasily with other discourses constituting my subjectivity. I rapidly worked to identify the gay idea as the product of a celebratory humanism with strong class articulations. Though this early exercise in deconstruction was not performed with the aid of 'theory' in its intellectualised versions, it nonetheless benefited from a stock of more informal knowledge. My critique of gayness was carried out with that dogged, relentless exposure of middle-class pretensions which those from petty-bourgeois origins will recognise. I was not entirely misguided, given the social profile of the pressure groups pushing for homosexual law reform and many of the prominent actors in the early days of gay liberation. There were strong links between reforming moral strategies, liberation or lifestyle politics and the transformations underway within the culture of the progressive middle classes during these years.[10] Such a scripting of gayness sat awkwardly with my own subject formation. Indeed, I resisted it, if at first only silently and sullenly. For not only did it signify disruption and violation of all of the paraphernalia of respectability, it polemicised for a self-consciously coherent sense of self which I could not share. Lower middle-class culture has historically carried both its own mechanisms of centring, often conceived around knowing your symbolic place, and its own experience of incoherence as a result of being spoken to simultaneously by both the major class groupings.[11] It was a formation at odds with the type of identity central to the early gay liberation movement.

Burdened with this legacy, I became a very reluctant convert to gay politics. Much more appealing for my own dispersed sense of identity were those 'continental' theorists who awarded top priority to the attack on humanism. I devoured structuralist Marxism, semiology and discourse theory with added nourishment precisely because they made personal sense. They combined the allure of 'scientific' rigour with a sustained critique of the fallacies of fixed subjectivity. Meanwhile, I was drawn to a career in formal politics, becoming a not very gay, but politically competent, Labour councillor in North London between 1986 and 1990. This involvement, among other things, fulfilled notions of ambition and respectability, bringing part of my life 'to order', as formal politics in its masculine versions so often does. At the time, my personal life commingled discourses of romantic love and lifestyle satisfaction with narratives of sexual transgression—a familiar structure in lives of professional men, the historical genealogy of which I have unravelled elsewhere.[12]

I have rehearsed this autobiographical fragment both to point out yet again the multiple and variable genres of homosexuality (others would inevitably produce quite different narratives) and to emphasise that receptivity to political discourse is in part dependent on the dynamics of subjectivity.[13]

The social vantage point of the actors in the queer drama has provided further evidence of the relationship between political agendas and the contours of self-identity. For if queers have reconstructed the history of modern homosexuality around a seismic break with gayness, they have done so via a characteristic view of the world. Glossing their profiles a little more concretely points to a distinctively metropolitan sense of self inhabited by those who negotiate the same social spaces of London, New York or Toronto, with their range of social and sexual pleasures.[14]

Characteristic cultural points of reference for queers have been a metropolitan image of the city and a mixture of traditional avant-garde and postmodern aesthetics. While the development of homosexual culture from the nineteenth century has been consistently associated with urban spaces of the modern city, queerness inhabits this social geography in distinctive ways. Part of the excitement for the queer agenda has been generated by the proliferation of urban sites of homosexuality since the 1970s, largely through commercial and entrepreneurial initiatives. But a different input reflects the particular social dislocations of late twentieth-century city living, rooted in infrastructural decline and cultural instability. The film-maker Derek Jarman, himself a vocal advocate of queer politics, encapsulated this social imagery in his autobiographical sketches, *Modern Nature*, 1991. Moving across the topography of urban life—first night receptions, HIV clinics, bar culture, deluxe consumption, sexual nocturnes on Hampstead Health—our hero celebrated the homosexual map of the metropolis.[15] Jarman's profile though is not entirely representative, for with the exception of those academics who have taken up queer theory, the majority of activists are 'on the margins' in an obvious socio-economic sense, while nonetheless accruing cultural capital. They are not part of the recognisable homosexual middle class; neither established professionals nor commercial entrepreneurs, but frequently members of a latter-day democratised bohemia. Contributors to Cherry Smyth's *Lesbians Talk Queer Notions*, 1992, written by both homosexual women and men, include independent film-makers, freelance journalists and writers, painters, poets and booksellers.[16] Students, themselves a migrant and transitory group, have also gravitated towards queer discourse. Queer commentators have tended to be unreflective about their own particular formation, often naturalising or celebrating it. Yet as always, politics is not put together in a vacuum, but by specifically constituted actors whose social profiles and visions of the world have effects on the formation of strategies.

In terms of my own identity, the early manifestations of queer activism were not likely to address me. Indeed I misread its agenda as the simple restatement of sexual essentialism, an attempt to reinvent the coherence of homosexuality, without noting the signs of a more complex debate about the construction of sexuality. With all its ambiguities, queerness has productively renewed long-standing discussions about the status of the homosexual identity and about how such a sense of self can be mobilised within a broader social and political field. But first the queer idea needs to be situated within the context of contemporary arguments about the homosexual.

Contemporary Discourses of Homosexuality

It is not of course accidental that the recent flurry of discourse over homosexuality has centred on the status of the *homosexual identity*. Given the historical yoking together of identity, biological processes and sexual object choice within modern systems of sexual organisation, many of the most hard fought battles of sexual politics have been waged on precisely this terrain. There have been many earlier examples of what is now termed identity politics: the reclamation of 'the spinster' within early twentieth-century British feminism, or the possibilities opened up for self-definition by the medicalised categories of the 'invert' and the 'lesbian' in broadly the same period.[17] In their self-conscious and inventive re-appropriation of an earlier label of subjective regulation, queer activists have worked with the principle of reverse discourse affirmation; turning a repertoire of regulation into a category of resistance. A similar case has been made for the lesbian category of 'the dyke'. New sexual personas are not assembled out of thin air, they have to be forged out of the current vocabularies available. The upsurge of activity around a queer identity has not taken place in a vacuum, but in the context of broader sexual speculations.

In Europe as in North America, the late 1980s and early 1990s has witnessed the crystallisation of new knowledges about homosexuality. From the medical profession, but this time from self-professed 'gay scientists', have come variants of biologism, through efforts to establish a relationship between sexual object choice and brain structure or genetic constitution—now argued for as a potentially positive factor in the struggle for minority civil rights.[18] At a different level, the impact of AIDS has led to a major focus of campaigning around the rights and identity of a community at risk, not simply from a virus, but from inadequate knowledge and treatment. In this respect, many HIV positive men have spoken about the ways in which being antibody positive itself confirms an enforced identity status.[19] Meanwhile in the realm of consumption, the ongoing expansion of male homosexual, and increasingly lesbian, culture around the exchange of goods and services has led to the consolidation of entrepreneurial networks dedicated to the reproduction of a 'homosexual lifestyle'. Via holidays and restaurants, shops and café-bars, insurance and legal services, it has now become possible to live a homosexual life in the large urban centres of Europe and North America. Steven Epstein has noted that in the US this commercial notion of a gay community (paralleling other genres of niche-marketing) has circulated its own quasi-essentialist identity around the idea of an ethnically-based interest group.[20] As a form of everyday commonsense it has sat somewhat awkwardly with the knowledge produced from a generation of academics and researchers. Here, despite the differing frames of reference, a dominant strand of argument has been to assert the relativism of homosexuality, both historically and in relation to different societal milieux. The 'social constructionist' paradigm, as it has come to be termed, has worked to deconstruct more unified and stable projections of the homosexual self.[21]

Finally, the identity factor has not been absent from the field of formal politics. In Britain and in US broadly left-of-centre parties and groupings continue to be pressed to enter into dialogue with the social movements. From these newer political activists has come a core demand for the recognition of rights and identities which are uneasily positioned within the collectivist traditions of both mainstream social democracy and labourism. Homosexuals have of course been only one of the growing list of identities claiming their place within political culture.

Reviewing these multiple variations on the theme of identity reveals that queer activism and theory is part of longer term discussions about the aetiology of homosexuality. Over the past decade, this has been taking place at the level of patterns and styles of life as well as more self-consciously in politics and theory. The status of the homosexual has been profoundly unstable since its modern inception in the 1960s—a result of differences within the community as much as the effects of official discourse. The eruption of the queer category represents the latest of these questionings.

The Construction of Sexuality: Binary Oppositions

Activists have remained deliberately and productively slippery over the status of the category queer, but they have been much more assertive about the system of modern sexuality within which queerness needs to be located. At its most grandiose this has been nothing short of a global account of the formation of the sexual across the binary polarities of heterosexuality/homosexuality. Such a dualism has appeared in fairly simple form in political slogans and rhetoric, but in much more sophisticated renderings from the recent work of cultural and literary theorists. Despite its global claims, it remains a highly specific account of sexual organisation. Binary oppositions have not encompassed the whole of the queer agenda; they have coexisted with more dispersed and plural renderings of sexuality. But the unitary politics of perversion has exercised considerable appeal. The rhetoric has not been without tongue-in-cheek irony. Here it is at its most camp on the British side of the Atlantic, from 'Homocult', the Manchester-based 'cell':

> HOMOCULTURE
> Our language is perversion
> Corruption Reclaiming Acting

Changing Surviving Subverting
Evolving Life
HETROTRASH
Their Language Is Conserving
Stagnating Lingering Death
QUEER
Love Yourself...[22]

Or in its more sexualised and romanticised Manhattan variant, from the anonymous manifesto, *I Hate Straights*:

Being queer means leading a different sort of life... It's about being on the margins, defining ourselves; it's about genderfuck and secrets, what's beneath the belt and deep inside the heart; it's about the night. Being queer is grassroots, because we know that every one of us, every body, every cunt, every heart and ass and dick is a world of pleasure waiting to be explored.[23]

This is queer power at its most outrageous and evangelical, but it nonetheless has enshrined a familiar reading of sexuality: queer against straight, perversion over normality, life as opposed to lingering death. For a number of writers the current upsurge of radicalism has marked a revival of the original agenda of 1960s homosexual liberation, which is seen to have been highjacked by the later gay agenda. Echoing Herbert Marcuse and other counter-culture liberationists from that decade, British activist Peter Tatchell has insisted that: 'queer emancipation is in the interests of heterosexuals, because it is about the rights of all humanity to experience the joys of queer desire without guilt or discrimination.' For Tatchell such pleasures are currently repressed by the institutionalised 'system of homophobia'.[24]

There have been some significant lines of convergence between the political language of queer activism and a growing body of sexual theory which has privileged transgression and perversion as cultural dominants in the organisation of Western societies. The connections have not been so much around an agreement on specific political agendas, but over a shared epistemological reading of sexuality. On both sides of the Atlantic much of this academic work has been broadly literary in its origins and framework, examining the ways in which texts have mediated, or refused, changing patterns of sexual behaviour via their representational coding. Eve Kosofsky Sedgwick's account of the complex rendering of male homosexuality within late nineteenth-century literary milieux in the *Epistemology of the Closet*, 1990, has been a recurrent point of reference for this corpus of writing. Rather than claiming familiar minority status for the homosexual theme, Sedgwick's narrative is premised on a much more all encompassing trope, namely that:

> many of the major modes of thought and knowledge in twentieth century Western culture as a whole are structured...by a chronic, now endemic crisis of homo/ heterosexual definition, indicatively male, dating from the end of the nineteenth century.[25]

This reading of the 'perverse implantation', the understanding that perversion is endemic to modern societies, was familiar from Michel Foucault's history of sexuality. But in the work of literary critics it has been elevated to even greater status as a quasi-anthropological principle of human culture. The 'perverse dynamic' of writers such as Wilde and Genet has also been claimed as a strategy of cultural resistance, turning and using transgression 'against the normative orders which demonise the sexual deviant'.[26]

Such accounts have delivered significant insights for our understanding of the mechanisms whereby perversity and the norm are mutually dependent and reinforcing. But they have also carried with them the ongoing burden of a binary reading of modern sexual regimes; if now a very complex binarism. There is a disabling inheritance from literary readings of culture here, evidenced both by a somewhat cavalier approach to history and an avant-gardist legacy. Via a series of characteristic slippages literary commentators move from identifying perverse structures *in texts*, to much more global pronouncements on the history of culture. In doing so they side-step many of the awkward questions of historical verification and periodisation. Moreover, in their reading of the literary careers of signficant homosexual men—notably Oscar Wilde—as dissident and transgressive, queer critics reproduce elements of a conventional modernist narrative, in which progressive male artists challenge tradition from the outside. In consequence the question of women's differential relation to avant-garde aesthetics remains obscured.

Just how specific this account of sexuality is becomes apparent when it is contrasted with a rather different narrative which is present in Foucault's work. Reviewing Foucault's writing on sexuality from the vantage point of over a decade, a crucial element in his account was the simultaneously global and local reading of sex. In *The History of Sexuality: Volume One*, alongside an emphasis on the specificity of discourse, Foucault drew attention to the broader lines of force which traversed particular fields: the inscription of sexuality within a politics of population, the persistence of the repressive hypothesis, the projection of sexual modernity around the constitution and governance of the self.[27] These were some of the larger networks of power. In positing sexuality in this way Foucault profoundly and irrevocably questioned common-sense understandings of what a history and politics of sexuality could be about. Foucault's system uncovered sex in the most unlikely places, as well as in more familiar areas: within sanitary science, household manuals and psychiatric principles. Sex intruded into the circuits of social government and inflected the tables of statistical classification, in addition to signifying bodily acts, identities and desires. Modern sexuality is in short a *dispersed field*, not a restricted one, organised around *multiple points of reference*. Within this framework Foucault identified a number of nodal points around which sexuality is fixed and power is exercised: the procreating couple, the masturbating child, the sexualised feminine body, as well as the pervert. The significance of these particular principles of power nomination have been much argued over, especially by feminists.[28] But Foucault's basic insistence is worth reiterating; that sexuality is plural, rather than simply articulated around any binary dualism.

In contrast the queer paradigm has tended towards a polarised codification of sex. It has privileged the principle of sexual dissidence as *the* epistemology of sexuality, in such a way that the pervert, as against the norm, has become the motif of sexual classification. What is performed is a reductionist slight of hand familiar from other quite different sexual philosophies. Sex is not now grounded in the family, nor in moral law, nor as a function of capitalism, but according to the binary principle of homo as opposed to heterosexuality. That such a conceptualisation has occurred within the most sophisticated forms of cultural analysis, as well as in political rhetoric, is a testament to the power of binary dualism within the history of nineteenth- and twentieth-century philosophy and social thought. The Hegelian legacy is prominent here, as is a more specific inheritance from one strand of Freudian psycho-analysis. Sexual theory is littered with reductionisms; they have proved equally unproductive, not least because they fail to grasp the plurality of sexual systems and force disabling choices around polarised oppositions.

The difficulties with such an approach were tabled in microcosm by one commentator to *Lesbians Talk Queer Notions*, who was interested in the value of queer categories, but who also felt partly fixed by her role as a mother. As British feminist and cultural critic Suzanne Moore put it:

> I don't think I could claim queer....While I want to embrace queer politics, some of the very basic demands of the Women's Liberation Movement have to be met— like childcare—but that's not very queer, is it? Not very exciting?[29]

What was being slyly raised here, was not only the issue of childcare *per se*, but the fact that procreation and the gendered rearing of children are an integral part of contemporary sexuality; they do not take place in some 'other' non-sexual domain. Such a conception of sexuality is one which queer activists might understandably refuse; defining it as part of a normative and hence heterosexual agenda. But rather than restating binary dualisms, it is important to grasp the multiple points of construction of modern sexuality *for all of us*. The political corollary of delimiting sex to a single principle ironically could be to reproduce a minority agenda for homosexuality. However exciting, however energetic, it is difficult to claim a broader based project for queerness. This is not simply due to its avant-garde stance, but because of its prescriptive reading of the sexual itself.

213

Plural Identities and Lifestyles

If one trajectory within queer theory has been towards the binary gloss on sexual systems, elsewhere the vision has been more positively plural. It should come as no surprise to discover that seemingly contradictory principles coexist inside the same social language. Foucault himself noted that discursive regularity was grounded in internal opposition and not simply conceptual uniformity. It is in its repertoire of lifestyle transgression that queerness has projected the image of a more plural culture of sexuality, in which the actors acknowledge power, but claim to utilise it as part of a fluid interchange of codes. Plurality, it has been argued, also enables homosexual men and women to enter into a sexual conversation which is long overdue: around lifestyles and sexual identities. And in their self-conscious positioning as being symbolically 'on the margins', queers have insisted that they are more able to confront the racial divisions within homosexual communities and to open up channels of access to people of colour.

Women have been understandably aware of a separate perspective on the queer agenda, given lesbianism's differentiated position within the history of homosexuality. The fact that British law has never defined the lesbian identity as illegal has involved a different stance on transgression, while feminist sexual politics has posed an ongoing challenge to libertarianism. Nonetheless, the renewed dialogue between lesbians and homosexual men has been a visible achievement of queer politics. This has taken place around AIDS activism and other campaigning work, as well as in argument and debate. A number of factors have precipitated this hesitant coming together around what we might term a practical lifestyle utopia. The generational issue has again been significant. The growing dissatisfaction of a younger generation of lesbians both with the failures of the women's movement to problematise heterosexuality adequately, and with the potential moralisms of political lesbianism, left some women in search of a different sense of sexual belonging. Sadomasochistic sex, 'leather', the pornographic and the obscene became key signifiers in an upsurge of lesbian sexual activity from the mid-1980s, as bars and clubs in London, New York and California began to produce distinctive sexual spaces for women orga-nised around transgressive sex. But 'SM' has also functioned in a more symbolic sense within lesbian culture, bringing forward an explicit, if at times embittered, recognition of the diversity of female sexuality.[30]

Coupled with this partial shift within lesbianism has gone a different type of sexual recomposition among homosexual men. The ongoing effects of AIDS and safer-sex injunctions to re-evaluate sexual practice, especially in relation to penetrative sex, have led to a modicum of self-consciousness on sexuality *per se* from younger men who have never known sex without the threat from AIDS. (It has also led simultaneously to an upsurge of unsafe sex among the same group of men in Britain.)[31] The overall result has been some pluralisation of the circuits of male homosexual desire (including a hypersexualisa-tion of the body's surface rather than fixation *with* the sexual act) and an inventive recasting of sexual meanings. Many of these codes have been prominent in the recent explosion of homosexual iconography within the mainstream media, as well as in the more immediate culture.

Finally, the popular impact of that most slippery of terms—postmodernism—has also stimulated forms of homosexual expression which are more multi-accented and more playful in their account of sexual difference. For postmodern iconography has not only transfixed recent academic debate, it has also entered many of the circuits of youth-orientated popular culture. Within homosexual milieux the impact of a postmodern aesthetic has been most frequently on display within fashionable metropolitan venues, often associated with dance music and designer drugs.[32] But its effects have also been visible outside the leading sectors of style. A partial turning away from fixed epistemologies of meaning (where in an older discourse, a leather jacket or a bunch of keys was tied to a specific sexual act or practice), the return of camp and other forms of irony as an expressive ritual, the popularity of 'mixed' venues for men and women where identities are less rigid—these cultural tropes have become stock-in-trade ways of living for a younger generation of homosexuals.

How have these various cultural factors shaped a more plural approach to sexual identity? Two recent manifestations of queer culture can serve to focus the debate: the work of the lesbian photographer Della Grace and the appearance of what has been collectively labelled queer cinema. It is not accidental that some of the more significant explorations around the homosexual identity have come from cultural practitioners working within representational forms. In photography as in cinema, long-standing traditions of artistic practice have consistently problematised the naturalness of identity and underlined the representational quality of sexual difference. Della Grace's spread of images in her photo collection *Love Bites*, 1991, projected queer lesbianism via transgressive female sexuality. One of these images, with the caption 'Lesbian Cock', depicted two lesbians kitted out in the paraphernalia of gay male desire. They were dressed in leather bikers' caps, even moustaches. One of the women posed with a dildo protruding from her crotch. There was a deliberate play on phallic power in the image (as well as a confrontationalist incitement to shock), with its connotations of cruising, casual sex and all the other accoutrements attached to these masculine scripts. Della Grace has argued that such representations—and their referents within the lesbian S/M scene—are more complex than the grafting of male sexuality onto the lesbian body.[33] The symbols of transgressive sex have been raided from the wardrobes of women sex-workers and post-punk fashion, as well as from gay men. For Grace, this has been about women actively appropriating a vocabulary of voyeurism and fetishism in a mutual exchange of power. The result has been both to expand women's access to sexual pleasure and to deconstruct gender identities.

Della Grace and the women's culture she references are not the first to foreground notions of transgressive lesbian desire. Gayle Rubin and the North American Samois collective were polemicising for a related form of 'SM' lesbian sex in the early 1980s.[34] But a comparison between the two moments is instructive. While Rubin and others were somewhat evangelical about their practice—and necessarily so given the charges from radical feminists—the newer cadre of lesbian queers have been more playful about their sexual aesthetic, indicative of a greater confidence and assurance.

A different exploration of plural representations has been

carried in queer cinema, a term which was first introduced at the 1991 Toronto Film Festival. Queer film and video makers have refused to be characterised by one dominant aesthetic or visual style, but their projects have been typically concerned with a non-functionalist rendering of sexual identity. Here, the impetus for change has come not so much from a reaction against restrictive codes of sexuality, as it has with Della Grace, but from a dissatisfaction with a fixed epistemology of cultural representation: the notion that gay film makers have a duty to project 'positive images' of homosexuality, to counter the negative effects of the conventional media.[35] Such an approach, which had its origins in the first wave of civil rights activism in the 1970s, has been opposed on the grounds that once again it reduces the complexities of sexual representation, refusing the way in which cinema, along with other cultural practices, can contribute to the exploration of identities. As the US film-maker, Tom Kalin, the director of *Swoon* has put it:

> Gender is not innate, it is a performance. We learn gender through a series of codes, and in a subtle way I wanted to gender-fuck, to propose disarray....I want us to take to task the feeling in the gay community that representation is instrumental.[36]

The emphasis on performativity produces its own sense of the constructed nature of sexuality. Hence, the self-conscious *bricollage* in Kalin's work, as in the texts of others who have espoused a queer profile. Prominent techniques include the deliberate use of camp and irony and the visual assembly of male homosexuality from disparate icons, such as 1920s Chicago gangsters, the silent film star Rudolph Valentino and the imagery of later road movies. Taken together these cultural representatives have worked to further destabilise the unity of homosexuality.

Conclusion: Identities, Avant-gardes and Formal Political Culture

How then to characterise the overall profile of queer activism? What is immediately apparent is that its sexual agenda is not systematically coherent, but consists of a set of divergent demands which unstably coexist together. These tensions reflect broader disagreements over the status of the modern homosexual. If the queer agenda has tended towards a reductive account of sexuality, organised around the dualism of heterosexuality versus homosexuality, then it has been much more plural about the homosexual subject itself. Here, queerness has constituted a more genuinely open-ended signifier, an umbrella term under which a range of transgressive identities could be rallied. At its most diverse, the implications are that the term queer has the potential to embrace not just homosexuals, but the many other identities which are outside normative sexual discourse: bisexuals, single-parents, celibates, the modern seemingly endless list of perversities. If this repertoire still works within the self-professed boundaries of the avant-garde, then it is a more expansive understanding of marginality than that delimited by conventional readings of homosexuality.

Such energetic conversations about sexual identity are part of a wider trajectory. For in microcosm queer discourse condenses the contradictory impulses contained within many strands of the new politics. What is at issue here is the status of subjectivity and its representation in the political arena. Queerness covers the whole spectrum of positions on the issue: from a relatively fixed conception of homosexuality to a much more fluid understanding of identity. These differences over the conception of social selfhood have erupted as a core debate within late twentieth-century political movements. In their most extreme form, notions of stable subjectivity confront a vision of dispersed and fractured personas as polarised positions. Stuart Hall, among others, has argued for a strategic resolution to the difficulties. Surveying the characteristic genres of racial identity forged in the Caribbean, he has drawn attention to the way in which these are: 'unstable points of identification....Not an essence but a positioning', which is not guaranteed by a single law of origin.[37] Within such an understanding, identities are concrete and material, the product of historically constituted discourses, but they are not innate. Hence identity politics becomes a matter of contingency, organised around a strategic rather than a naturalised essentialism.

A parallel argument has been developed by certain strands

of European and North American feminism. These have drawn on the vocabulary of poststructuralism to problematise any simple notion of the category 'woman' or 'woman's experience' as the point of departure for late twentieth-century sexual politics.[38] Insisting that appeal to the twin concepts of identity and experience has been ultimately disabling, in that it quickly degenerates into a divisive debate about *which* women and *whose* experience, a more fluid understanding of the self has been claimed as a more productive basis for a progressive politics of gender. Such ideas have been coherently thought through on the terrain of formal politics by Ernesto Laclau and Chantal Mouffe. They have floated the concept of 'radical democratic citizenship' as a term which might bridge the often competing demands of different social groups, without crystallising around exclusive notions of identity and individual rights.[39]

At a general level of political theory and debate such positions appear to assemble a convincing case, having the advantages of relative logical consistency and a persuasive sense of political pragmatism. But a number of obstacles remain for the practical progress of such politics. The first of these centres on the structures of the dominant culture of formal democracy, with which identity politics at some stage or other in its journey is forced to engage. The second difficulty concerns the representativeness of the vision of pluralism projected within such a programme. Both issues confront the queer project. It is worth spending some time reviewing these problems by way of conclusion, in order to confront the political realities facing this strategy for progressive change.

It is a truism, but one worth reasserting, that the dominant political cultures in almost all of the major democracies remain profoundly suspicious of the radical pluralist agenda, with its emphasis on diversity and the relativisation of identities and value systems. This may appear as a contradiction in terms, given that a touchstone of post-war democratic theory and practice has been a plural conception of interest groups, adjudicated by citizens via the circuits of democratic choice. But the perceived disruptiveness of a more accentuated pluralism lies in its challenge to a number of the foundations on which democratic political culture has been built. Such difficulties crucially have to do with democracy's understanding of political subjects and the discourse of meaning and rationality which they are assumed to speak. Formal political culture is still almost exclusively organised around fixed epistemologies, conceived within what is in reality an early twentieth-century system of political representation. A cornerstone of this structure remains the fiction of a fixed and stable political self. As all groups who have been historically constituted as 'minorities' know from practical experience parliamentary democracy has only taken serious cognisance of their demands when they have defined themselves as rights-based pressure groups, projecting a coherent subjectivity to claim recognition. There have been few if any recent political movements which have successfully mobilised around the more fluid discourses of contingency and plural identity in their engagement with formal politics. The 'revisionist' strand of British social democracy in the 1960s, led by figures such as Tony Crosland and Roy Jenkins, moved some way towards the relativisation of value systems and a contingent notion of social morality, in the interests of freedom and civilised tolerance. But this was pluralism 'from above', and it continued to be grounded in the firmest rhetoric of self-belief by these men from the dominant political class.[40] Identity politics continues to face the realities of a political system which is not easily disposed to relativise its own values.

There are in fact strong historical and cultural continuities between the moral project of 1960s social democrats and the new pluralist agenda. One of the links centres on the relationship of both of these political discourses to their social fields of legitimation. Posing an unfashionably Gramscian question here delivers significant if potentially uncomfortable results. The discourse of progressive democrats in the 1960s retained strong articulations with one particular constituency, notably with sections of the progressive middle class. Without posing the relationship between political discourse and class formations in a reductionist way, it could be demonstrated that the current agendas of pluralism and deconstruction retain links with this fraction. It is, for example, not simply a matter of intellectual fashion that such issues are high on the agenda of academics and social and media professionals. For the pluralist project dramatises many of the broader social and personal anxieties experienced by these groupings. The difficulty for pluralism as a political agenda is that of constructing a broader based appeal for such a programme, beyond representing the interests of a sectional group. Just as I described my own autobiographical rejection of 1960s progressive radicalism, there is no reason to assume that contemporary versions of this language can command support across multiple social constituencies.

The point of rehearsing these difficulties is not simply to sound the note of political pessimism, nor is it to argue for a return to a pressure group or civil rights discourse for homosexuality, or for any other of the new political movements. It is rather to inject a more urgent sense of the political realities facing the pluralist project. There needs to be further thought given to the issue of translating what are a sophisticated set of intellectual concepts into the *language of politics*. As the queer debate has demonstrated, this is the other agenda amid all of the enthusiasm and excitement of claiming identity.

(11)

Hegemony Trouble

The Political Theories of Judith Butler, Ernesto Laclau and Chantal Mouffe

Anna Marie Smith

Judith Butler's *Gender Trouble*[1] has been widely recognised as a ground-breaking contribution to feminist theory and lesbian and gay studies. Her conceptualisation of gender as a performative construction, as the effect of practices which take place in complex fields of oppressive forces and resistances, poses a radical challenge to the various gender reductionisms which limit feminist thought. It should be noted, however, that Butler's text also constitutes a contribution to political theory, namely the theory of hegemony. Butler's use of this term throughout her text marks her rejection of domination and liberation theories in favour of a Foucauldian approach to power relations. In this respect, Butler has much in common with Ernesto Laclau and Chantal Mouffe. Like Butler, Laclau and Mouffe have appropriated poststructuralist and psychoanalytic categories in their attempt to theorise contemporary political strategies. While Butler lacks Laclau and Mouffe's background in the Gramscian Marxist tradition, and Laclau and Mouffe have only briefly mentioned the feminist debates on gender and sexuality, their theoretical and political positions are remarkably similar. I shall show that while these theorists 'get into trouble' in their elaboration of the theory of hegemony, they do so at different moments, and that they could in fact draw on each other's work to move beyond these difficulties.

Laclau and Mouffe's theory of hegemony[2] can be located as a critical response to the failures of the class-centric thinking which has shaped leftist strategising. The class-centric approach can be summarised in terms of three basic arguments: the social is fundamentally structured in terms of two classes, the working class and the bourgeoisie; the working class is the historical vehicle of revolutionary change; and that insofar as actual workers fail to engage in revolutionary strategies, intellectuals operate as the necessary supplement to the working class by leading it towards its own true consciousness. Against this model, Laclau and Mouffe insist on the 'de-centring' of class: they argue that we cannot predict whether or not class will operate as a predominant form of identification, over other forms, in any particular context. With the de-centring of class, it becomes possible to argue that class may be lived in terms of race in some contexts[3] or in terms of sexuality in others. Laclau and Mouffe also argue that we cannot predict the political tendency of a social agent based on its class element: a movement consisting largely of working-class persons is just as likely, but only as likely, to be as racist, sexist and homophobic as movements in which bourgeois individuals constitute the majority. Laclau and Mouffe's de-centring of class is widely misunderstood as a dismissal of class. This mis-reading may be especially appealing in the context of the American myth of capitalism's triumph over socialism. However, post-Marxism is not the same as the bourgeois fantasy of post-socialism, just as the critique of gender reductionism is not the same as the sexist fantasy of post-feminism. Post-Marxism attempts to draw out the most democratic aspects of the Marxist tradition, and to insert them into a political theory which is suited to the complexities of contemporary identity games. (I am using the term identity games not to dismiss their seriousness, but to draw an analogy between strategies around identity and Wittgenstein's category of language games. We cannot stand outside the field of identity strategies, which implies in turn that even though we never actually fully occupy positions, we are always positioned, and that our impossible identity claims have position effects.)

Laclau and Mouffe in fact offer an extremely useful approach to class for lesbian, gay and bisexual studies. If the political is no longer regarded as an expression of the economic, and identity games cannot be analysed in terms of *a priori* class categories, then there is no legitimate reason to dismiss sexuality as a 'marginal issue'. Sexuality may indeed operate as the site in which consent is organised for authoritarian projects. In my own research, for example, I have argued that the demonisation of queerness in Britain from 1984 to 1990 was central to the legitimation of Thatcherism. This demonisation of queerness, most notably in the form of Section 28, which prohibited the promotion of homosexuality, drew on the new right tradition of demonising the 'enemies within' in general, and the new racism tradition in particular.[4] Class-centric thinking would rule out this kind of analysis from the start. With Laclau, Mouffe and Stuart Hall, I would argue that Thatcherism can only be understood in terms of a theory of hegemony.

Hegemony emerges in Laclau and Mouffe's text as a formation which is constructed through the contingent practice of articulation. Articulation involves the linking together of disparate forces, elements and positions. As a contingent practice, there is nothing predetermined about articulation; every articulated ensemble is unique and contextually specific. Thatcherism, for example, has been described by Stuart Hall as the juxtaposition of free market individualism, monetarism, anti-statism, anti-unionism, racist law and order campaigns, xenophobic nationalism, pro-family traditionalism, and anti-lesbian and anti-gay moralism.[5] Although Thatcherism can be located in terms of many different traditions, its specificities are unique to the particular context of British politics in the late 1970s and 1980s. Each of the elements in this articulated ensemble was to some extent transformed through its articulation. Thatcherism's attack on the lesbian and gay community, for example, was not exactly the same as previous attacks, for it was shaped by the new racism of the British right wing. It is precisely this constitutive aspect of articulation which sets hegemony apart from coalition theories. The formation of a hegemonic bloc does not involve the mere combination of pre-constituted elements. For Laclau and Mouffe, articulations do not operate outside of, or in addition to, pre-constituted identities; identities, and the social itself, are nothing but the effects of articulation.

There are, however, several arguments in Laclau and Mouffe's text which are incompatible with their theory of hegemony. They rightly argue that the term 'new social movements' inappropriately groups these struggles together merely because they are not defined in terms of class.[6] They insist that the specific form of the anti-sexist, anti-racist, and anti-heterosexist struggles depends on specific articulations, such that it becomes impossible to take the 'progressiveness' of any of these struggles for granted.[7] They do recognise the differences which can emerge within each of these struggles,[8] such as the possibility of a racist feminism, or even a feminism which claims to be democratic and, in its promotion of censorship, has authoritarian effects.[9] Laclau and Mouffe nevertheless state that the task of the left is to '[expand] the chains of equivalents between the different struggles against oppression'[10]. Although they envision an alternative hegemonic bloc in which the 'autonomy' of the articulated struggles is at least partially preserved, and although they call for the formation of a new common sense in which the advance of one struggle would never be made at the expense of another,[11] they do not pay sufficient attention to the fact that we are infinitely distanced from this ideal in the current juncture. They state that the 'equivalential articulation between anti-racism, anti-sexism and anti-capitalism...requires a hegemonic construction which, *in certain circumstances*, may be the condition of consolidation of each one of these struggles.'[12]

In many contexts, however, exactly the opposite is required. Where lesbians are confronted, for example, with an utterly non-negotiable wall of sexism from gay men, the consolidation of our lesbian struggles may in fact depend on the pursuit of a different, and equally impossible, goal: the organisation of an autonomous lesbian space. In the case of racial differences, it would certainly not be legitimate for white activists to instruct people of colour that their interests are best served by working with existing white organisations. Resistances should always be informed by the principle of the interdependency of oppression—that anti-queerness depends on sexism which depends on racism which depends in turn on class privilege—but we can only determine the best forms of resistance within specific contexts, and this evaluation will obviously yield different results from different positions. June Jordan, in an interview with Asian-British feminist Pratibha Parmar, comments, 'I would say about coalitions what I said about unity, which is what for? The issue should determine the social configuration of politics.'[13] Chela Sandoval places a similar emphasis on the contextualisation of strategic decisions. She calls for the formation of an oppositional consciousness which would create 'the opportunity for flexible, dynamic and tactical responses'. She states,

> Third world feminists are calling for...a new subjectivity, a political revision that denies any *one* perspective as the answer, but instead posits a shifting tactical and strategic subjectivity that has the capacity to re-centre depending upon the forms of oppression to be confronted.[14]

Although Laclau and Mouffe do recognise that strategic decisions should be made in terms of specific contexts, they nevertheless compromise this contextualisation by constructing a myth of an anti-authoritarian hegemonic bloc. Jordan and Sandoval, by contrast, are far more sceptical about unification strategies. Their emphasis on temporary and tactical unities, and on the contextualisation of resistances, is precisely the sort of strategic approach which is compatible with Laclau and Mouffe's non-essentialist conception of the social.

Laclau and Mouffe also pay virtually no attention to the phantasmatic aspect of the construction of identities. As Slavoj Zizek rightly points out, spaces such as 'the nation'—which excludes the unassimilable black immigrant—and 'the family'—which excludes dangerous queerness—are phantasmatic spaces. Laclau and Mouffe argue that political differences take the form of antagonistic relations. Each of the opposed camps regards the other as blocking its project to become fully itself; in a sense, each side blames the other for its own failure in self-realisation. It is true that the British new right often blames blacks and queers for the weaknesses in white Britishness, but this is not the whole story. Unassimilable blackness and dangerous queerness should not be simply regarded as antagonistic enemies—they are more usefully understood as symptom figures.[15] The British new right has made profound investments in these figures: anti-lesbian and gay discourse, for example, cannot be analysed in terms of the 'homophobia' model, for anti-queer bigots are simultaneously repulsed by and obsessed with homosexuality. Indeed, the Thatcherite

obsession with homosexuality yielded excessive representations—the devotion of entire parliamentary debates, national
news stories and editorials to homosexuality. These
symptomatic representations were profoundly ambiguous. On
the one hand, they contributed to the escalation in queer-
bashing and anti-queer discrimination. On the other hand, the
Thatcherite demonisations politicised sexuality and brought
queerness out onto the terrain of official and public discourse in
an unprecedented manner. Thousands of activists seized upon
these conditions as an historical opportunity and organised a
whole range of resistances against the Thatcherite measures.[16]
It should be noted that although Zizek usefully theorises the
symptomatic aspect of demonisations, his approach virtually
ignores the entire question of power. From Zizek's perspective,
we do not know, and it does not even matter, why this
particular blackness and/or queerness at this particular
moment becomes a symptom figure.

Butler shares Jordan and Sandoval's scepticism about
unification strategies. Against Laclau and Mouffe's tendency
towards homogenising difference, Butler remains deeply
suspicious about simple prohibitions and singular identities.
Unlike Zizek, Butler confronts psychoanalytic theories with
genealogical interrogations and deconstructive contextualisa-
tions. However, her theory has also been widely read as
promoting voluntaristic and individualistic solutions to heterosexism. By comparing Butler's theory of hegemony with that of
Laclau and Mouffe, it can be shown that this reading is an
inaccurate caricature which neglects the most important
aspects of her work.

Like Laclau and Mouffe's *Hegemony and Socialist Strategy*,
Gender Trouble deploys deconstructionist tactics to undermine
essentialism. Laclau and Mouffe weaken the reductionist argument that the economic determines the ideological by showing
that the frontier between these two spheres is always violated,
that the development of economic technologies, for example, is
always shaped by political concerns. Butler takes aim at the
essentialist sex/gender dualism, in which sex is posited as the
prediscursive, and gender is relegated to the secondary terrain
of social interpretation. Following Foucault, Butler de-natur-
alises sex by locating sex as a fictitious nature which legitimates

the extension and intensification of disciplinary strategies. By showing the strategic character of sex categorisation, Butler undermines the sex-as-nature versus gender-as-social-construction dualism.

These theoretical interventions have important political consequences. If one's fundamental identity were already determined in the economic sphere, and if politics were, in the last instance, absent from the economic, then politics would be reduced to struggles between already-constituted subjects. If sex were already given, and gender were an 'expression' of sex, then feminist struggles would remain trapped within the confines of contemporary sex/gender systems. As Gayle Rubin argues in her essay, 'The Traffic in Women', the costs of this sex/gender system are enormous.[17] Butler reiterates Rubin's contextualisation of the apparently natural compulsory heterosexual order as the *hegemonic* sex/gender system. For Butler, sex is not pre-political, it is a political fiction. For Laclau, Mouffe and Butler, then, politics is not a power struggle between natural subjects, it is a struggle around the very process of constructing and contesting identity. Where Laclau and Mouffe criticise the dangerous fantasy of a Revolution which would simultaneously return us to an original state and bring about the dissolution of politics, Butler notes the totalitarian possibilities of Wittig's theory of the recovery of an original nature for women.[18] By rejecting the fantasy of recovering a repressed nature, and of standing outside representational politics, Butler echoes Laclau and Mouffe's insistence that there is nothing outside the discursive. Instead of proposing utopias which would inevitably have exclusionary effects, Laclau, Mouffe and Butler argue that the moment of the last challenge to identity is infinitely postponed. Again, this infinite postponement of closure is not merely an interesting theoretical problem; the vulnerability of even the most hegemonic formations to contestation is precisely the condition of democracy.

A further analogy can be drawn between Laclau and Mouffe's conception of articulation and Butler's conception of the performative character of gender. Articulations are not merely added to an underlying structure; the social orders into which we are thrown are nothing but sedimented articulation effects. Butler similarly states, 'That the gendered body is performative suggests that it has no ontological status apart from the various acts which constitute its reality.'[19] Because gender is nothing but the sedimented effects of repeated practices, it is purely contingent: the apparently 'natural' and 'unnatural' actually have the same ontological status. Every 'original' is actually the copy of a copy, there is no absolutely 'true' gender which can be used as a neutral standard to dismiss 'false' genders, and so on. The articulations, or performatives, which constitute the social are therefore contingent: they are neither external additions to, nor the determinations of, an underlying necessity.

Contingency, however, does not mean that 'anything goes'. In technical terms, it is important to distinguish between the accidental and the contingent. If performatives were accidental—utterly random, wholly outside any rationality—then Butler would be promoting an apolitical voluntarism. Throughout the text, however, Butler effectively counters the 'anything goes' approach. She admits that 'parody by itself is not subversive'.[20] For Butler, gender practices are 'regulatory' in the sense that gender identities are always constituted in terms of normative ideals which have exclusionary effects.[21] To paraphrase Norma Alarcón, becoming 'woman' always takes the form of becoming 'this particular woman', not only in opposition to 'that particular man', but also in opposition to 'that particular woman' who is positioned differently in terms of race and class.[22] Butler explicitly emphasises this exclusionary and overdetermined character of gender identities: in the opening pages of her text, she argues that the advance of the universalistic conceptions of 'woman' and patriarchy have racist implications. Her initial references to the racial regulation of gender are not sustained throughout the text. She nevertheless consistently places performative practices within the context of asymmetrical power relations. Commenting on de Beauvoir, she states, 'Gender is the repeated stylization of the body, a set of repeated acts within a highly rigid regulatory frame that congeal over time to produce the appearance of substance, of a natural sort of being.'[23]

Butler's argument can be usefully read through Laclau's more recent phenomenological conception of hegemony.[24]

Laclau argues that an articulation becomes hegemonic to the extent that it operates as a horizon. Because it is wholly contingent, the institutionalisation of a particular articulation can only be accomplished through the violent suppression of alternatives. Habitual repetitions of the hegemonic articulation conceal the traces of that violent suppression; over time, the repetitions install the hegemonic articulation as the only possible coherent formation. The hegemonic articulation gradually loses its appearance as one alternative among many, and begins to operate as the rule which establishes an ahistorical and apolitical distinction between intelligibility and unintelligibility.[25] To borrow the language of Thatcherism, hegemony does not depend on popularity, it depends on the normalisation of the idea that there is no alternative. In Britain in the 1980s, it became almost impossible to speak about politics—including queer and anti-queer discourse—outside the Thatcherite framework.

Butler's critique of gender essentialism is also framed within a politicised phenomenology. She argues that in psychoanalytic theory, the symbolic 'claims to be intelligibility'.[26] Genders and sexualities which defy the compulsory heterosexual framework are ruled 'out of order': they are supposed to be unrepresentable and unthinkable. Like Laclau, Butler practises reactivation: not a Husserlian return to origins and essences, but a return to an awareness of the contingency of that which represents itself as necessity. Reactivation is in this sense the return to the political, the exhibition of the violent forces, marginalisations, and hierarchies at work at the very core of every tranquil nature. Butler therefore attempts to show the historical and political character of the hegemonic delimitations of the 'thinkable' sexes and genders. She states that her aim is 'not to celebrate each and every new possibility qua possibility, but to redescribe those possibilities that already exist, but which exist within cultural domains designated as culturally unintelligible and impossible'.[27]

Butler and Laclau do of course take different theoretical routes. For example, Butler's critique of the conception of a social order which can establish itself as *the* order of representation draws on the Foucauldian theory of the creative and differentiating effects of the law. Laclau turns to Wittgenstein on this point: although we cannot stand outside all language games, the rules in language games 'only exist in the practical instances of their application—and are consequently modified and deformed by them'.[28] Butler and Laclau both arrive at the same place, namely the insistence that even the most naturalised orders and rules of intelligibility remain vulnerable to subversions which would at least partially escape total domestication.

Butler differs from Laclau on three important points. First, she suggests that coalitions would have less exclusionary effects if their participants accepted a model of temporary, fragmented and incomplete forms of unity.[29] This theory is problematic because it depends upon a self-conscious refusal of the will to identity. Although unification strategies should always be analysed in terms of specific contexts, it should also be recognised that even with the best intentions, we are always caught up in the will to identity and are always being used to advance exclusionary strategies. In Laclau's terms, consensus always involves coercion,[30] and a consensus around fragmentation would not constitute a special case.

Although Laclau's theoretical arguments are often highly abstract, he nevertheless consistently attempts to situate them in terms of historical research. His method of working through contemporary political histories is particularly evident in his exchange with Aletta Norval on apartheid in South Africa.[31] Butler, by contrast, does not give sufficient attention to the specific contexts of her examples of subversion. One of her examples involves a hypothetical 'neighbourhood gay restaurant'. Its owners announce that the restaurant is closed for vacation by putting out a sign which says, 'she's overworked and needs a rest'. Butler describes the sign as a 'very gay appropriation of the feminine'.[32] She states that the sign does not constitute a 'colonizing "appropriation" of the feminine' because this evaluation would depend on the erroneous assumption that the feminine belongs to women.[33] Butler should note here, as she does elsewhere, that there are many different kinds of gay appropriations of the feminine. Surely an evaluation of the colonising effects of this particular appropriation should take into account the racial, gendered and sexual aspects of the relations around the sign: the restaurant's management-staff relations, its marketing strategy, its place within the spatial-political relations within the neighbourhood and so on.

Finally, Butler promotes the permanent problematisation of 'identity' through subversive appropriations. She states, 'The more insidious and effective strategy it seems is a thoroughgoing appropriation and redeployment of the categories of identity themselves, not merely to contest "sex", but to articulate the convergence of multiple sexual discourses at the site of "identity" in order to render that category, in whatever form, permanently problematic.'[34] Laclau would agree that every dislocation of a hegemonic space opens up possibilities which had been relegated to the residual sphere of the unthinkable. He insists, however, that re-spacialisations are inevitable; for Laclau, hegemonic strategies take the form of the spacialisation of temporality.[35] In other words, identity claims construct spaces: they give us the sense of being located within a partially bounded order whose incomplete frontiers operate simultaneously as the defences against disruption and the limits of our freedom. We cannot remain in the non-spacialisable moment outside all identity claims: every subversion of a hegemonic space depends on the resources of marginalised spaces, and the defence of the possibilities which are opened up through subversion depends in turn on the construction and reinforcement of alternative spaces. To return to Butler's restaurant, the display of this sign in a public place would be impossible without the collective struggles which had created the space for the restaurant in the first place—the resistances of queer entrepreneurs against the police, government authorities, straight business associations and so on; of the queer publications, which provide advertising space, against the legal system and the mainstream press; of the 'alternative' neighbourhood inhabitants, the queers, students, artists, drug dealers, prostitutes and so on, against the inner city developers and the pro-family local government forces. The restaurant sign is actually located within this tradition of struggling to define space, and has its own effects in terms of taking space. In this brief analysis, I have placed Butler's hypothetical gay restaurant in the context of the 1980s spatial-political relations of the gay neighbourhood on Church Street in Toronto, Canada. Purely hypothetical examples are not very useful in political theory; theoretical formulations should always be developed through some sort of encounter with the complexities of a specific historical situation. Although Butler's text is clearly informed by contemporary lesbian, gay, bisexual and trans-gender struggles, the theory/practice encounter is not analysed in sufficient detail.

In any event, a significant difference remains between *Gender Trouble* and the Laclau-Mouffe project. Laclau and Mouffe regard identity formation both as an enabling strategy and as a dangerous disciplining of difference, while Butler tends to emphasise the latter moment and to neglect the first. Laclau and Mouffe offer a double analysis of the politics of identity: the ways in which all identities are always open to problematisation, subversion, parody, and so on, and the ways in which the political terrain is always simultaneously re-spacialised through new articulations or identity claims. Butler concentrates on problematisation without adequately addressing re-spacialisation. The inextricability of subversion and spacialisation, or re-citation and re-situation, can actually be found in the Derridean conception of iteration which is central to Butler's and Laclau's theories of resistance. For Derrida, signification takes the 'form' of iteration, the repetition of past repetitions in which an irreducible difference is always introduced between every repetition. Any statement which appears to be 'nonsensical' or 'illogical' can be disengaged from the context in which it appears impossible, and re-engaged in another context such that it functions as a meaningful statement. No single context can establish itself as the only possible context: every mark can be endlessly re-cited. In other words, that which appears to be unthinkable can be re-situated as thinkable through the subversion of hegemonic discourse. However, Derrida also explicitly links re-citation with the process of engendering new contexts:

> Every sign...can be *cited*, put between quotation marks; in so doing it can break with every given context, engendering an infinity of new contexts in a manner which is absolutely illimitable.[36]

'*Engendrer*', the verb used by Derrida in the French original,[37] has three meanings: to procreate; to cause, create, determine and produce; and third, from geometry, to describe or produce a closed figure through self-displacement, such as a perpendicular line which 'engenders' a cone. Re-citation, the breach of a context through displacement, is inextricably linked with re-situation, the construction of new partially bounded figures or spaces. Iteration should therefore be read not as a permanent problematisation, but as multiple re-citations which necessarily involve endless re-constructions of temporary and precarious spacial contexts.

By promoting permanent problematisation, even as a regulative idea, Butler forecloses several important strategies. We can only take responsibility for the ways in which we are positioned, however imperfect that positioning may be, if we recognise that we are always caught up in identity claims. The effects of identity claims are undecidable; in some cases, such as the erasure of lesbian-ness in official discourse on sexuality,[38] impossible claims to occupy positions are absolutely vital to resistance strategies. The permanent problematisation approach may be a useful response to the representation of white gay male-ness as a hyper-sexual excess, but it may have limited value for lesbians, bisexual women and gay men of colour who are struggling against erasure. It should also be noted that authoritarian discourses often cope quite well with problematisations. In Britain in the 1980s, it was often the Thatcherites who would engage in subversive re-appropriations and who would lecture the left on its essentialist conception of natural political subjects. In that context, it was absolutely crucial that resistance strategies entailed not only the weakening of hegemonic horizons of intelligibility but also direct collective struggles to defend alternative spaces.

(12)

Pluralism, Solidarity, and Change

Anne Phillips

In the catalogue of revisions and recoveries that describes contemporary radical thought, few items stand out so starkly as the new attitude towards plurality and difference.[1] The themes associated with difference have become particularly fashionable—as evidenced in various strands of feminist and postmodernist thought—and it would seem that pluralism has also redeemed itself. Paul Hirst's book on *Representative Democracy and Its Limits* contains a chapter explicitly devoted to the retrieval of pluralism;[2] a recent collection on *Dimensions of Radical Democracy* is ordered around the project of a 'radical and plural democracy';[3] and contemporary work in political philosophy positively groans under the weight of diversity, plurality and difference. Out of favour for many years, pluralism is now being yoked to its radical opposite as a kind of anti-establishment, anti-conformism, registering our refusal to pretend we are the same.

This marks a major shift in attitude. Through much of the preceding decades, pluralism served as a warning sign to all good radicals, who would then gather themselves up to do battle against its complacent defence of the status quo. In the world of political theory, for example, pluralism was closely associated with attacks on the excesses of utopian thinking: it was linked with Karl Popper's contrast between the open and the closed society;[4] or with Isaiah Berlin's contrast between negative and positive freedom.[5] Pluralism took issue with any tradition of political thought that seemed to anticipate the perfectibility of the human condition, and its practitioners identified a dangerous utopianism or more drastic totalitarianism in all such grandiose ideals. The arguments were all on the side of moderation, and for those who felt themselves tussling with the injustices and inadequacies of present societies, the easy accusations of 'utopianism' or 'totalitarianism' seemed a route to political passivity. Pluralism equalled scepticism; scepticism led to a failure of imagination. The philosophers of pluralism were abandoning all hopes for the future just because of some risks that might accompany change.

The kind of pluralism that developed in political science or political sociology took a different form, but here too it gained itself a sorry reputation as apologetics for the status quo. Generations of students were introduced to the divide between pluralism and Marxism; countless essays were written querying the false complacencies of the first or the outdated simplicities of the second. As pluralism developed (particularly within American political science), it was perceived as a direct challenge to 'ruling class' or 'elite' theories of the state: an approach that stressed the dispersal rather than the concentration of power; that talked of the checks and balances exerted by competing interest groups; that implied all was well in contemporary democracy.

Radicals regarded this as poor analysis made even worse by its limited ambition. In stressing the complex differentiation of society into a variety of interest groups, pluralist theory was thought to underplay—indeed deny—the more fundamental binary divide between classes. In conceiving of democracy as adequately safeguarded by the presence of multiple elites, it was said to gloss over systematic and sustained inequality. In accepting a vision of politics as activated solely through group interest, it was said to legitimate a sordid particularism in which no group looked beyond its own private and material advantage. Pluralism seemed to be telling us that our own sense of democratic impotence was irrelevant so long as it was sufficiently shared, and that human beings were not made for solidarities any wider than the group. Radicals argued forcefully against each point.[6]

The gulf was often based on mutual misrecognition, but this was hardly—at the time—to the point. Robert Dahl, for example, was frequently (and correctly) cited as a leading exponent of pluralist theories of democracy, but it was rarely perceived that 'the theorist in question, far from being a died-in-the-wool reactionary, is far to the left of the American political spectrum'.[7] As this comment indicates, Dahl's position on the political spectrum is now more precisely delineated, and this retrieval is itself symptomatic of a larger development. The deep gulf between pluralism and the left is being bridged, and part of the background to this convergence is to be found in the realm of political sociology, and the increasingly subtle revisionism Marxism had to practise in order to cope with the absence of a clear ruling class.[8] The dominance of class itself was challenged through the work of feminists, who proposed new theories of patriarchy or the sex/gender system, and developed alternative analyses of the basis of oppression and the formation of political identity.[9] Class unity, it was claimed, never did override sexual, national, religious or ethnic division. It was simply perverse to seek to explain male power over women or the rise of fascism or the brutalities of racism without reference to non-class forces.

These revisions already shifted the focus of analysis towards a more plural understanding of social division and political forces, but it is developments in the realm of normative political thought that have brought about the final recuperation. Particularly important here is the increased insistence on a multiplicity of perspectives and values: a growing recognition that, while individuals may and do change their beliefs and values, there is nothing that guarantees convergence over some basic or unifying concerns. Some of this pressure comes from those who seek their inspiration in pre-Enlightenment traditions;[10] more of it from those who look beyond the Enlightenment to explore what is increasingly described as postmodernism.[11] A significant contribution comes from feminist theory, which in exploring the masculine bias of universalising theory has ended up endorsing much of the postmodern critique.[12]

A dominant tradition in contemporary political thought now stresses contingency, contestation and change. A plurality of convictions is seen as both inevitable and permanent, and in terms already familiar from the arguments of earlier pluralists,

THE LESSER EVIL AND THE GREATER GOOD

today's theorists warn against the illicit imposition of one view as if it were the only and necessary truth. The implication—for example, in Richard Rorty's work—is not that we must give up on our most cherished beliefs, more that we should recognise their status as beliefs that are valid for ourselves. The corollary, of course, is that others may hold very different beliefs with equal legitimacy and conviction, and that there is no final reference point in either logic or history that will resolve potential dispute. Consider here the growing importance of Islam in world politics, which has forced Western intellectuals to reconsider the tensions between a secular humanism and religious modes of thought. Or think of the grotesque consequences of a socialism that anticipated the ending of 'significant difference' by refusing to permit variation, and threatened in the process the very validity of socialist ideals.[13] Whether we welcome the ensuing relativism or not, few would now want to be associated with a politics that refuses to recognise alternatives, or claims to know the solutions in advance.

This 'moral pluralism' has coincided with the second major element in contemporary pluralist thinking: the growing distrust of monolithic solutions. As socialists came to terms with the crisis and collapse of the centralised economies, those who were not already there moved towards some version of a 'mixed' economy: arguing for a combination of state enterprises, co-operative and small-scale private enterprises;[14] and refusing the either/or conflict between the market and the plan.[15] Much the same pattern has characterised recent rethinking on the nature and development of democracy. There is by now a virtually unanimous consensus on the importance of multi-party competition, and the main defining feature of radical democracy is that it presses for still more diversity.[16] The arguments add up to more than a defence of local democracy against a bureaucratic centre, for what they emphasise are the multiple avenues through which people will choose to exercise their autonomy and control, and the necessary and desirable variation. Politics cannot and should not be standardised; there can be no one set of answers to all anticipated and unforeseen problems.

The final element in the recuperation of pluralism—and this is the one that comes closest to the mainstream tradition in political science—is the growing emphasis on the political significance of sub-groups that are defined through gender, ethnicity, religion, disability, sexuality, language and so on. This development has been very much informed by the emergence and theorisation of the so-called 'new social movements', whose point of reference has been identities other than class.[17] How new these movements are remains a moot point (which I shall not try to resolve), but they have certainly achieved a novel impact on the development of left theory. As recently as the 1960s and 1970s, radicals still tended to regard forms of political mobilisation that were based around ethnicity, gender or sexuality as politically immature: early moments in consciousness, not yet dignified by the discovery of class. Since then, the declining vitality of an explicitly class politics has combined with the sustained energy of these alternative social movements to encourage a more positive assessment of their role. In drawing out the implications of this new politics, people have distanced themselves still further from the binary simplicities of an earlier age. They have come to speak far more confidently of the value to be attached to heterogeneity, diversity and difference.[18]

Pluralism and Solidarity

The pluralism in these new developments is considerably more radical than the mainstream pluralism it echoes, but part of the problem I want to consider is that where it is more radical, it is also more disruptive of traditional solidarity. As already noted, one recurrent complaint levelled against mainstream pluralist theory was that it glossed over systematic political inequality. Celebrating the dispersal rather than the concentration of power, it failed to come to terms with the sustained exclusion of marginal groups from any kind of power at all. The new pluralism can hardly be held to account for this same failing. Many exponents of the new pluralism have explicitly concerned themselves with identifying and empowering hitherto marginalised groups, stressing the inequalities that regulate relations between different social or cultural groups, and proposing new forms of democracy that can validate and empower people as

239

members of their specific social groups. Far from disparaging the group basis of such mobilisations (as in a century of socialist distaste for women's self-organisation as women) such theorists treat social heterogeneity as both necessary and positive. Far from ignoring systematic social inequality (as in the blander versions of mainstream pluralism) such theorists will support the self-organisation of women, of black people, of disabled people, of lesbians and gay men; will encourage caucuses of such groupings within whatever organisations they find themselves; and in the most fully developed versions, have called for new democratic procedures that will ensure additional representation for all oppressed groups.[19] This is a proactive, not a laissez-faire pluralism. It therefore escapes the standard critique of the older pluralism that it attaches insufficient weight to the problems of political equality.

But then precisely because of this, it leaves itself more exposed to the other critique: that in conceiving politics as a matter of competition between groups (each pressing for its own advantage), pluralism has abandoned any hope of common or unifying concerns. Theorists of the older pluralism happily rejected what they saw as the inappropriate politics of a common interest; and the absence of any over-arching forms of social cohesion gave them no particular cause for concern, partly because their pluralism was premised on interest rather than identity groups. Exponents of the earlier pluralist democracy typically conceived of people as mobilised around a variety of temporary concerns: politically passive for most of their lives; paper members, perhaps, of a number of associations or pressure groups; springing into occasional and temporary action only under exceptional conditions, when they perceived their interests as directly under threat. In such a scenario, it hardly mattered that people's loyalties and solidarities were restricted to a locality or a group. Most people were thought to have a number of overlapping associations or interests, none of which was all-embracing or dominant, few of which were intensely felt. Where political mobilisation follows this pattern, democracy may well remain tolerant and stable. The relative apathy of the constituent groups is enough to keep the society firmly on the road.

This kind of argument is less readily available to the

exponents of the new pluralism. Because these make more serious claims in terms of empowering previously marginalised voices—because they are more radically egalitarian in their aims—they are also more vulnerable to criticism for encouraging division and fragmentation. The new pluralism homes in on identity rather than interest groups: not those gathered together around some temporary unifying concern—to defend their neighbourhood against a major road development, to lobby their representatives against some proposed new law— but those linked by a common culture, a common experience, a common language. These links are often intensely felt, and more important still, are often felt as opposition and exclusion. Identity groups frequently secure their identity precisely around their opposition to some 'other', focusing on a past experience of being excluded, and sometimes formulating a present determination to exclude. Serious division and fragmentation then become far more probable within a pluralism that sets out to empower each such voice.

This is part of the problem I want to address. Insofar as radicals concern themselves (as they surely should) with the unequal distribution of power and influence, they have to consider non-class group differences and identities as a legitimate basis for political organisation. They have to acknowledge, that is, the importance of autonomous organisation for groups that perceive themselves as disadvantaged or oppressed. They have to consider the role of caucuses in strengthening the voice of such groups, and explore the forms of additional representation that might be required to deliver an equality of power. But in doing this, they may be validating an exclusive and fragmented politics that leaves little space for the development of a wider solidarity. The politics that develops from this may block future alliances for change. The retrieval of pluralism thus presents radicals with a problem that does not figure for their mainstream precursors, for the problem of solidarity only arises in traditions that deal in prospects for change. The political context out of which the new pluralism has emerged (socialist, feminist, anti-racist, etc.) is one that necessarily concerns itself with the conditions under which people join together in common cause over common oppressions, and is rightly preoccupied with those circumstances that will generate alliances for change. The kinds of questions posed by such radicals recurrently return to this ground. What is it that enables people to see beyond the specificities of their own life (each one unique in its own way) towards what might be shared experiences and goals? What kind of ideas or experiences promote this? What is likely to get in its way?

Solidarity has long been conceived as the opposite of difference: something that develops when and because difference disappears. The new pluralism has little time for this older teleology of transition, encouraging a far more positive celebration of what earlier activists had considered partial or parochial or lesser. But as far as prospects for solidarity are concerned, this more celebratory notion of group difference looks considerably less hopeful. Instead of seeking out some common ground with those who are like us only in parts of their identity, or discovering our own limits and partialities in the recognition of other points of view, we may find ourselves propelled towards a more exclusionary assertion of precisely what makes us different. It is hard to see the bases for wider solidarity in this.

I want to approach this question from two different angles, both of which may push the discussion further along. The first involves considering the only tradition in mainstream pluralism that has seriously engaged with identity politics. I have noted that most theories of pluralist democracy deal with interest-based—or perhaps ideas-based—groups, and do not consider the additional plurality of groups whose association arises from a common culture or a common identity. The major exception to this is consociationalism, a term developed by Arendt Lijphart to describe the institutional practices of those European countries that have been characterised by linguistic and religious division. What lessons, if any, can be learned from this tradition? What light does it cast on the problems of group difference and solidarity?[20]

In the second section, I turn to discussions of tolerance and justice, considering Susan Mendus's discussion of *Toleration and the Limits of Liberalism*[21] and Iris Young's recent discussion of 'Justice and Communicative Democracy'.[22] In both cases, the emphasis is on validating difference, but within a public arena that can encourage interaction and change. I raise here what may prove to be a particularly difficult issue, relating to the asymmetry between dominant and subordinate groups. If one of the values in recognising difference is that it obliges dominant groups to reconsider the partiality of their own position, is there an equal injunction on subordinate groups to reconsider their own perspectives?

Consociationalism

The most obvious point of comparison between consociationalism and the new pluralism is that consociational democracy—later redescribed as 'consensus democracy'—deals in group divisions of a non-class nature. Arendt Lijphart sets out to consider the problems of democracy in plural societies that are characterised by 'segmental cleavages' of 'a religious, ideological, linguistic, regional, cultural, racial or ethnic nature'.[23] He addresses, that is, some (though by no means all) of the group divisions that are highlighted in the new pluralism.

His fundamental starting point is that patterns of majoritarian rule are inappropriate to such societies. The winner-takes-all principle (most graphically illustrated in the electoral systems of Britain and the USA) ensures the dominance of the party that captures the largest single share of the votes; and while this principle may be perfectly acceptable in a society that enjoys a recurrent see-saw between two competing parties, it is both undemocratic and dangerous in a plural society that contains 'virtually separate subsocieties with their own political parties, interest groups, and media of communication'.[24] The problem is not so much that majoritarianism excludes minority *opinions*, for most people will accept it as part of the working principles of democracy that the policies preferred by a majority should take precedence over policies that have only minority support. The problem arises when these differences of opinion coincide with more fundamental communal differences that have locked people into their own 'subsociety' and discouraged association between different groups. In such cases, each minority remains permanently a minority, while each majority remains securely in power.

One frequent (and by no means disreputable) response is to look to such social or educational or political developments as might break down entrenched barriers between communities, arguing that this will then shift the grounds of political division onto less troubled—but perhaps more 'substantial'—terrain. From Lijphart's perspective, such initiatives are often wishful thinking: 'The integration of a deeply divided society may not be possible at all and certainly cannot be achieved in a reasonably short time.'[25] Where this is so, the real choices will come down to either power-sharing between divided communities, or else partition along subcultural lines.

There are two things to note here, both of which limit the relevance of consociationalism to the more general problems I have raised. The first is that Lijphart and others have concerned themselves only with those group divisions which are *already* expressed in political parties, or will emerge as such under conditions of free association. The basic framework of consociational theory is set by the issue of stability, and the question is not how to empower groups that have been excluded from politics, but how to deal with those who have generated their own political organisations. This is compelling enough if all one cares about is stability (why make things more difficult by identifying groups that have not bothered to identify themselves?) but then has little to say on the issue of equality between different groups. It does not tackle, for example, the corrosive consequences of powerlessness and marginalisation, and the ways these can inhibit the development of any group identity that differs from the dominant norm. And because it sets the stakes so high, requiring of groups not only that they have a strong sense of themselves and their own interests but that they form their own political party as well, it excludes from consideration most of the groups that figure in arguments of the new pluralism. (Consider, by contrast, Iris Young's tentative list for contemporary America: 'women, blacks, Native Americans, Chicanos, Puerto Ricans and other Spanish-speaking Americans, Asian Americans, gay men, lesbians, working-class people, poor people, old people, and mentally and physically disabled people'.[26]) The most marginalised will be as marginal in a consociational democracy as they are anywhere else; neither the theory nor the practice is about equalising democratic weight.

The second point to note is one repeatedly made in the literature: that consociationalism is not so much about democracy as about accommodation between political elites. The power sharing mechanisms advocated by Lijphart and others depend crucially on the co-operation of political leaders, who work to moderate what might otherwise be explosive tensions between their respective communities. Deals are struck between these leaders in conditions of confidence and secrecy that conduce to political accommodation, and each leader undertakes to deliver the support of his segment for whatever the final deal. As one of the more vocal critics puts it: 'Consociation boils down in practice to a conservative cartel of ethnic elites sharing power by giving priority to their class over their ethnic interests. The success stories are few; the problems are many; and the democracy is largely a fiction.'[27]

In thinking about the lessons that can be drawn from the theory and practice of consociationalism, it is important to recognise that the elitism here is no accident, but built into the whole approach. The more divided the society, the more potentially explosive the tensions; but then the deeper the segregation, the more powerful will be each segment's elite. A group that is only loosely unified, across a range of overlapping—and perhaps conflicting—identities and interests, is likely to throw up competing leaderships, and this will undermine the conditions for consociational success. The most favourable conditions for a stable consociational democracy are those in which the leadership of each group has unchallenged authority, due to the internal cohesion of the segment itself, or more generally (as in Lijphart's first analysis of the politics of accommodation in the Netherlands) because of the deferential nature of the political culture. The greater the internal democracy of any specific community, the more likely it is that members will query the deal that their leaders have struck. What the elites had considered a happy compromise between 'their' community and the others may fail to win enough popular support.[28]

Note one important consequence of this. Lijphart has

argued—and in his own terms the argument is entirely coherent—that it does not matter if consociational devices shore up
and strengthen divisions between segments. Since power sharing will encourage the proportional distribution of resources
and offices between the different segments, this will most
likely increase social segmentation, and initially intensify the
plural divisions. No problem, says Lijphart, for this potential
increase in plural conflict will paradoxically enhance the
chances for consociational success. If the subcultural identity
becomes even more important in each individual's life, then the
power and authority of the group's leaders will correspondingly
increase, and it will be even easier to deliver the support of the
followers en bloc. Internal democracy may diminish; fragmentation increase; any wider solidarity become a meaningless joke.
As far as political stability is concerned, however, the chances
will be better than ever. The bitterness and bigotry of group
closure simply do not figure as issues in this, for they are
considered compatible with a stable democracy.

If we approach the question from the angle of the new
pluralism, the risks of group closure become that much more
severe. No radical will favour forms of group representation
that deliver power to an unquestioned authority: the spokes-
people (usually spokes*men*) of each tightly knit and exclusive
community. So if the new pluralism also works to intensify a
closed and oppositional politics, based around the narrow self-
perceptions of divided and competing groups, it does not have
the escape route of elite moderation. It has to think far more
seriously than any of its mainstream counterparts about the
way that group representation can entrench a politics of
competitive exclusion. It has to consider whether it is worth the
candle to ditch the blander universalisms of the Enlightenment
if this leads straight to the politics of the enclave. The new
pluralism cannot resort (as do the theorists of mainstream
pluralism) to a happy vision of groups that are at odds with one
another on some issues, but still reach a compromise on others,
because it wants to engage with the more intensely felt politics
of excluded and identity-driven groups. Nor can it retreat (as do
the analysts of consociational democracy) to an unflappable
tolerance of group rigidity, because it must keep worrying
away at the conditions that will generate change.

Tolerance, Justice and Difference

For those working within an explicitly radical framework, the emphasis has been rather different. In her discussion of liberal perspectives on tolerance, for example, Susan Mendus explores the limits of a 'live and let live' approach to difference, arguing that liberal theories come up against intractable problems in defining the legitimate scope for toleration. The crucial contrast she draws between liberal and socialist perspectives is that the former emphasise the private spaces within which difference can flourish, while the latter concern themselves with a more public process of generating a wider community. She argues that the first part of the socialist impetus towards tolerating difference is simply a pragmatic one, based on a clearer understanding than is common in the liberal tradition that people do not simply 'choose' their membership of sub-groups. Socialists will see personal ideals as alterable, but not simply the objects of choice, and because of this strong sense of individuals as products of their circumstances, will find intolerance an inappropriate reaction. Mendus goes on, however, to argue that this pragmatic impetus towards toleration can be welded to a more positive moral account. Because socialists aspire to a sense of loyalty and belonging, 'they require both more and less toleration than do liberals':[29] more, because toleration is then a necessary component in the development of larger loyalties; less, because the kind of permissive toleration that simply lets people get on with their own business is not enough to generate the sense of belonging. Socialists are engaged on a moral quest for a wider community and solidarity, and members of sub-groups will never achieve the requisite sense of belonging if they are simply enjoined to carry on in their own private world. Nor, however, will they achieve this sense of belonging if they feel they are being asked to give up one identity in order to take on some other.

In contrast to consociationalism, the argument is explicitly premised on change. Mendus is rejecting that frozen tolerance of difference in which each community or sub-group just carries on in isolation from all others; she is thus implicitly rejecting consociational mechanisms which deal only in the 'fair' distribution of power between groups that will remain different and hostile. She presents difference more as a challenge, something that challenges dominant groups to reassess their own values and perspectives, but also challenges subordinate and excluded groups to go beyond sectarian loyalties. The ultimate goal is a wider sense of belonging, which is why difference can be neither denied nor simply left as it is.

A recent paper by Iris Young reiterates the argument she made in *Justice and the Politics of Difference* for specific representation for oppressed or disadvantaged groups, but puts it in the context of a discussion of justice and communicative democracy. Where the older pluralism of interest groups concerns itself only with the representation of *interests*, the communicative theory of democracy emphasises a process of transformation and change. Decisions are arrived at, not through backstage pressure or the anonymous casting of votes, but through direct interchange and discussion. In the process, participants may move from a narrow conception of their individual or group self-interest towards a concern with justice: indeed in order to be taken seriously in any democratic discussion, 'a person must transform his or her claim from "I want" to "I am entitled to" and offer some justification of this claim'.[30]

Thus in societies characterised by group division and inequality, the combined emphasis on discussion and group representation can be expected to transform the politics of dominant groups.

> Group representation unravels the false consensus that cultural imperialism may have produced, and reveals group bias in norms, standards, styles and perspectives that have been assumed as universal or of highest value. By giving voice to formerly silenced or devalued needs and experiences, group representation forces participants in discussion to take a reflective distance on their assumptions and think beyond their own interests. When confronted with interests, needs and opinions that derive from very different social positions and experience, persons sometimes come to understand the limitations of their own experience and perspective for coming to a conclusion about the best

policy for everyone. Coupled with the knowledge that the perspectives expressed by oppressed groups also carry a specific vote, and thus that they cannot be ignored if the whole body is to come to a decision, such enhanced communication best promotes just outcomes.[31]

In both arguments, the emphasis is on public interaction between different groups, and the ways that difference then encourages a process of self-reflection and change. But the real force of the argument lies in the way that difference can alter the perspectives of dominant groups: this is where it appears most unambiguously positive. In considering the cultural imperialism of Western traditions, or the patriarchal assumptions of Enlightenment thought, or just the more self-regarding narrowness of groups who have a current monopoly on resources and power, it is easy enough to regard enforced exposure to alternative perspectives as a positive development. If the confrontation with difference disrupts or undermines the unthinking certainties of dominant groups, then all to the good. We need not presume in advance that there is nothing of value in their beliefs or ideals—but we have good reason to expect them to be limited and partial and biased. In such contexts, difference can and should generate change: encouraging a reassessment of what may prove unfounded complacencies; and forcing people to reconsider what may be false generalisations from a very limited base.

But what of the more recently and perhaps still tentatively formulated assumptions of what are still subordinate groups? A confrontation that may seem thoroughly desirable in respect of the previously unchallenged dominance of narrowly unrepresentative groups appears less straightforwardly progressive in respect of those who have barely edged their way onto the public domain. Are these too to be 'disrupted' and 'undermined' and 'forced' to think more widely than themselves? Or should we say that where there is an existing asymmetry in power, there should also be an asymmetry in what is demanded? So perhaps men should have to confront their gender bias, but women shouldn't yet face this injunction? Perhaps white Americans should be exposed to criticism for referring only to the 'canon' of white Americans, but black Americans shouldn't yet be required to be equally even-handed? To deny the difference between dominant and subordinate groups is to fall back into the complacencies of the older pluralism, and most radicals would want to avoid that conclusion. Is the implication that difference should only work to 'challenge' what are dominant groups—inviting perhaps a more modest 'self-reflection' among those who remain outside the fold?

In one sense this is a false dilemma, for groups that feel themselves excluded in the current distribution of resources or power have usually adopted a language of entitlements or justice, knowing full well that they have no chance with the simpler assertions of 'I want'. To this extent, they are already in the business of communicating with others across the boundaries of difference, and are unlikely to need reminding that there are groups that are different from themselves.[32] The problem arises only where the mounting frustration among members of marginalised groups produces a more defiant sense of closure. Oppressed or marginalised or disadvantaged groups may then feel themselves propelled into a more exclusionary or separatist politics that simply refuses to recognise the concerns of those they feel have too long ignored their own. Once this happens, dominant groups are only too happy to feel themselves absolved from the pressure to reassess their own behaviour and beliefs.[33] Group division can then rigidify in a pattern that lends itself to more consociational solutions. The prospects for cross-group communication diminish, and it seems that the best we can hope for is a fairer distribution of resources and power. This is not an outcome to be welcomed by anyone who looks towards transformation and change.

What this indicates to me is that a radical perspective on democracy and difference must start from, but cannot remain exclusively within, the project of political equality. The systematic inequalities between dominant and subordinate groups provide us with a major part of any radical agenda, and direct our attention to the kinds of mechanisms that might be necessary to deal with existing asymmetries in power. But whatever form these mechanisms take (thus quota systems to guarantee a fairer distribution of political representation, or official caucuses to increase a sub-group's political weight, or some other of a range of alternatives) these will only contribute to a wider sense of solidarity if they work within the assumption of transformation and change. The problem, after all, is not just how to achieve a fairer distribution of resources and power between groups we expect to remain hostile, or contemptuous of one another. The problem is how to generate that more comprehensive understanding that validates the worth of each group. If we had this already, we would not be discussing this problem: it is clearly an outcome dependent on change.

Despite my anxieties on the subject, it seems clear that no group can remain immune from this process. It may be more unambiguously satisfying to disrupt or undermine the complacencies of dominant groups, but the challenge must inevitably be mutual, to both dominant *and* subordinate groups. The oppressed have no monopoly on good behaviour; being a victim is not a guarantee of right. Groups necessarily exist in relationship to one another, and whatever bias or partiality we perceive in one group, it is all too likely to be mirrored in some aspect of the opposing camp. It is in the nature of groups to be partial, and this applies whether they currently enjoy power or not.

What we can say, however, is that the process of mutual challenge is neither defensible nor very likely to happen without initiatives that tackle the asymmetry in power. Failing these, it does indeed seem inappropriate to call on subordinate or marginalised groups to adjust themselves to what may be the prejudices of those with more power; and failing these, it will be hard to impress on the dominant that they must listen to an opposing voice. In this sense, genuine and substantial political equality is the *sine qua non* of a plural society. For any radical, however, it is the beginning rather than the end of the project, for the ultimate goal remains the forging of common cause across the boundaries of difference. Exponents of the older pluralism can bask in a happy neutrality over the 'interests' their interest groups press: no need for criticism or judgement or future directions for change. Those immersed in the new pluralism cannot follow this same route. They cannot rely on the live and let live maxim as a way of resolving problems of difference; nor rest content with consociational procedures that may shelter each group from the process of mutual challenge and change. The intractability of difference should not be viewed as an intractability of *particular differences*, and insofar as each social group defines itself in relation to (and often in opposition to) some other, its sense of itself is necessarily fluid and liable to be transformed. While difference must be recognised and equality guaranteed, none of the differences is set in stone.

It is important, however, that this more dynamic sense of differences as changing, recomposing, in some cases dissolving, should not lead us to a new version of the older myths of homogeneity. Particular differences can and do go away; solidarities can and are forged across what looked like formidable barriers. This is not to say that difference *per se* will disappear, or that if we only work hard enough on our mutual understanding we will converge on some single set of shared ideals. What distinguishes a radical perspective on democracy is not its anticipation of future homogeneity and consensus, but its commitment to a politics of solidarity and challenge and change.

Notes and References

1 Values, Diversity and Social Theory
Jem Thomas

1. Charles Taylor, *Sources of the Self*, Cambridge University Press, Cambridge, 1989, p.61.
2. For example: Guy Oakes, *Weber and Rickert*, MIT Press, Cambridge, MA, 1988, p.135; Roger Brubaker, *The Limits of Rationality*, George Allen and Unwin, London, 1984, p.87; Alasdair MacIntyre, *Whose Justice? Which Rationality?*, Duckworth, London, 1988, ch.XIX.
3. 'On the Very Idea of a Conceptual Scheme', *Proceedings and Addresses of the American Philosophical Association*, 1974; reprinted in Donald Davidson, *Inquiries into Truth and Interpretation*, Oxford University Press, Oxford, 1984, essay 13.
4. Jean-François Lyotard, *The Postmodern Condition*, translated by Geoff Bennington and Brian Massumi, foreword by Fredric Jameson, Manchester University Press, Manchester, 1984, p.47.
5. Ibid., p.8.
6. Martin Albrow, *Max Weber's Construction of Social Theory*, Macmillan, London, 1990, p.244.
7. A.J. Ayer, *Language, Truth and Logic*, Victor Gollancz, London, 1936, ch.6. The phrases are from David McNaughton, *Moral Vision*, Basil Blackwell, Oxford, 1988, p.17.
8. J.L. Mackie, *Ethics*, Penguin Books, Harmondsworth, 1977, pp.48–9.
9. Contrast with the very misleading claim to the exact contrary in Guy Oakes's introduction to Georg Simmel, *The Problems of the Philosophy of History*, translated and edited by Guy Oakes, The Free Press, New York, 1977, pp.9–11.
10. Max Weber, *Roscher and Knies*, translated with an introduction by Guy Oakes, The Free Press, New York, 1975, p.251, n.47.
11. Albrow, *Max Weber's Construction of Social Theory*, op.cit., p.8, seems to me quite

right to suggest that the influence of Dilthey is as marked as that of Rickert in Weber's work; this seems especially the case with the opening chapter of Max Weber, *Economy and Society*, edited by Guenther Roth and Claus Wittich, University of California Press, Berkeley, 1978.

12. Clifford Geertz, *The Interpretation of Cultures*, Basic Books, New York, 1973, ch.1.

13. Weber, *Economy and Society, op.cit.*, p.4.

14. Ibid., pp.956-8.

15. Max Weber, *The Methodology of the Social Sciences*, translated and edited by Edward A. Shils and Henry A. Finch, with a foreword by Edward A. Shils, The Free Press, New York, 1949, p.7.

16. Ibid., p.131.

17. Barry Hindess, *Philosophy and Methodology in the Social Sciences*, The Harvester Press, Hassocks, 1977, p.48.

18. Cf. Weber, *The Methodology of the Social Sciences, op.cit.*, p.107.

19. Ibid., p.112.

20. Weber, *The Methodology of the Social Sciences, op.cit.*, pp.83-4, 'Undoubtedly all evaluative ideas are "subjective"....And they are, naturally, historically variable in accordance with the character of the culture and the ideas which rule men's minds. But it obviously does not follow from this that research in the cultural sciences can only have results which are "subjective" in the sense that they are *valid* for one person and not for others. In other words, the choice of the object of investigation and the extent or depth to which this investigation attempts to penetrate into the infinite causal web, are determined by the evaluative ideas which dominate the investigator and his age. In the *method* of investigation, the guiding "point of view" is of great importance for the *construction* of the conceptual scheme which will be used in the investigation. In their *mode* of use, however, the investigator is obviously bound by the norms of our thought just as much here as elsewhere. For scientific truth is precisely what is *valid* for all who *seek* the truth.'

21. A.N. Prior, 'The Autonomy of Ethics', *The Australasian Journal of Philosophy*, vol.38, no.3, December 1960, pp.199-206, gives analogous valid is/ought deductions.

22. Guenther Roth and Wolfgang Schluchter, *Max Weber's Vision of History*, University of California Press, Berkeley, 1979, p.5.

23. Weber, *The Methodology of the Social Sciences, op.cit.*, p.15.

24. Max Weber, *Gesammelte Aufsätze zur Wissenschaftslehre*, vierte Auflage, herausg. von Johannes Winckelmann, J.C.B. Mohr (Paul Siebeck), Tübingen, 1973, p.612.

25. Cf. Heinrich Rickert, *The Limits of Concept Formation in Natural Science*, translated and edited by Guy Oakes, Cambridge University Press, Cambridge, 1986, p.10.

26. Cf. Lawrence Scaff, *Fleeing the Iron Cage*, University of California Press, Berkeley, 1989, esp. ch.3.

27. The former because the openness of science to testing depends on it; the latter because science's findings are to be available to policy makers and therefore stand logically prior to evaluative and policy decisions.

NOTES AND REFERENCES

28. Weber, *The Methodology of the Social Sciences, op.cit.,* pp.58–9.
29. R.M. Hare, *The Language of Morals,* Clarendon Press, Oxford, 1952, Part III.
30. Bernard Williams, *Ethics and the Limits of Philosophy,* Fontana Paperbacks and William Collins, 1985, pp.140 and 218.
31. Ibid., pp.129 and 140.
32. Donald Davidson, *Essays on Action and Events,* Clarendon Press, Oxford, 1980, p.216.
33. Taylor, *Sources of the Self, op.cit.,* p.58.
34. Weber, *The Methodology of the Social Sciences, op.cit.,* p.11.
35. Cf. McNaughton, *Moral Vision, op.cit.,* p.61.
36. Mackie, *Ethics, op.cit.,* pp.38–42.
37. The term is from John McDowell, 'Values and Secondary Qualities', in Ted Honderich (ed.), *Morality and Objectivity,* Routledge and Kegan Paul, London, 1985, pp.110–29. I am strongly indebted to McDowell throughout this section.
38. Taylor, *Sources of the Self, op.cit.,* p.504.
39. Ibid., p.99.

2 Richard Rorty's Ironist Liberalism
Simon Thompson

1. Jean-François Lyotard, *The Postmodern Condition,* Manchester University Press, Manchester, 1984, p.xxiv.
2. Ibid., p.xxiii.
3. For useful discussions of this idea see: David Harvey, *The Condition of Postmodernity,* Oxford University Press, Oxford, 1989, pp.44–7; G. McLellan, 'The Enlightenment project revisited' in Stuart Hall et al. (eds), *Modernity and Its Future,* Polity Press, Cambridge 1992; Stephen White, *Political Theory and Postmodernism,* Cambridge University Press, Cambridge, 1991, pp.4–7.
4. White, *op. cit.,* ch.1.
5. Richard Rorty, 'Feminism and Pragmatism', *Radical Philosophy,* no.59, Autumn 1991, p.7.
6. Rorty, 'Habermas, Derrida, and the Functions of Philosophy', unpublished manuscript, 1991, p.1, n.1.
7. Richard Rorty, *Contingency, Irony and Solidarity,* Cambridge University Press, Cambridge, 1989, p.46; see also his 'Habermas, Derrida, and the Functions of Philosophy', p.20.
8. Rorty, *Contingency, Irony and Solidarity,* p.xv.
9. Rorty, ibid., p.xvi. Laclau and Mouffe's notion of a '*radical and plural democracy*' embraces some of the same sort of ideas. Thus they argue that a democracy exists insofar 'as it refuses to give its own organization and its own values the status of a *fundamentum inconcussum*. There is democracy as long as there exists the possibility of an unlimited questioning'. Rather than being defined simply as a particular set of institutional arrangements, democracy must therefore be seen as 'a certain inflection, a certain "weakening" of the type of validity attributable to any organization and any value'. This

weakening of validity widens 'the area of the strategic games that it is possible to play,' and thus widens 'the field of freedom.' See: Ernesto Laclau and Chantal Mouffe, *Hegemony and Socialist Strategy*, Verso Press, London 1985, p.187. Since freedom is seen as the opportunity to transform any set of circumstances, the project of radical democracy is like Rorty's liberal utopianism at least in as much as it involves an attempt to perpetuate the possibility of change rather an attempt to achieve a final and fixed state of affairs.

10. Rorty, 'Feminism and pragmatism', *op.cit.*, p.10.

11. It could be argued that a further strength of ironist liberalism lies in its avoidance of the dangers posed by the search for certainty. Thus Laclau and Mouffe argue that '[e]very attempt to establish a definitive suture and to deny the radically open character of the social which the logic of democracy institutes, leads to what Lefort designates as "totalitarianism"; that is to say, to a logic of construction of the political which consists of establishing a point of departure from which social can be perfectly mastered and known'; Laclau and Mouffe, *op.cit.*, p.187.

12. For further details of Rorty's account see for example: *Contingency, Irony and Solidarity*, pp.59–60, 194–5.

13. Ibid., p.190.

14. Richard Rorty, 'The Contingency of Community', *London Review of Books*, 24 July 1986, p.10.

15. Karl Popper, *Conjectures and Refutations*, Routledge and Kegan Paul, London 1972, p.357.

16. Richard Bernstein, *The New Constellation*, Polity Press, Cambridge, 1991, p.272.

17. Ibid., pp.280–1.

18. Ibid., pp.278–9.

19. Ibid., p.272.

20. Sabina Lovibond, 'Feminism and Pragmatism: A Reply to Richard Rorty', *New Left Review*, no.193, 1992, p.60.

21. Ibid., p.61.

22. Rorty, *Contingency, Irony and Solidarity*, p.7.

23. Rorty, 'Feminism and Pragmatism', pp.4–5.

24. Rorty, *Contingency, Irony and Solidarity*, *op.cit.*, p.9.

25. Ernesto Laclau, *New Reflections on the Revolution of Our Time*, Verso Press, London 1990, p.219.

26. Richard Bernstein, 'One Step Foward, Two Steps Backward: Richard Rorty on Liberal Democracy and Philosophy', *Political Theory*, vol.15, no.4, 1987, p.547.

27. Ibid., p.552.

28. Ibid., p.554.

29. Ibid., p.550.

30. Note that in focusing on these criticisms of Rorty's ethnocentrism, I have neglected a number of other criticisms which are no doubt equally worthy of consideration. For example, I do not have space to consider Fraser's charge that Rorty's social theory is 'hypercommunitarian' in that it 'homogenizes social space, assuming, tendentiously, that there are no deep

social cleavages capable of generating conflicting solidarities and opposing "we's'". See: Nancy Fraser, 'Solidarity or Singularity? Richard Rorty between Romanticism and Technocracy', in A. Malachowski (ed.), *Reading Rorty*, Basil Blackwell, Oxford, 1990, pp.314-5.

31. Richard Rorty, 'Habermas and Lyotard on Postmodernity' in R. Bernstein (ed.), *Habermas and Modernity*, Polity Press, Cambridge, 1985, p.197.

32. Michel Foucault, *The Foucault Reader*, Penguin, Harmondsworth, 1986, p.385. This passage is quoted in Bernstein, 'One Step Foward, Two Steps Backward', p.554; and discussed in Rorty, *Contingency, Irony and Solidarity*, pp.64-7.

33. Rorty, ibid., p.44.

34. Rorty, 'The Priority of Democracy to Philosophy', in M. Peterson and K. Vaughan (eds), *The Virginia State of Religious Freedom: Two Hundred Years After*, Cambridge University Press, Cambridge, 1988, p.279, n.33.

35. Ibid., p.266.

36. Ibid., pp.266-7; and see: John Rawls, *A Theory of Justice*, Oxford University Press, Oxford, pp.553-4.

37. Rorty, 'The Priority of Democracy', *op.cit.*, p.269.

38. Richard Rorty, 'Solidarity or Objectivity?', in J. Rajchman and C. West (eds), *Post-analytical Philosophy*, Columbia University Press, New York, 1985, p.11. Compare Rawls's remark that democratic people 'take pride in distinguishing themselves from nondemocratic people' in his 'The Priority of Right and Ideas of the Good', *Philosophy and Public Affairs*, vol.17, no.4, 1988, p.271.

39. Richard Rorty, 'Thugs and Theorists: A Reply to Bernstein', *Political Theory*, vol.15, no.4, 1987, p.578, n.20.

40. Ibid., p.575, n.4.

41. Ibid., pp.565-6. Note that this was written after the start of Gorbachev's programme of *perestroika*, but before the revolutions of 1989-90.

42. Rorty, *Contingency, Irony and Solidarity*, *op.cit.*, p.93.

43. Ibid., p.198. Here Rorty's position can be usefully compared to that of Walzer, who argues that '[i]nsofar as we can recognize moral progress, it has less to do with the discovery or invention of new principles than with the inclusion under the old principles of previously excluded men and women. And that is more a matter of (workman-like) social criticism and political struggle than of (paradigm-shattering) philosophical speculation.' See: Michael Walzer, *Interpretation and Social Criticism*, Harvard University Press, Cambridge, MA, 1987, p.27.

44. Foucault, *The Foucault Reader*, *op.cit.*, p.385.

45. Rorty, 'Thugs and Theorists', *op.cit.*, p.575, n.4.

46. Ibid., p.568.

47. Ibid., p.565.

48. Ibid., p.566.

49. Rorty, 'The Priority of Democracy to Philosophy', p.259.

50. For details of what he calls the 'liberal ideal of political legitimacy' see: Jeremy Waldron, 'Philosophical Foundations of Liberalism', *Philosophical Quarterly*, vol.37, no.147, 1987, pp.127-50.

51. Rorty, *Contingency, Irony and Solidarity*, *op.cit.*, p.xvi.

52. Ibid., p.192.
53. I would argue that on this account of ethnocentrism, the ironist liberal need not endorse Rorty's contention that Nietzsche and Loyola are 'mad' since we cannot get anywhere with them in political discussion. I believe that Rorty's is far too simple an account of political disagreement, since, for example, it is possible fundamentally to disagree with someone's politics and yet not think them mad. Think of the relevant differences of degree and of kind between animal rights activists, neoconservatives, Catholics, Serbian nationalists, Chinese communists and so on. On the possibility of reasonable disagreement see in particular: Rawls, 'The Domain of the Political and Overlapping Consensus', *New York University Law Review*, vol.64, no.2, 1989, pp.233–55.
54. Rorty, *Contingency, Irony and Solidarity, op.cit.*, p.196.
55. Of course, as Jeffrey Weeks pointed out to me, it is then pertinent to ask what should be done with these people now excluded from the group with which I identify. I don't think that there any general answer can be given to this question. Some groups can be tolerated, others must be suppressed, and so on. This is not an issue which I can take up here.

3 Between the Devil and the Deep Green Sea
Rosemary McKechnie and Ian Welsh

1. Ulrich Beck, *Risk Society: Towards a New Modernity*, Sage, London, 1992
2. Especially Anthony Giddens, *The Consequences of Modernity*, Polity Press, Cambridge, 1991; *Modernity and Self Identity*, Polity Press, Cambridge, 1991.
3. Throughout the 1970s large scale scientific and technical developments became the focus for sporadic though intense public demonstrations highlighting the importance of public risk acceptance for modernist visions. See for example: Dorothy Nelkin and Michael Pollak *The Atom Besieged*, MIT Press, London, 1981; Mary Douglas, *Risk According to the Social Sciences*, Routledge, London, 1986.
4. David Pearce et al., *Decision Making for Energy Futures*, Macmillan, London, 1979. For a theoretical consideration of commensurability see: Thomas in this volume.
5. Brian Wynne, *Rationality and Ritual: The Windscale Inquiry and Nuclear Decisions in Britain*, BSHS, Chalfont St Giles, 1982.
6. See for example: Andrew Ross, *Strange Weather*, Verso, London, 1991, esp. ch.2; Donna Harraway, 'The Bio-politics of Postmodern Bodies: Determinations of Self in Immune System Discourse', *Differences*, vol.1, no.1, 1989, pp.3–43; Emily Martin, 'The End of the Body?', *American Ethnologist*, vol.18, 1991, pp.121–40.
7. For example Michael Fitzpatrick and Don Milligan link the risks of radioactive fallout and other environmental contaminants and sexual practices. See: *The Truth About the Aids Panic*, Junius, London, 1987, p.39.
8. Tony Juniper in FOE campaigning letter, March 1993.
9. Martin Albrow, *Globalization, Knowledge and Society*, Sage, London, 1990, p.9.

NOTES AND REFERENCES

10. We are grateful to Peter Jowers for clarifying comments on areas where we tended to reproduce this tendency in an earlier version of this work.

11. Examples of such processes can be found in Arjun Appadurai, 'Disjuncture and Difference in the Global Cultural Economy' in Mike Featherstone (ed.), *Global Culture: Nationalism, Globalization and Modernity*, Sage, London, 1990, pp.295–310.

12. See: Anthony Giddens, *The Consequences of Modernity*, op.cit., pp.35–48; Ulrich Beck, *Risk Society*, op.cit., p.77. See also: Ulrich Beck, 'From Industrial Society to the Risk Society: Questions of Survival, Social Structure and Ecological Enlightenment', *Theory, Culture and Society*, vol.9, 1992, pp.97–123.

13. Beck, *Risk Society*, op.cit., p.70.

14. Ibid., pp.34–6.

15. Ibid., p.34.

16. Ibid., p.27. But see also: Ulrich Beck 'The Anthropological Shock: Chernobyl and the contours of the risk society', *Berkeley Journal of Sociology*, vol.9 no.3, 1987, pp.153–65.

17. Beck, *Risk Society*, op.cit., pp.47–53.

18. Ibid., p.71.

19. Ibid., p.53.

20. Ibid., p.70.

21. Ibid.

22. Giddens, *The Consequences of Modernity*, op.cit., p.53.

23. For a discussion of the functionalist tendencies in Giddens work see: R. Robertson, *Globalization*, Sage, London, 1992, esp. ch.9. Scott Lash offers another interpretation in 'Reflexive Modernization: The Aesthetic Dimension', *Theory, Culture and Society*, vol.10, 1993, pp.1–23.

24. Beck, *Risk Society*, op.cit., p.165.

25. Ibid., p.168. Giddens, *Modernity and Self-Identity*, op.cit., p.57.

26. Ibid., p.175.

27. Ibid., p.176.

28. These accounts set the development of scientific thought in its sociocultural context, examining how science is shaped by social forces and in turn contributes to the values of the societies it is part of. Thus scientific definitions of problem areas has always been intertwined with socio-cultural and moral definitions. See for example: P. Treichler, 'AIDS, HIV and the Cultural Construction of Reality', in G. Herdt, S. Lindenbaum (eds), *The Time of AIDS: Social Analysis, Theory and Method*, Sage, London, 1992; L. Jordanov, *Sexual Visions: Images of Gender in Science and Medicine between the Eighteenth and Twentieth Centuries*, Harvester, Hemel Hempstead, 1990.

29. Jeffrey Weeks, 'Post-Modern AIDS?' in T. Boffin and S. Gupta (eds), *Ecstatic Antibodies*, Rivers Oram Press, London, 1991, p.134.

30. Ibid.

31. The similarities and differences between the social history of AIDS and that of previous stigmatising (often sexually transmitted) diseases is discussed in A.M. Brandt, *'No Magic Bullet'*, Oxford University Press, 1985; E. Fee and D.M. Fox (eds), *AIDS: The Burdens of History*, University of California Press, Berkeley, 1989; V. Berridge, 'Aids: History and Contemporary History', in Herdt and Lindenbaum (eds), *The Time of AIDS*, op.cit.

32. See: G.M. Oppenheimer, 'In the Eye of the Storm: The Epidemiological Construction of AIDS', in Fee and Fox (eds), *AIDS: The Burdens of History*, *op.cit.*

33. See: R. Frankenberg, 'One Epidemic or Three?: Cultural, Social and Historical Aspects of the AIDS Pandemic', in P. Aggleton, G. Hart and P. Davies (eds), *AIDS: Social Representations, Social Practices*, Falmer Press, Basingstoke, 1991; A.M.Brandt, 'AIDS: From Social History to Social Policy', in Fee and Fox, *AIDS: The Burdens of History*, *op.cit.*

34. A critique of the way the concept 'culture' has developed within epidemiological and policy perspectives has emerged from the works of anthropologists who were called on to penetrate those 'cultures' perceived as most 'other'. See: M. Singer, 'AIDS and US Ethnic Minorities: The Crises and Alternative Anthropological Responses' in *Human Organisation*, vol.51, no.1, 1992; N. Glick Schiller, 'What's Wrong with this Picture? The Hegemonic Construction of Culture in AIDS Research in the United States' in *Medical Anthropology Quarterly*, vol.6, no.3, 1992, pp.237–54.

35. In G. Herdt et al., 'AIDS on the Planet: The Plural Voices of Anthropology' in *Anthropology Today*, vol.6, no.3, 1990, p.12.

36. P. Bourdieu, *Language and Symbolic Power*, Polity Press, Cambridge, p.166.

37. See: P. Bourdieu, 'Le Nord et Le Midi: Contribution a une analyse de l'effet Montesquieu' and 'L'Identité et la Représentation. Elements pour une réflexion critique sur l'idée de region', in *Actes de la Recherche en Science Sociale*, vol.35, 1980, pp.21–5, 63–72.

38. Z. Bauman, *Modernity and the Holocaust*, Polity Press, Cambridge, 1989, p.18.

39. P. Treichler, 'AIDS, Gender and Biomedical Discourse', in Fee and Fox, *AIDS: The Burdens of History*, *op.cit.* p.213.

40. Ibid.

41. For a succinct analysis of the inadequacies and implicit evaluations associated with the category 'Prostitute' see: S. Day, 'Prostitute Women and AIDS: Anthropology', in *AIDS* 2, 1988, pp.421–8; similarly for drug-users and their partners see: S. Kane and T. Mason, '"IV Drug-Users" and "Sex Partners": The Limits of Epidemiological Categories and the Ethnography of Risk', in Herdt and Lindenbaum (eds), *The Time of AIDS*, *op.cit.*

42. M. Singer, 'AIDS and US Ethnic Minorities', *op.cit.*

43. Kane and Mason, '"IV Drug-Users" and "Sex Partners"', *op.cit.*; E. Quimby, 'Anthropological Witnessing for African Americans: Power, Responsibility and Choice in the Age of AIDS', in Herdt and Lindenbaum (eds), *The Time of AIDS*, *op.cit.*

44. E. Quimby, 'Anthropological Witnessing for African Americans', *op.cit.*

45. Beck reasserted this position repeatedly at the conference 'Risk Society: Modernity and the Environment', Centre for the Study of Environmental Change, Lancaster University, 29 May 1991.

46. See for example: Brian Wynne, 'Knowledges in Context', *Science Technology and Human Values*, vol.5, 1991, pp.111–21; and 'Misunderstood Misunderstandings: Social Identities and Public Uptake of Science', *Public Understanding of Science*, vol.1, 1992, pp.281–304.

47. Giddens, *Modernity and Self Identity*, *op.cit.* For an anthropological account see: Rosemary B. McKechnie, 'Insiders and outsiders: identifying experts on

home ground', in Alan Irwin and Brian Wynne (eds), *Misunderstanding Science*, Cambridge, forthcoming, 1994.

48. In this manner proposals to locate a nuclear reactor on a remote Northumberland beach provided the motivation to create an extensive alliance to oppose the transport of spent nuclear fuel through London. For further discussion see: Ian Welsh, *British Nuclear Power: Protest and Legitimation*, unpublished PhD thesis, Lancaster, 1988. Forthcoming as *Nuclear Power: Generating Dissent*, Routledge. For a consideration of aesthetics see Jowers this volume.

49. For example, a public inquiry inspector dismissed objectors' evidence into a reactor siting decision by reference to his holiday memories of the location as a child. See: Ian Welsh, 'The NIMBY syndrome: Its Significance in the History of the Nuclear Debate in Britain', *British Journal for the History of Science*, vol.26, 1993, pp.15-32.

50. This is a tendency present not only in the work of Beck and Giddens but also Scott Lash and John Urry, *The End of Organised Capitalism*, Polity Press, Cambridge, 1987.

51. Where detailed consideration of 'new' social movement activity has taken place there is often an imposition of a set of theoretical ambitions which distorts the material. Perhaps the biggest victim in this sense is the work of Alan Touraine which sought a replacement for Marx's proletariat in a social movement which would contest the means of cultural reproduction and domination seized by an autonomous technocracy. See: Alan Touraine, *The Voice and The Eye*, 1981, *Anti-Nuclear Protest*, Cambridge University Press, 1983, 'New Social Movements', *Social Research*, 1985. Melluci's field work in this area also relates weakly to his overall theoretical concerns, though remaining fluid enough to express the diversity and hybridity to be encountered in social movement formations. See: Alberto Melucci, *Nomads of the Present*, Radius, London, 1989, and Amy Bartholomew and Margit Mayer's excellent review article 'Nomads of the Present: Melucci's Contribution to New Social Movement Theory', *Theory, Culture and Society*, vol.9, 1992, pp.141-59. For an excellent review of these and other issues concerning the use of new social movements see: Rudiger Schmitt-Beck, 'A Myth Institutionalised: New Social Movements in Germany', *European Journal of Political Research*, vol.21, 1992, pp.357-83.

52. Giddens, *Modernity and Self Identity*, op.cit., p.38.

53. Ibid., pp.39-40, emphasis in original.

54. Ibid., pp.51-64.

55. Ibid., ch.7 is a stunning example of this.

56. Giddens, *The Consequences of Modernity*, op.cit.

57. Beck, *Risk Society*, op.cit., p.54.

58. Ibid., pp.160-5.

59. See: Derek Wall, *Green History*, Routledge, 1993.

60. Gro Harlem Brundtland, *Our Common Future*, World Commission on Environment and Development, Oxford, 1987. See also: Linda Starke, *Signs of Hope*, Oxford University Press, Oxford, 1990 for a review of progress towards achieving the objectives of the Brundtland Report.

61. Marien, *Futures*, 1992.

62. Andre Gorz, *Ecology as Politics*, Pluto Press, London, 1987 edn, p.3.
63. For example in the UK the Council for the Preservation of Rural England and the Green Alliance produced *Putting Our Own House in Order*, CPRE, London, 1992. The subtitle 'The UK's Responsibility to the Earth Summit' was part of a clear exhortation to the government for action.
64. Peter M. Haas et al., 'The Earth Summit: How Should We Judge Success?', *Environment*, vol.34, October 1992, pp.6–11, 26–33, *op.cit.*, p.29.
65. For a detailed consideration of this position see: Warwick Fox, *Towards a Transpersonal Ecology*, Shambala, London, 1990.
66. J.G. Speth, 'A Post-Rio Compact', *Foreign Policy*, vol.88, Fall 1992, pp.145–9; W.A. Nitze, 'Swords into Ploughshares: Agenda for Change in the Developing World', *International Affairs*, vol.69, 1993, pp.39–53.
67. *The Ecologist*, vol.22, November/December 1992, p.122.
68. For a discussion of this see: Mark Imber, 'Too Many Cooks? The Post-Rio Reform of the United Nations', *International Affairs*, vol.69, 1993, pp.55–70.
69. For a general account of what cultural theory could contribute see: M. Douglas, and M. Calvez, 'The Self as Risk-Taker: A Cultural Theory of Contagion in Relation to AIDS', in *The Sociological Review*, vol.38, no.3, 1990, pp.445–64; for a more grounded account of the shifting development of understanding of the risks associated with HIV within the cultural context of health beliefs, political and economic background see: P. Farmer, 'Sending Sickness: Sorcery, Politics, and Changing Concepts of AIDS in Rural Haiti', in *Medical Anthropology Quarterly*, vol.4, no.1, pp.6–27.
70. See: D. Richardson, 'AIDS Education and Women: Sexual and Reproductive Issues' in P. Aggleton, P. Davies and G. Hart (eds), *AIDS: Individual, Cultural and Policy Dimensions*, Falmer Press, Basingstoke, 1990; B.G. Schoepf, 'AIDS, Sex and Condoms: African Healers and the Reinvention of Tradition in Zaire', in *Medical Anthropology*, vol.1114, 1992, pp.225–42.
71. Beck, *Risk Society*, *op.cit.*, p.158.
72. Giddens, *Modernity and Self Identity*, *op.cit.*, p.221.
73. Anthony Giddens, *The Nation State and Violence*, Polity Press, Cambridge, 1985.
74. Vandana Shiva, *The Ecologist*, vol.22, November/December 1992.

4 Ordering The City
Judith Squires

1. Kevin Robins, 'Prisoners of the City: Whatever could a Postmodern City be?', *New Formations*, no.15, Routledge, London, 1991, p.19.
2. R. Moore, 'Open and Shut', *New Statesman and Society*, 12 October 1990, p.27.
3. The communitarian perspective I refer to is to be found in Michael Sandel, *Liberalism and the Limits of Justice*, Cambridge University Press, Cambridge, 1982 and Alasdair MacIntyre, *After Virtue*, Duckworth, London, 1981; the postmodern perspective in Iris Marion Young, *Justice and the Politics of Difference*, Princeton University Press, Princeton, 1990; the radical pluralist

perspective in Chantal Mouffe, *The Return of the Political*, Verso, London, 1993.

4. Jürgen Habermas, *The Structural Transformation of the Public Sphere*, trans. T. Burger, MIT Press, Boston, 1989, originally 1962.

5. Jane Jacobs, *The Death and Life of Great American Cities*, Random House, New York, 1961, p.50.

6. Richard Sennett, *The Fall of Public Man*, Faber and Faber, London, 1986.

7. Hannah Arendt, *The Human Condition*, Chicago University Press, Chicago, 1958, p.180.

8. C. Baudelaire, 'The Salon of 1845' in *Art in Paris 1845-1862*, Phaidon Press, Oxford, 1965.

9. Ibid., pp.31-2.

10. Italo Calvino, *Invisible Cities*, Picador, London, 1972.

11. Janet Wolff, 'The Invisible Flaneuse: Women and the Literature of Modernity', in A. Benjamin (ed.), *The Problems of Modernity*, Routledge, London, 1989.

12. M. Berman, *All That Is Solid Melts Into Air*, Verso, London, 1983.

13. T. McEwan, *McX*, pp.27-8.

14. Thomas More, *Utopia*, Logan and Adams, Cambridge texts, 1989.

15. Elizabeth Wilson, *The Sphinx In The City*, Verso, London, 1991, p.9.

16. See: David Harvey, *The Condition of Postmodernity*, Blackwell, Oxford, 1989.

17. I borrow this term from Robins, 'Prisoners of the City', *op.cit.*

18. M. Castells, *The Informational City*, Basil Blackwell, Oxford, 1989, p.348.

19. Paul Virilio, as discussed by McKenzie Wark in *Arena*, no. 82, 1988.

20. Jean Baudrillard, 'The Ecstasy of Communication', in Hal Foster (ed.), *Postmodern Culture*, Pluto Press, London, 1985.

21. John Lichfield, 'No Particular Place to Live', *Independent*, 15 November 1992, p.8.

22. Ibid., p.11.

23. Ibid., p.9.

24. Doreen Massey, 'A Place Called Home?', *New Formations*, no.17, Summer 1992, Lawrence and Wishart, London.

25. David Harvey, *The Condition of Postmodernity*, *op.cit.*

26. Fredric Jameson, *Postmodernism: or the Cultural Logic of Late Capitalism*, Verso, London, 1991.

27. Kevin Robins, 'Tradition and Translation: National Culture in its Global Context', in J. Corner and S. Harvey (eds), *Enterprise and Heritage*, London, Routledge, 1991, p.41.

28. Massey, 'A Place Called Home', *op.cit.*, p.9.

29. Suzanne Moore, *Looking For Trouble*, Serpent's Tail, London, 1991, p.210.

30. L. Mumford, 'Theory and Practice of Regionalisation', *Sociological Review*, 20, 1928.

31. P. Cooke, 'Modernity, Postmodernity and the City', *Theory, Culture and Society*, 4, 1988, pp.114-15.

32. F. Bianchini and H. Schwengel, 'Re-imagining the city', in Corner and Harvey (eds), *Enterprise and Heritage*, *op.cit.*

33. D. Harvey, *The Condition of Postmodernity*, *op. cit.*, p.83.

34. *An Urban Renaissance: The Role of the Arts in Urban Regeneration*, London, The Arts Council, 1987.
35. Ibid.
36. Ibid.
37. D. Ley, 'Modernism, Postmodernism and the Struggle for Place', in J. Agnew and J. Duncan (eds), *The Power of Place*, Unwin Hyman, Boston, MA, 1989, p.33.
38. M. Featherstone quoted in Robins, 'Tradition and Translation', *op.cit.*, p.7.
39. Ron McCarthy in C. Gardner and J. Shepard (eds), *Consuming Passions*, Unwin Hyman, London, 1989.
40. Quoted in Lichfield, 'No Particular Place to Live', *op.cit.*, p.11.
41. Roy Boyne and Ali Rattansi (eds), Introduction to *Postmodernism and Society*, Macmillan, Basingstoke, 1990, p.21.
42. Wilson, *The Sphinx in the City, op.cit.*, p.152.
43. Arendt, *The Human Condition*, Chicago University Press, Chicago, 1958, p.52.
44. Maurizio Passerin d'Entreves in Chantal Mouffe (ed.), *Dimensions of Radical Democracy*, Verso, London, 1992, p.151.
45. Quoted in d'Entreves, ibid., p.151.
46. Seyla Benhabib, *Situating the Self*, Polity Press, Cambridge, 1992, p.90.
47. Ibid., p.91.
48. Ibid., p.91.
49. Ibid., p.94.
50. Young, *Justice and the Politics of Difference, op.cit.*, p.97.
51. Richard Sennett, *Uses of Disorder*, Penguin, Harmondsworth, 1971, p.36.
52. Young, *Justice and the Politics of Difference, op.cit.*, Princeton University Press, Princeton, 1990.
53. M. Foucault, *Power/Knowledge*, ed. C. Gordon, Harvester Press, Brighton, 1980, p.152.
54. Habermas, *The Structural Transformation of the Public Sphere, op.cit.*
55. Young, *Justice and the Politics of Difference, op.cit.*
56. D. Harvey, 'Social Justice, Postmodernism and the City', unpublished paper.
57. Harvey, ibid.
58. Ibid.
59. Ibid.
60. Jane Jacobs, *The Death and Life of Great American Cities, op.cit.*
61. Raymond Williams, 'The Metropolis and the Emergence of Modernism', in E. Timms and D. Kelley (eds), *Unreal City*, Manchester University Press, Manchester, 1985, p.19.

5 Symbolic Antagonism, Police Paranoia and the Possibility of Social Diversity
Sean Watson

1. Policeman, 35, twice married, 12 years' experience, uniformed PC on inner city division of large British constabulary, middle class background, grammar school education. Interviewed in 1988. Apart from the exceptions noted, all the interviews quoted in this paper were conducted by the author as part of an ongoing research project.
2. Policeman, 23, married, five years' experience plus two and a half years as cadet; uniformed PC on city division of a large British constabulary, middle-class background, comprehensive education. Interviewed in 1988.
3. Policeman, 40, divorced, 22 years' experience, plainclothes sergeant in Criminal Intelligence Unit in city division of a large British constabulary, educated at technical school. Interviewed in 1988.
4. American officer working in the narcotics field commenting on marijuana use. Quoted by Jock Young, 'The Role of the Police as Amplifiers of Deviance, Negotiators of Reality and Translators of Fantasy', in S. Cohen (ed.), *Images of Deviance*, Pelican, Harmondsworth, 1971.
5. Mary Douglas, *Purity and Danger*, Routledge, London 1978, p.3.
6. A notable exception to this of course is Horkheimer and Adorno's analysis of authoritarian and anti-semitic ideology. Theodor Adorno, Else Frenkel-Brunswick, Daniel J. Levinson, R. Nevitt Sanford, *The Authoritarian Personality*, Norton, New York, 1969. Max Horkheimer and Theodor W. Adorno, *The Dialectic of Enlightenment*, Allen Lane, London, 1973, pp.168–208.
7. Policeman, 40, divorced, 22 years' experience, plain clothes sergeant in Criminal Intelligence Unit in city division of large British constabulary, educated at technical school. Interviewed in 1988.
8. Policeman, 25, married, two years as cadet, six and a half as regular. Uniformed PC on inner city division of large British constabulary. Interviewed in 1988.
9. Slavoj Zizek, 'The Undergrowth of Enjoyment', *New Formations*, no.9, Winter 1989, pp.7–29.
10. This phenomenon in which the actual qualities of the out-group are relatively unimportant, since their perceived qualities are derived from paranoid projection, is dealt with in detail by Adorno in his account of anti-semitic ideology in Adorno et al., *The Authoritarian Personality*, op.cit. and by Horkheimer and Adorno in *The Dialectic of Enlightenment*, op.cit.
11. 'Targeting' is the practice whereby an individual will be picked out as particularly inherently troublesome. Resources will then be targeted on that individual in the hope of 'getting a job on him' (in other words amassing sufficient evidence to pin a crime on him). So the perception of the individual as a 'dangerous individual' (Michel Foucault, 'The Dangerous Individual', in Michel Foucault, *Politics, Philosophy, Culture*, Routledge, London, 1990) precedes legally valid knowledge of his behaviour. These 'dangerous' qualities are projected onto him and then 'a job' is sought in

order to legally rationalise this projection. This practice is not some sort of unofficial aberration in police practice, it is a key official strategy employed, in particular, by Crime Investigation Departments and Crime Intelligence Units. This strategy is dependent for its sense on the discourses of 'delinquency' in which crime is accounted for as the product of an out-group of inherently dangerous and morally retarded individuals; Foucault (ibid., 1990 pp.125–52) and Pasquino (P. Pasquino, 'Criminology: The Birth of a Special Knowledge', in Graham Burchell, Colin Gordon and Peter Miller (eds), *The Foucault Effect: Studies in Governmentality*, Harvester/Wheat-sheaf, London, 1991, pp.235–50) have both given indispensable accounts of the constitution of these discourses. Also Michel Foucault, *Discipline and Punish*, Penguin, London, 1979, pp.257–93. They have not however sufficiently accounted for the affective attractiveness of such potentially paranoid discourse.

12. Policeman, 25, married, two years as cadet, six and a half as regular. Uniformed PC on inner city division of large British constabulary. Interviewed in 1988.
13. Policeman, 28, married, seven years in the army, five and a half years police. Uniformed PC on attachment to 'Street Offences' unit of inner city division of large British constabulary. Interviewed in 1988.
14. Policeman, 38, seven years in the army, married with children, fourteen years in police. PC on attachment to the Youth Liaison team of inner city division of large British constabulary. Interviewed in 1988.
15. Michael Rustin, *The Good Society and the Inner World*, Verso, London, 1991.
16. Victor Burgin, 'Paranoiac Space', *New Formations*, no.12, Winter 1990, pp.61–75.
17. Ibid. p.67, from S. Freud, 'Psycho-Analytic Notes on an Autobiographical Account of a Case of Paranoia', 1911.
18. Ibid. Also Madan Sarup, *Jacques Lacan*, Harvester Wheatsheaf, London, 1992, pp.107–10.
19. Quoted by Burgin, *op.cit.*, p.65, from S. Freud 'Psycho-Analytic Notes on an Autobiographical Account of a Case of Paranoia', 1911.
20. Slavoj Zizek, *For They Know Not What They Do: Enjoyment as a Political Factor*, Verso, London, 1991.
21. Anthony Giddens, *Modernity and Self Identity*, Polity Press, Cambridge, 1991, pp.35–69.
22. For example, Sarup, *Jacques Lacan, op.cit.*, p.104. Also Ernesto Laclau, *New Reflections on the Revolution of Our Time*, Verso, London, 1990, pp.211–12.
23. Ibid., pp.207–8.
24. The use of a developmental explanation of existential trust/anxiety makes it unduly individualistic, psychologistic and static. It would imply that an individual's level of trust/tolerance was fixed throughout life (subsequent to very early developmental stages) regardless of social context. Whilst it may be argued that a basic substratum of existential trust/anxiety is laid down very early on, to argue that subsequent social context is irrelevant is plainly unsustainable. To premise a 'normalising' schema on such a developmental model both compounds the initial error and introduces a further, questionable, political dimension.

25. Ernesto Laclau has recently devoted much attention to the issue of symbolic antagonism/dislocation (*New Reflections, op.cit.*, pp.39–60). I shall return to consider the significance of his claims in relation to this paper in my conclusions.

26. Rustin, *The Good Society, op.cit.*, pp.57–84.

27. Burgin, *Paranoic Space, op.cit.*, p.67.

28. Ibid., p.67.

29. Sir Kenneth Newman, *The Principles of Policing and Guidance for Professional Behaviour*, Public Information Department of the Metropolitan Police, London, 1985.

30. Ibid., p.9.

31. Michel Foucault, 'Governmentality', in Graham Burchell, Colin Gordon and Peter Miller (eds), *The Foucault Effect, op.cit.*

32. Newman, *Principles of Policing, op.cit.*, p.9.

33. See: also Ian Hacking, 'How Should we do the History of Statistics?', in Graham Burchell, Colin Gordon, Peter Miller (eds), *The Foucault Effect, op.cit.*

34. Foucault, 'Governmentality', *op.cit.*, pp.102–3.

35. Newman, *Principles of Policing, op.cit.*, pp.102–3.

36. Ibid., p.13.

37. Ibid., p.11.

38. Alan Silver, 'The Demand for Order in Civil Society: A Review of Some Themes in the History of Urban Crime, Police, and Riot', in David Bordua (ed.), *The Police: Six Sociological Essays*, John Wiley, New York, 1967.

39. Slavoj Zizek, 'The Undergrowth of Enjoyment', *New Formations*, no.9, Winter 1989, pp.7–29; Slavoj Zizek, *The Sublime Object of Ideology*, Verso, London, 1989; Slavoj Zizek, *For They Know Not What They Do: Enjoyment as a Political Factor*, Verso, London, 1991; Slavoj Zizek, 'Eastern Europe's Republics of Gilead', *New Left Review*, no.183, 1992, pp.50–62.

40. Ibid., p.57.

41. Policeman, thirty five, married, middle class background, grammar school educated, twelve years' experience, uniformed PC in inner city division of large British constabulary. Interviewed in 1988.

42. Policeman, thirty five, married, working class background, seven years' experience, uniformed sergeant in inner city division of large British constabulary. Interviewed in 1988.

43. Egon Bittner, 'Florence Nightingale in Pursuit of Willie Sutton: A Theory of the Police', in H. Jacobs (ed.), *The Potential for Reform of Criminal Justice*, Sage, London, 1974; Egon Bittner, *The Functions of the Police in Modern Society*, Jason Aronson, New York, 1975.

44. It is for this reason that Egon Bittner's analysis of policing in the United States can be generalised to analysis of policing throughout the rest of the modern, industrial, capitalist world.

45. Newman, *Principles of Policing, op.cit.*, p.12.

46. Ibid., pp.12–13.

47. Ibid., p.14.

48. Laclau, *New Reflections, op.cit.*, pp.39–60.

49. Ibid., pp.43–4.

50. Jean F. Lyotard, *The Postmodern Condition*, Manchester University Press,

Manchester 1986. Jean F. Lyotard, *The Inhuman*, Polity Press, Cambridge, 1991. Richard Rorty, *Contingency, Irony and Solidarity*, Cambridge University Press, Cambridge, 1989.

51. See: Peter Jowers work on the sublime in Kant, Rorty and Lyotard in this volume.

52. Peter Jowers in this volume outlines the way in which Lyotard, via Kant, articulates the possibility of overcoming moments of sublime horror through the imagination and the eventual symbolisation of the initially unsymbolisable sublime horror/symbolic dislocation. This avenue is not open to the police officer, however. Any attempt to overcome imaginatively the antagonisms at the heart of the police subject would subvert the role of the police officer as guarantor of social passivity and thus undermine the conditions for ontological security and imaginative hybridisation in the rest of the population.

53. E.C. Hughes, 'Good People and Dirty Work', in E.C. Hughes, *The Sociological Eye*, Chicago, Aldine, Chicago, 1971.

6 Bodies, Boundaries and Solidarities
John Bird

1. Z. Bauman, *Modernity and Ambivalence*, Polity Press, London, 1991, pp.137-8.
2. R. Young, 'Transitional phenomena', in B. Richards (ed.), *Crises of the Self*, Free Association Books, London, 1989, p.37.
3. S. Zizek, *Looking Awry—An Introduction to Jacques Lacan through Popular Culture*, MIT Press, New York, 1991, pp.165-6.
4. There is much discussion of the terms 'race', 'racism' and 'ethnicity'; F. Anthias ('Connecting "race" and ethnic phenomena', *Sociology*, vol.26, no.3, 1992, pp.421-38), provides one possible clarification. Arguing that ethnicity always involves exclusion, she sees ethnicity becoming racism where culture is seen as 'a static and reified expression of collective or national identity...[and where there is a] pecking order of cultures...[and where contact with some] is desirable and leav[es] indelible blotches on the purity of "national" culture' (p.435). This racism involves social organisation which separates, guarantees and maintains differential treatment.
5. M. Klein, 'Notes on some Schizoid Mechanisms', *International Journal of Psychoanalysis*, 27, 1946, pp.99, 110; *The Writings of Melanie Klein, vol.3: Envy and Gratitude and Other Works*, Hogarth Press, London, 1975.
6. E. Durkheim, *The Division of Labour in Society*, Free Press, New York, 1964; E. Durkheim and M. Mauss, *Primitive Classification*, Cohen and West, London, 1969; E. Durkheim, *The Elementary Forms of the Religious Life*, Allen and Unwin, London, 1971.
7. Z. Bauman, *Modernity and the Holocaust*, Polity Press, London 1989; Bauman, *Modernity and Ambivalence, op.cit.*
8. It is not the intention here to take up the debate surrounding Barker's work (M. Barker, *The New Racism*, Junction Books, London, 1981), in which he postulates a new racism which stresses differences in ways of life, as

NOTES AND REFERENCES

opposed to the old, with its stress upon imputed biological differences. It is certainly part of the logic of the position I am putting forward that the references to differences associated with bodies—sex, disease, dirt, food— remain central to ethnic differences. The very term 'ethnic cleansing' resonates with this. Put another way, biological differences are always a potential nodal point in structures and discourses of racial and ethnic difference.

9. J. Dollard, *Caste and Class in a Southern Town*, Yale University Press, New York, 1937.
10. M. Rustin, *The Good Society and the Inner World: Psychoanalysis, Politics and Culture*, Verso, London, 1991.
11. Young, 'Transitional Phenomena', *op.cit.*
12. H. Bhabha, 'Introduction', F. Fanon, *Black Skin, White Masks*, Pluto Press, London, 1986; H. Bhabha, 'The Other Question: Difference, Discrimination and the Discourse of Colonialism', in F. Barker (ed.), *Literature, Politics and Theory*, Methuen, London, 1986. There is a common concern here to read Fanon and others through the work of Lacan.
13. Z. Bauman, *Modernity and Ambivalence*, *op.cit.*, p.24.
14. M. Klein, *Love, Guilt and Reparation*, Virago Press, London 1988.
15. M. Douglas, *Purity and Danger*, Routledge, London, 1966.
16. Bauman, 1991, *op.cit.*
17. P. Mestrovic, *The Coming Fin de Siècle*, Routledge, London, 1991.
18. E. Durkheim, *op.cit.*, especially chapter 7.
19. Durkheim, *The Division of Labour in Society*, *op.cit.*
20. W. Pickering, *Durkheim's Sociology of Religion*, Routledge, London, 1984.
21. Durkheim, *The Division of Labour in Society*, *op.cit.*, pp.85–6.
22. J.-P. Sartre, *Portrait of an Anti-Semite*, Secker and Warburg, London, 1948.
23. B. Richards (ed.), *Crises of the Self*, Free Association Books, London, 1989, pp.1–23.
24. Bauman, 1991, *op.cit.*
25. Giddens indicated in discussion of a paper delivered at the University of Bristol (February 1993) that the terms optimism and pessimism were inappropriate to a late modern, risk-based society.
26. A. Giddens, *The Transformation of Intimacy*, Polity Press, London, 1992.
27. Bauman, *Modernity and the Holocaust*, *op.cit.* and Bauman, *Modernity and Ambivalence*, *op.cit.*
28. Giddens, *The Transformation of Intimacy*, *op.cit.*, pp.181–2.
29. Bauman, *Modernity and the Holocaust*, *op.cit.*, p.58.
30. Ibid., pp.61–2.
31. Ibid., p.217.
32. Bauman, *Modernity and Ambivalence*, *op.cit.*, p.15.
33. Klein, *Envy, Gratitude and Other Essays*, *op.cit.*
34. Douglas, *Purity and Danger*, *op.cit.*
35. R. Hinshelwood, *A Dictionary of Kleinian Analysis*, Free Association Books, London, 1989, pp.410–14.
36. F. Fanon, *Black Skin, White Masks*, Pluto Press, London, 1986, p.13.
37. H. Segal, *Klein*, Fontana, London, 1979, p.133.

269

38. C.F. Alford, *Melanie Klein and Critical Social Theory*, Yale University Press, London 1989.
39. Bauman, *Modernity and Ambivalence, op.cit.*, pp.259–60.
40. C. West, 'Interview with Cornell West', in A. Ross, *Universal Abandon: The Politics of Post Modernity*, Edinburgh University Press, Edinburgh, 1988, p.277.
41. Bauman, 1991, *op.cit.*, pp.250–1.
42. Bauman, 1991, *op.cit.*, p.243.
43. Z. Bauman, *Intimations of Postmodernity*, Routledge, London, 1992, pp.198–200.
44. M. Maffesoli, 'The ethics of aesthetics', in *Theory, Culture and Society*, 8, 1991, p.11.
45. A. Elliot, *Social Theory and Psychoanalysis in Transition*, Blackwell, London 1992. S. Zizek, 'Eastern Europe's republic of Gilead', in *New Left Review*, 1992.

7   New Foundations
Chetan Bhatt

I would like to thank Robert Mitchell, Hansa Chudasama, John Solomos, Ruth Frankenberg and Lata Mani for comments on an earlier draft.

1. Leonie Jameson, 'A Shropshire *samosa sur l'herbe*', *Independent*, 9 September 1992.
2. See for example: Akbar Ahmed, *Postmodernism and Islam*, Routledge, London, 1992.
3. This essay will concentrate mainly on examples of black political agency which have been identified as a return to ethnicity, religion or 'fundamentalism'. Frequent references are made to examples of that agency inside and outside the west, and the essay eclectically moves its focus from non-western movements to black western ones, but this should not be taken as demonstrating an essential identity between diverse manifestations of that agency in different geographical locations. Further, the focus on these manifestations is not to overlook other contemporary black political agency, including resistance to the former in and outside the west which have been investigated elsewhere, or black anti-racist and black feminist agency which has been documented elsewhere. It has become traditional to say that 'black' refers to (the anti-racist anti-imperialist class unity) of people in Britain of African and Asian descent, and this is the convention used even though the manifest content of the essay implies that those taxonomies, however politically desirable or necessary to fight for, are tentative.
4. Paul Gilroy, *There Ain't No Black in the Union Jack: the cultural politics of 'race' and nation*, Hutchinson, London, 1989.
5. World Hindu Council.
6. Indian People's Party.
7. National Volunteer's Organisation.
8. See for example: 'From resistance to rebellion: Asian and Afro-Caribbean

struggles in Britain' in A Sivanandan, *A Different Hunger: Writings on Black Resistance*, Pluto Press, London, 1982.

9. See: Fredric Jameson's discussion of Iranian Islamic 'fundamentalism' as a postmodern phenomenon in *Postmodernism, or the Cultural Logic of Late Capitalism*, Verso, London, 1991. Choueiri makes a useful distinction, in the context of Islamic movements, between 'revivalist' Islam (an eighteenth and nineteenth century phenomenon, whose product is contemporary Wahhabism and the Saudi state), 'reformist' Islam, an urban intellectual movement vigorously opposed to Islamic tradition that tried to accommodate Islam with Western philosophies and cultures, and 'radical Islam', a novel twentieth century phenomenon which grew in direct reaction to the nation-state and which 'does not revive or reform [but] creates a new world and invents its own dystopia'. Choueiri argues, correctly, that all these movements can be accurately described as 'fundamentalist'. Youssef M. Choueiri, *Islamic Fundamentalism*, Pinter Publishers, London, 1990.

10. *Times of India*, 13 October 1988.

11. A far-right conception of 'Hinduness', the 'essence' of being a Hindu.

12. The precise meaning of essentialism as the tendency which imputes an essence to an object has become confused in these recent debates. Essentialism is used in this sense (as in the view that there are inherent essences to the male and female genders, or to particular 'races'). However, there appear to be at least three other ways it is used. One is the designation as essentialist any discourse which makes a monologic claim (such as the only social contradiction is between classes or between genders), which should be more properly viewed as determinist. Second, the view that all social contradictions can be explained by some primary social contradiction is frequently seen as essentialist but is more accurately viewed as reductionist. However, these two vague uses are trivial in comparison with a third tendency which calls 'essentialist' any discourse which makes an absolutist or sometimes any truth claim. This is, of course, problematic, since all statements, including relativistic ones, are in weak or strong senses claims to truth. It is from this third tendency that the view arises of all identities as essentialist, since those subject to those identities all claim some truth about themselves. The problem with this tautological view is that it reads the manifest content of a stated identity synchronically as a text, rather than acknowledge the historical complexities of the social, economic and cultural formations within which agents share and recreate their identities. Many political discourses which are pejoratively described as essentialist are frequently not so. For example, the revolutionary feminist position that heterosexuality or patriarchy is the prime and only real social contradiction cannot *necessarily* imply that all men have an essence for that would negate the idea of any revolutionary feminist political strategy (except an untenable absolute separatism) since all men are inherently unchangeable.

13. Jenny Bourne's 'Cheerleaders and Ombudsmen: the Sociology of Race relations in Britain' in *Race and Class*, vol.11, no.4, spring 1980, and A. Sivanandan, 'RAT and the degradation of Black Struggle' in *Race and Class*, vol.16, no.4, Spring 1985 are the best examples of this tendency.

14. For example, Tariq Modood has written on how the category 'black' at best excludes or at worst actively discriminates against South Asians. He calls for a specific South Asian identity separate from 'black' which encompasses all those who identify with 'the heritage of the civilisations of old Hindustan prior to the British conquest [roughly] those people who believe that the Taj Mahal is an object of their history'. However, many Hindu revivalists want to destroy the Taj Mahal and all other symbols of pre-colonial Moghul rule, as they represent the period of the 'slavery of Hindus under Muslims', thus abruptly terminating that imagined community. See: Tariq Modood, '"Black" racial equality and Asian identity', *New Community*, vol.14, no.3, 1988.

15. The RSS's second leader, Madhav Golwalker, openly supported Aryan National Socialism in Germany and was an admirer of Hitler.

16. This issue is highly pertinent to contemporary struggles against the dynamic sacralisation, or 'ethnicisation' of civil societies. See: for example, Achin Vaniak's discussion of 'communalism' in India in his *The Painful Transition: Bourgeois Democracy in India*, Verso, London, 1989.

17. This highly important relation between cultural political movements and new technologies of mass communication, including the mass visual and aural media, satellite communications and computer networks, needs further research. See: Michael Benedict (ed.), *Cyberspace: First Steps*, MIT, Cambridge, MA, 1991.

18. K.N. Panikkar, 'A historical overview', in Sarvepalli Gopal (ed.), *Anatomy of a Confrontation*, Penguin India, New Delhi, 1991. Romila Thapar argues in the same volume that the desire to reinvent Hinduism around Ramjanmabhumi in Ayodhya is to provide Hinduism with a founding sacred text (Valmiki's *Ramayana*), an original Jerusalem (Ayodhya), a prophet or teacher (Ram, as a reincarnation of Vishnu), an ecclesiastical infrastructure (the VHP's new *dharma*) and the conversion of a larger body of people to the new religion (by extending the influence of *Ramabhakti* beyond its cult followers). Thapar identifies arguments that this convergence is towards a form of Semitic religion.

19. The indescribable energy and force of cosmic creation, in Hindu mythology.

20. The 'rule of Ram' or 'Ram's kingdom', a utopian state of peace and harmony.

21. Mahabharat is a mythical formation, but it also means 'India' in revivalist discourse.

22. Quoted in M. Ruthven, *A Satanic Affair: Salman Rushdie and the Rage of Islam*, Chatto & Windus, London, 1990.

23. Doreen Massey, 'A Global Sense of Place', *Marxism Today*, June 1991.

24. See: Lata Mani and Ruth Frankenberg, 'Crosscurrents, crosstalk: race, "postcoloniality" and the politics of location', *Cultural Studies*, April 1993.

25. See: Toni Morrison (ed.), *Raceing Justice, Engendering Power*, Pantheon, New York, 1992.

26. *Newsweek*, 11 May 1992.

27. Michael Omi and Howard Winant, *Racial Formation in the United States*, Routledge, London, 1986.

NOTES AND REFERENCES

28. *Daily Telegraph*, 6 April 1992.
29. *Eastern Eye*, 15 October 1991.
30. Ron Simmons, 'Some thoughts on the challenges facing black gay intellectuals' in Essex Hemphill (ed.), *Brother to Brother: New Writings by Black Gay Men*, Alyson, Boston, 1991.
31. Shabbir Akhtar, *Be Careful with Muhammad!*, Bellew, London, 1989.
32. *Independent*, 24 July 1992.
33. The Blackburn riot was the spark to a number of riots in northern England in July 1992.
34. See: David Harvey, *The Condition of Postmodernity*, Blackwell, Oxford, 1989 and Edward W. Soja, *Postmodern Geographies: the Reassertion of Space in Critical Social Theory*, Verso, London, 1989.
35. Giovanni Arrighi, Terence K. Hopkins and Immanuel Wallerstein, *Antisystemic Movements*, Verso, London, 1989.

8 Why do Empty Signifiers Matter to Politics?
Ernesto Laclau

1. Ernesto Laclau and Chantal Mouffe, *Hegemony and Socialist Strategy: Towards a Radical Democratic Politics*, Verso, London, 1985.

9 Towards the Politics of a 'Lesser Evil'
Peter Jowers

1. Jean-François Lyotard, 'Interview with J.F. Lyotard', *Diacritics*, 14, 1984, p.19.
2. 'Interview', *op.cit.*, p.21. His neologism *differend* is discussed below.
3. David Carroll, *Paraesthetics*, Methuen, London, 1987, p.183.
4. Jean-François Lyotard, *The Postmodern Condition: A Report on Knowledge*, Manchester University Press, 1986, p.77.
5. Ibid.
6. The term derives from Jean-François Lyotard, 'The Sublime and the Avant-Garde', in A. Benjamin (ed.), *The Lyotard Reader*, Basil Blackwell, Oxford, 1989, p.206.
7. David Harvey, *The Condition of Postmodernity*, Polity Press, Cambridge, 1991.
8. Jean-François Lyotard, *The Differend*, Manchester University Press, Manchester, p.140.
9. Jean-François Lyotard, *The Postmodern Condition, op.cit.*, p.xxv.
10. See: Paul Crowther, *The Kantian Sublime*, Oxford University Press, Oxford, 1989, pp.7–19, and Jean-François Lyotard, 'The Sublime and the Avant-Garde', *op.cit.*, pp.200–6.
11. Lyotard, *The Differend, op.cit.*, p.119.
12. See: below for a short explication of this term.
13. Lyotard, *The Postmodern Condition, op.cit.*, p.xxv, my emphasis.

14. The locus classicus for Kant's discussion of analogy is in Immanuel Kant, *Critique of Judgement*, Harper Press, New York, 1951, Section 59, pp.221–5.
15. Jean-François Lyotard, *The Differend*, op.cit., p.65–6. Lyotard is showing how the formal rules of classical logic have only restricted applicability as types of conjunction.
16. D. Carroll, *Paraesthetics*, op.cit., p.183–4.
17. Mary McClosky, *Kant's Aesthetics*, Macmillan Press, London, 1987, p.1, writes of many of Kant's remarks in the third critique as being 'forbiddingly obscure'. This is a commonly held view. I seek to make it less so.
18. Richard Rorty, *Contingency*, Cambridge University Press, Cambridge, 1989.
19. Ibid., pp.32, 46–7.
20. Ibid., p.59.
21. For an extremely concise but well put statement of this plurality of possible histories see: Gianni Vattimo, *The End of Modernity*, Polity Press, Cambridge, 1988, pp.1–15.
22. Jean-François Lyotard, 'Judiciousness in dispute, or Kant after Marx', *The Lyotard Reader*, ed. A. Benjamin, Basil Blackwell, Oxford, 1989, p.352. Here Lyotard explores why we need to break with Hegelian inspired philosophies of history, and of course the famous incredulity towards 'metanarratives' so central to his *Postmodern Condition*.
23. Lyotard, *The Postmodern Condition*, op.cit., p.10, my emphasis.
24. Some controversy surrounds how 'phrase' should be translated. See: G. Bennington, *Lyotard: Writing the Event*, Manchester University Press, Manchester, 1988, pp.123–4 and G. Van Den Abeele, in Lyotard, *The Differend*, p.194.
25. Lyotard, *The Differend*, op.cit., p.66. 'For there to be no phrase is impossible, for there to be *And a phrase* is necessary....To link is necessary, but how to is not.'
26. Lyotard, *The Differend*, op.cit., p.27, my emphasis.
27. Ibid., p.33.
28. Ibid., p.42.
29. Ibid., pp.45–6.
30. Ibid., p.64.
31. Ibid., p.131. For a commentary see: David Carroll, *Paraesthetics*, op.cit., p.176.
32. Immanuel Kant, *The Critique of Judgement*, op.cit., p.14. Lyotard uses the term abyss instead of gulf see: *The Differend*, op.cit., p.130.
33. I discuss below how both Rorty and Lyotard reject the metaphysics of the subject upon which this distinction is founded and yet still need to take the relation between is and ought seriously.
34. Lyotard, *The Differend*, op.cit., pp.130–3.
35. Lyotard, 'Interview', op.cit. p.18.
36. Lyotard, *The Postmodern Condition*, op.cit., p.82.
37. Richard Rorty, op.cit., p.125.
38. See: Immanuel Kant, *Critique of Judgement*, Introduction, 'Of the Critique of Judgement as a means of combining the two parts of philosophy into a whole', pp.13–14. See also: *The Lyotard Reader*, op.cit., pp.325–8.
39. Kant, *Critique of Judgement*, op.cit., Introduction, Section 4, p.16.
40. Lyotard, *The Differend*, op.cit., p.63.

41. Ibid., p.138.
42. Lyotard, *The Lyotard Reader*, *op.cit.*, p.331.
43. Paul Guyer's magisterial work, *Kant and the Claims of Taste*, Harvard University Press, Cambridge, MA, 1979, self-consciously ignores Kant's discussion of the sublime. Guyer's interest is in Kant's development of a priori synthetic judgements which can be the subject of 'publicly valid discourse'. The detailed reasons for this exclusion of the sublime are given in footnote 2, p.399. He argues that Kant's discussion of the sublime is 'a supplement' to that of beauty, that the sublime does not allow for intersubjectivity and that it is safe to assume 'that his analysis of this particular aesthetic merit will not be of much interest to modern sensibilities'. That is about as wrong as you can get! For a valuable and concise discussion of Kant's views on the public nature of reason see: Onora O'Neill, 'Vindicating Reason', in Paul Guyer, *The Cambridge Companion to Kant*, Cambridge University Press, Cambridge, 1992, pp.280-308.
44. See: Immanuel Kant, *The Critique of Judgement*, Section 24, p.85.
45. Ibid., Section 26, p.95.
46. See: Lyotard, *The Differend*, *op.cit.*, p.88, for a brilliant discussion of 'examples'.
47. For the close similarities of this *demand* to the primary *call* which institutes ethical obligation see: Lyotard, *The Differend*, op.cit., pp.107-27.
48. Terry Eagleton, *The Ideology of the Aesthetic*, Basil Blackwell, Oxford, 1990, pp.95-6. Brilliant as this work is, I cannot subscribe to its unreconstructed 'metaphysical' Marxism.
49. For a similar discussion see: J.M. Bernstein, *The Fate of Art: Aesthetic Alienation from Kant to Derrida and Adorno*, Polity Press, Cambridge, 1992, p.53 where he argues that 'the transcendental legislation of reason and understanding is an equivalent to a repression of the political'.
50. Immanuel Kant, *The Critique of Judgement*, op.cit., Section 23, p.82, my emphasis.
51. Ibid., Section 23, p.83.
52. Lyotard, *The Inhuman*, Polity Press, Cambridge, 1991, pp.136.
53. Is this sense of loss of control why feelings of the sublime, contrary to Paul Guyer's estimate, become so central to all the discussions of postmodernism?
54. Immanuel Kant, *The Critique of Judgement*, op.cit., Section 23, p.84.
55. Ibid., Section 28, p.101.
56. All these are scattered through the text but perhaps their most clustered and dense appearance comes in Section 29 where real agitation can be sensed as Kant grapples with the interaction of the sublime and religiosity in his attempt to distinguish rational religion from fanaticism. See: ibid., Section 29, pp.111-20.
57. Ibid., Section 28, p.100, my emphasis.
58. Ibid., Section 26, p.93.
59. Ibid., Section 27, p.97, my emphasis.
60. See: J.M. Bernstein. *The Fate of Art*, op.cit., pp.179 on this point.
61. Immanuel Kant, *The Critique of Judgement*, op.cit., Section 29, p.116, his emphases.

62. For a beautiful evocation of the sensory basis of the art-work see: Lyotard, *The Inhuman, op.cit.*, pp.140–1.
63. Jean-François Lyotard, from 'Amnesis of the visible, or candour' in *The Lyotard Reader, op.cit.*, pp.224–6.
64. Jean-François Lyotard, 'The sublime and the avant-garde' in *The Lyotard Reader, op.cit.*, p.204.
65. Ibid., pp.197–8.
66. Ibid., p.202.
67. See: Lyotard, *The Inhuman, op.cit.*, p.3.
68. Lyotard, *The Postmodern Condition, op.cit.*, p.78.
69. J.M. Bernstein argues this is how Kantian aesthetics ought to be regarded and claims it accounts for powerful currents in Heidegger's thought.
70. For the two moods of the sublime see: Jean-François Lyotard, *The Postmodern Condition*, pp.77–82.
71. Lyotard, *The Differend, op.cit.*, p.84.
72. Ibid., p.111.
73. Ibid., p.116.
74. Ibid., p.160.
75. Ibid., p.138.
76. Ibid., p.141.
77. Ibid., pp.103–4.
78. Ibid., p.179.
79. See particularly: Lyotard, *The Inhuman, op.cit.*, pp.191–204.

10 Essentialism Revisited?
Frank Mort

Thanks to Lucy Bland, Robert Kincaid and Chris Waters for their help and advice with this piece.
1. Pierre Bourdieu, *Homo Academicus*, trans. Peter Collier, Polity Press, London, 1988, pp.174–81. For a useful gloss on Bourdieu's conception of the intellectual field see: Scott Lash, *The Sociology of Postmodernism*, Routledge, London, 1990, ch.9.
2. Jean Baudrillard, *Le miroir de la production, ou L'illusion critique du matérialism, Galilée*, Paris, 1985; *America*, trans. Chris Turner, Verso, London, 1989.
3. For analysis of the difficulties involved in the take-up of American strategies by British queer activists see: Richard Smith, 'Papering over the cracks', *Gay Times*, May 1992, p.29.
4. On the generational divisions opened up by the term queer see: Alan Sinfield, 'What is in a Name?' *Gay Times*, May 1992, p.25. On the broader challenge posed to the established gay community by queer activism see: Peter Tatchell, 'Do us a favour—call us queer', *Independent on Sunday*, 26 July 1992; Melanie Phillips, 'Politics of the New Queer', the *Guardian*, 23 June 1992, p.19; Keith Alcorn, 'Queer and Now', *Gay Times*, May 1992, p.20; Cherry Smyth, *Lesbians Talk Queer Notions*, Scarlet Press, London, 1992, p.19.
5. For specific discussion of queerness in the context of a cultural politics of

race see: Pratibha Parmar and Isaac Julien, 'Queer Questions', *Sight and Sound*, September 1992, p.21.

6. See especially: Derek Jarman, 'Queer Questions', *Sight and Sound*, September 1992, pp.34–5. Jarman questions the assumed community of interests implied in the usage of the term gay, together with its simplistic understanding of aesthetic sensibility.

7. For some of the most significant attempts to weave autobiographical narratives into broader post-war British cultural histories see: Carolyn Steedman, *Landscape for a Good Woman: A Story of Two Lives*, Virago, London, 1986; Raphael Samuel, 'The Lost World of British Communism', *New Left Review*, no.154, November/December 1985, pp.3–53; 'Staying Power: The Lost World of British Communism, Part Two', *New Left Review*, no.156, March/April 1986, pp.63–113; Janice Winship, *Inside Women's Magazines*, Pandora, London, 1987.

8. Edward Thompson, *William Morris: Romantic to Revolutionary*, Merlin Press, London, 1977, p.791.

9. For autobiographical accounts which explore class cultural narratives of the post-war period, though not in their gendered dimensions see: Richard Hoggart, *A Sort of Clowning: Life and Times, volume 2: 1940–59*, Oxford University Press, Oxford, 1991; *An Imagined Life: Life and Times, volume 3: 1959–91*, Chatto and Windus, London 1992; Raymond Williams, *Border Country*, Chatto and Windus, London, 1960. For feminine versions which specifically explore the gendered dynamics of respectable working-class/ lower-middle-class culture see: Valerie Walkerdine, 'Dreams from an Ordinary Childhood', in Liz Heron (ed.), *Truth, Dare or Promise: Girls Growing Up in the Fifties*, Virago, London, 1985, pp.63–77.

10. For analysis of the relationship between reforming moral strategies and progressive middle-class culture in the 1960s see: Stuart Hall, 'Reformism and the Legislation of Consent', in National Deviancy Conference (ed.), *Permissiveness and Control: The Fate of the Sixties Legislation*, Macmillan, London, 1980, pp.1–43; Jeffrey Weeks, *Sex, Politics and Society: the Regulation of Sexuality since 1800*, Longman, London, 1981, chapters 12 and 13. For commentaries from 'inside' the culture of reformism see: Susan Crosland, *Tony Crosland*, Coronet, London, 1983; Roy Jenkins, *A Life at the Centre*, Pan, London, 1992, pp.175–213. Jenkins's account of 1960s liberalism is noticeably cool in retrospect.

11. For historical accounts of the formation of the lower middle class and the skilled working class see: Geoffrey Crossick (ed.), *The Lower Middle Class in Britain, 1870–1914*, Croom Helm, London, 1977; Robert Gray, *The Labour Aristocracy in Victorian Edinburgh*, Clarendon Press, Oxford, 1976.

12. Frank Mort, *Dangerous Sexualities: Medico-moral Politics in England since 1830*, Routledge and Kegan Paul, London, 1987, pp.47–53, 83–6. For a detailed account of one specific professional biography see: Leonore Davidoff, 'Class and Gender in Victorian Britain: Arthur J. Munby and Hannah Cullwick', *Feminist Studies*, vol.5, no.1, 1979, pp.89–133; Derek Hudson, *Munby, Man of Two Worlds: The Life and Diaries of Arthur J. Munby 1828–1910*, Abacus, London, 1974.

13. For recent explorations of the concept of political culture see: John Gibbins

(ed.), *Contemporary Political Culture: Politics in a Postmodern Age*, Sage, London, 1989.

14. For an anti-consumerist critique of queerness as an exclusively metropolitan phenomenon see: Paul Hegarty, 'I consume, therefore I am queer', *Rouge*, Issue 11, 1992, pp.11–12; also C. Smyth, *Lesbians Talk Queer Notions*, *op.cit.*, p.34.

15. Derek Jarman, *Modern Nature: The Journals of Derek Jarman*, Vintage, London, 1991; *At Your Own Risk*, Vintage, London, 1993. Jarman's autobiographical sketches celebrate a humanist discourse of coherent subjectivity rather than its postmodern fracturing.

16. C. Smyth, *Lesbians Talk Queer Notions*, *op.cit.*, p.6.

17. For the reclamation of the term 'spinster' by early twentieth-century British feminists see: Sheila Jeffreys, *The Spinster and her Enemies: Feminism and Sexuality 1880–1930*, Pandora, London, 1985; Lucy Bland, *Banishing the Beast: English Feminism and Sexual Morality, 1885–1918*, Penguin, Harmondsworth, forthcoming. For similar appropriations of the 'invert' and 'lesbian' see: Lillian Faderman, *Surpassing the Love of Men: Romantic Friendship and Love between Women from the Renaissance to the Present*, Women's Press, London, 1985; *Odd Girls and Twilight Lovers*, Penguin, Harmondsworth, 1992.

18. Simon LeVay, self-professed American 'gay scientist', has conducted experiments on the possible relationship between sexual object choice and brain structure. LeVay argues that proof of the biological nature of homosexuality would aid civil rights recognition in the USA, given that the American Supreme Court grounds its rulings on the discrimination of minorities in a conception of biological immutability.

19. See for example: Max Navarre, 'Fighting the Victim Label', in Douglas Crimp, *AIDS: Cultural Analysis Cultural Activism*, MIT Press, Cambridge, MA, 1989, pp.143–6; Jonathan Grimshaw, 'The Individual Challenge', in Erica Carter and Simon Watney (eds.), *Taking Liberties. AIDS and Cultural Politics*, Serpent's Tail, London, 1989, pp.213–18;

20. Steven Epstein, 'Gay Politics, Ethnic Identity: The Limits of Social Constructionism', *Socialist Review*, nos 93–94, 1988, pp.21, 37. See: also John D'Emilio, 'Capitalism and Gay Identity', in Anne Snitow, et al. (eds), *Powers of Desire: The Politics of Sexuality*, Monthly Review Press, New York, 1983, pp.177–206; *Sexual Politics, Sexual Communities: The Making of a Homosexual Minority in the United States, 1940–1970*, University of Chicago Press, Chicago, 1983.

21. Examples of academic work which has adopted a social constructionist approach would include: Mary McIntosh, 'The Homosexual Role', *Social Problems*, vol.16, no.2, 1968, pp.182–92; Jeffrey Weeks, *Coming Out: Homosexual Politics in Britain from the Nineteenth Century to the Present*, Quartet, London, 1977; J. D'Emilio, *Sexual Politics*, *op.cit.*; Kenneth Plummer (ed.), *The Making of the Modern Homosexual*, Hutchinson, London, 1981.

22. HOMOCULTURE, fly poster, quoted in A. Sinfield, 'What's in a Name?' *op.cit.*, p.27.

23. 'I Hate Straights', quoted in K. Alcorn, 'Queer and Now', *op.cit.*, p.21.

24. P. Tatchell, 'Do us a favour—call us queer', *op.cit.*

25. Eve Kosofsky Sedgwick, *The Epistemology of the Closet*, University of California

Press, Berkeley, CA, 1990, p.1. For other literary accounts which work within parallel frameworks see: Joseph Bristow (ed.), *Sexual Sameness: Textual Differences in Lesbian and Gay Writing*, Routledge, London, 1992.

26. Jonathan Dollimore, *Sexual Dissidence: Augustine to Wilde, Freud to Foucault*, Oxford University Press, Oxford, 1991. Dollimore analyses the significance of the perverse dynamic, whose genealogy is traceable historically from Augustinean theology through early modern literary culture to its twentieth century manifestations in Freud and Foucault. In his study of Wilde and Genet he argues that both writers embrace the 'paradoxes of the perverse', utilising a conception of transgression against normative discourse.

27. Michel Foucault, *The History of Sexuality Volume 1: An Introduction*, trans. Robert Hurley, Pantheon Books, New York, 1979, chapter 2.

28. For feminist critiques and rereadings of Foucault see: Irene Diamond and Lee Quinby (eds), *Feminism and Foucault: Reflections on Resistance*, Northeastern University Press, Boston, 1988; Naomi Schor, 'Dreaming Dyssymmetry: Barthes, Foucault and Sexual Difference', in Alice Jardine and Paul Smith (eds), *Men in Feminism*, Methuen, New York, 1987, pp.98–110; Judith Walkowitz, *City of Dreadful Delight: Narratives of Sexual Danger in Late-Victorian London*, Chicago University Press, Chicago, 1992, pp.1–13.

29. Suzanne Moore, quoted in C. Smyth, *Lesbians Talk Queer Notions*, op.cit., p.34.

30. See: Pat Califia, *Sapphistry: The Book of Lesbian Sexuality*, The Naiad Press, New York, 1980; Samois (ed.), *Coming to Power: Writings and Graphics on Lesbian S/M*, Samois, Berkeley, CA, 1981.

31. After a rapid drop in the number of cases of sexually transmitted diseases in the mid to late 1980s among homosexual men, the government's Public Health Laboratory Service Aids Centre has reported significant increases since 1988. Researchers also report on accelerated HIV infection rates among gay men under twenty five in London since 1991, 'Young gays risk HIV as cases rise', the *Guardian*, 12 February 1993.

32. See for example: the magazine *FF* and the related London club venues 'FF' and 'Trade'.

33. Della Grace, *Love Bites*, Gay Men's Press, London, 1991. For similar recent arguments about lesbian perversity see: Carol Queen, 'When the Lights Changed', *Taste of Latex*, vol.1, no.4, Winter, 1990–91; *Quim*, Issue 3, Winter 1991.

34. See especially: Gayle Rubin, 'The Leather Menace: Comments on Politics and S/M', in Samois (ed.), *Coming to Power*, op.cit., pp.192–225.

35. Examples of queer cinema would include Christopher Münch, *The Hours and the Times*, 1991; Laurie Lynd, *RSVP*, 1991; Paul Verhoeven, *Basic Instinct*, 1992; Tom Kalin, *Swoon*, 1992; Gregg Araki, *The Living End*, 1992. For analysis of the phenomenon see: *Sight and Sound*, September 1992, pp.30–9.

36. Tom Kalin, *Sight and Sound*, ibid., p.36.

37. Stuart Hall, 'Cultural Identity and Diaspora', in Jonathan Rutherford (ed.), *Identity: Community, Culture, Difference*, Lawrence and Wishart, London, 1990, p.226. For similar analysis of the formation of national and racial difference see: Benedict Anderson, *Imagined Communities: Reflections on the Origin and Rise of*

Nationalism, Verso, London, 1982; Edward Said, *Orientalism*, Penguin, Harmondsworth, 1985.

38. See for example: Joan Scott, *Gender and the Politics of History*, Columbia University Press, New York, 1988; Denise Riley, *'Am I That Name?' Feminism and the Category of Women in History*, University of Minnesota Press, Minneapolis, 1988; Judith Butler, *Gender Trouble: Feminism and the Subversion of Identity*, Routledge, Chapman and Hall, New York, 1990; Judith Butler and Joan Scott (eds), *Feminists Theorize the Political*, Routledge, London, 1992.

39. Ernesto Laclau and Chantal Mouffe, *Hegemony and Socialist Strategy: Towards a Radical Democratic Politics*, Verso, London, 1983; C. Mouffe, 'Feminism, Citizenship and Radical Democratic Politics', in J. Butler and J. Scott (eds), *Feminists Theorize the Political, op.cit.*, pp.369–84.

40. For the social democratic project of moral relativisation see especially: C.A.R. Crosland, *The Future of Socialism*, Jonathan Cape, London, 1956, pp.515–29; *The Conservative Enemy: A Programme of Radical Reform for the 1960s*, Jonathan Cape, London, 1962, pp.237–41.

11 Hegemony Trouble
Anna Marie Smith

1. Judith Butler, *Gender Trouble*, New York, Routledge, 1990.
2. Ernesto Laclau and Chantal Mouffe, *Hegemony and Socialist Strategy*, London, Verso, 1985.
3. This is a paraphrase of Stuart Hall's formulation, which he presents in his 'Race, Articulation and Societies Structured in Dominance', UNESCO, *Societies Structured in Dominance*, Paris, UNESCO, 1980, p.341.
4. I have presented this research in 'A Symptomology of an Authoritarian Discourse: The Parliamentary Debates on the Prohibition of Homosexuality', *New Formations*, no.10, Summer, 1990, pp.41–65.
5. Stuart Hall and Martin Jacques (eds), *The Politics of Thatcherism*, London, Lawrence and Wishart, 1983; and Stuart Hall, *The Hard Road to Renewal*, London, Verso, 1988.
6. Laclau and Mouffe, *Hegemony and Socialist Strategy, op.cit.*, p.159.
7. Ibid., pp.168–9.
8. Ibid., p.168.
9. These are my examples.
10. Laclau and Mouffe, *Hegemony and Socialist Strategy, op.cit.*, p.176.
11. Ibid., pp.183–4.
12. Ibid., p.182, emphasis added.
13. June Jordan, interviewed by Pratibha Parmar, in Parmar, 'Black Feminism: The Politics of Articulation', in Jonathan Rutherford (ed.), *Identity: Community, Culture, Difference*, London, Lawrence and Wishart, 1990, p.112.
14. Chela Sandoval, 'Feminism and Racism: A Report on the 1981 National Women's Studies Association Conference', in Gloria Anzaldúa (ed.), *Making Face, Making Soul*, San Francisco, Aunt Lute Foundation Books, 1990, pp.66, 67.

NOTES AND REFERENCES

15. Slavoj Zizek, *The Sublime Object of Ideology*, London, Verso, 1989.
16. For recent developments in lesbian and gay activism in Britain see: Ken Plummer (ed.), *Modern Homosexualities: Fragments of Lesbian and Gay Experience*, London, Routledge, 1992; and Cherry Smyth, *Lesbians Talk Queer Notions*, London, Scarlet Press, 1992.
17. Gayle Rubin, 'The Traffic in Women: Notes on the "Political Economy" of Sex', in Rayna Reiter (ed.), *Toward an Anthropology of Women*, New York, Monthly Review Press, 1975, pp.157–210.
18. Butler, *Gender Trouble, op.cit.*, p.118.
19. Ibid., p.136.
20. Ibid., p.139.
21. Ibid., p. 24, 16.
22. Norma Alarcón, 'The Theoretical Subject(s) of *This Bridge Called My Back*, and Anglo-American Feminism', in Gloria Anzaldúa (ed.), *Making Face, Making Soul: Haciendo Caras: Creative and Critical Perspectives by Women of Color*, San Francisco, Aunt Lute Foundation Books, 1990, pp.361–2.
23. Butler, *Gender Trouble, op.cit.*, p.33.
24. Ernesto Laclau, *New Reflections on the Revolution of Our Times*, London, Verso, 1990.
25. Ibid., pp.33–5.
26. Butler, *Gender Trouble, op.cit.*, p.56.
27. Ibid., p.149.
28. Laclau, *New Reflections on the Revolution of Our Time, op.cit.*, p.22.
29. Butler, *Gender Trouble, op.cit.*, p.14–15.
30. Laclau, *New Reflections on the Revolution of Our Time, op.cit.*, pp.171–3.
31. Ibid., pp.135–75.
32. Butler, *Gender Trouble, op.cit.*, p.122.
33. Ibid., p.123.
34. Ibid., p.128.
35. Laclau, *New Reflections on the Revolution of Our Time, op.cit.*, p.42.
36. Jacques Derrida, 'Signature, Event, Context', translated by Samuel Weber and Jeffrey Mehlman, *Limited Inc.*, Northwestern UP, Evanston, 1988, p.12. Emphasis in original.
37. Jacques Derrida, 'Signature, évenement, contexte', *Marges de la Philosophie*, Paris, Les Éditions de Minuit, 1972, p.381.
38. I have discussed British official discourse on lesbianism in 'Resisting the Erasure of Lesbian Sexuality: A Challenge for Queer Activism', in Ken Plummer (ed.), *Modern Homosexualities: Fragments of Lesbian and Gay Experiences*, London, Routledge, 1992, pp.200–13.

12 Pluralism, Solidarity, and Change
Anne Phillips

I am indebted to comments by Susan Mendus, some of whose formulations have crept into my revised version.

1. A longer version of this essay is published in Anne Phillips, *Democracy and*

Difference, Polity Press, Cambridge, UK, and Pennsylvania State University Press, Pennsylvania US, 1993.

2. Paul Hirst, *Representative Democracy and Its Limits*, Polity Press, Cambridge, 1990.

3. Chantal Mouffe (ed.), *Dimensions of Radical Democracy: Pluralism, Citizenship, Community*, Verso, London, 1992.

4. Karl Popper, *The Open Society and Its Enemies*, Routledge and Kegan Paul, London, 1945.

5. Isaiah Berlin, *Four Essays on Liberty*, Oxford University Press, Oxford, 1969. For a recent discussion of 'The Pluralism of Isaiah Berlin' see: Perry Anderson, *A Zone of Engagement*, Verso, London, 1992.

6. The literature is immense, but key contributions were P. Bachrach and M.S. Baratz, 'The Two Faces of Power', *American Political Science Review*, vol.56, no.4, 1962; G. Duncan and S. Lukes, 'The New Democracy', *Political Studies*, vol.11, no.2, 1963; and C. Pateman, *Participation and Democratic Theory*, Cambridge University Press, Cambridge, 1970, esp. ch.1.

7. Paul Hirst, *Representative Democracy*, *op.cit.*, p.56.

8. See for example: N. Poulantzas, *Classes in Contemporary Capitalism*, New Left Books, London, 1975; G. Carchedi, *On The Economic Identification of Social Classes*, Routledge and Kegan Paul, London, 1976; E. Olin Wright, 'What is Middle about the Middle Class?', in J. Roemer (ed.), *Analytical Marxism*, Cambridge University Press, Cambridge, 1986.

9. For an overview of these debates see: M. Barrett, *Women's Oppression Today*, second edition, Verso, London, 1988.

10. Alasdair MacIntyre is the main example of this. See his: *After Virtue*, Duckworth and Sons, London 1981; and *Whose Justice? Whose Rationality?*, University of Notre Dame Press, Notre Dame, 1988.

11. For example, Richard Rorty, *Contingency, irony and solidarity*, Cambridge University Press, Cambridge, 1989.

12. See the essays collected in Linda Nicolson (ed.), *Feminism/Postmodernism*, Routledge, London, 1990; and Anne Phillips, 'Universal Pretensions in Political Thought', in Phillips, *Democracy and Difference*, *op.cit.*

13. This is particularly powerfully argued in A.J. Polan, *Lenin and the End of Politics*, Methuen, London, 1984.

14. See: Alec Nove, *The Economics of Feasible Socialism*, George Allen and Unwin, London, 1983.

15. David Miller, *Market, State and Community: Theoretical Foundations of Market Socialism*, Clarendon Press, Oxford, 1989.

16. John Keane, *Democracy and Civil Society*, Verso, London, 1988, p.xiii.

17. R. Dalton and M. Kuechler (eds), *Challenging The Political Order: New Social and Political Movements in Western Democracies*, Polity Press, Cambridge, 1990.

18. One of the best examples is Iris Marion Young, *Justice and the Politics of Difference*, Princeton University Press, New Jersey, 1990.

19. Ibid.

20. In *Justice and the Politics of Difference*, *op.cit.*, Iris Young briefly notes the parallels between her own vision of group representation and the European experience of consociationalism, noting however, that 'European Models of consociational democratic institutions...cannot be removed from the con-

NOTES AND REFERENCES

text in which they have evolved, and even within them it is not clear that they constitute models of participatory democracy', p.191. See also: Jane Mansbridge, *Beyond Adversary Democracy*, Basic Books, New York, 1980, for an exploration of consociational principles of equalising political outcomes.

21. Susan Mendus, *Toleration and the Limits of Liberalism*, Macmillan, Basingstoke, 1989.

22. Iris Marion Young, 'Justice and Communicative Democracy', in Roger Gottlieb (ed.), *Tradition, Counter-Tradition, Politics: Dimensions of Radical Philosophy*, Temple University Press, Philadelphia, 1993.

23. Arendt Lijphart, *Democracy in Plural Societies: A Comparative Exploration*, Yale University Press, New Haven, 1977, pp.3–4. The central theses of consociational democracy are developed in Lijphart's analysis of *The Politics of Accommodation: Pluralism and Democracy in the Netherlands*, University of California Press, Berkeley, 1968; and subsequently refined through his *Democracies: Patterns of Majoritarian and Consensus Government in Twenty-One Countries*, Yale University Press, New Haven, 1984. His study on *Power-Sharing in South Africa*, Policy Papers in International Affairs, University of California Press, Berkeley, 1985, proposes a consociational constitution for South Africa, and includes an extended discussion of his critics. See also: Lijphart, 'Democratic Political Systems: Types, Cases, Causes, and Consequences', *Journal of Theoretical Politics*, vol.1, no.1, 1989.

24. Lijphart, *Democracy in Plural Societies*, op.cit., p.22.

25. Arendt Lijphart, 'The Northern Ireland Problem: Cases, Theories, and Solutions', *British Journal of Political Science*, vol.5, no.1, 1975, pp.83–106.

26. Iris Marion Young, 'Polity and Group Difference: A Critique of the Ideal of Universal Citizenship', *Ethics*, 99, 1989, p.261.

27. Pierre L. van den Berghe, 'Protection of Ethnic Minorities: A Critical Appraisal', in Robert G. Wirsing (ed.), *Protection of Ethnic Minorities: Comparative Perspectives*, Pergamon Press, Oxford, 1981, p.349.

28. This was a point that Brian Barry developed in his 'Political Accommodation and Consociational Democracy', *British Journal of Political Science* vol.5, no.4, 1975, where he argues that divisions based on ethnic identity may be less amenable to consociational management than those based around religion, because the former do not provide the same undisputed authority basis for 'the' leaders.

29. Mendus, *Toleration and the Limits of Liberalism*, op.cit., p.158.

30. Iris Marion Young, 'Justice and Communicative Democracy', op.cit., p.158.

31. Ibid., p.23.

32. Thus, for example, those concerned with measures to increase the political representation of black Americans have noted that it is impossible to rely only on increasing their numbers: when a group is in a numerical minority, its chances of transforming the political agenda depend on securing broader coalitions with white liberals. See: Rufus P. Browning, Dale Rogers Marshall and David H. Tabb (eds), *Racial Politics in American Cities*, Longman, New York and London, 1990; and Lani Guinier, 'Voting Rights and Democratic Theory: Where Do We Go From Here?', in Bernard Grofman and Chandler Davidson (eds), *Controversies in Minority Voting: The Voting Rights Act in Perspective*, The Brookings Institution, Washington DC, 1992.

33. Something like this seems to have happened in the arguments on US campuses over the content of the undergraduate curriculum: the so-called 'political correctness' debate. There is an extraordinary level of indignation among those who feel their cherished traditions under attack from a wave of 'minority' charges; and while I too hate to be attacked by students, I cannot but feel that the catalogue of inappropriate demands has been collated in order to absolve people from changing what they teach. There is a certain amount of bad faith in employing what may well be the closed dogmatism of one's critics as a way of evading responsibility for questioning and reviewing oneself. I am aware that I speak from the relatively safe harbours of British universities—but whatever may be the 'excesses' of those currently challenging the canon, these should not serve to excuse myopic practices among dominant groups.

Index

INDEX